Rottenkid: A Succulent Story of Survival

"Brigit Binns may have had a hard-drinking actor for a father and a mother of dangerous exuberance, but she is the star of her life story. This child of Hollywood writes with an observant honesty, telling of hard times and harrowing psychological troubles with surprising humor and heart. You will come away from this book with great admiration for her spirit and great affection for her."

—Rick Kogan, Legendary *Chicago Tribune* columnist,
radio personality, and noted author

· · · ·

"A grounded remembrance of an outwardly glittering Hollywood upbringing. Binns' self-aware and wry writing will interest readers who grew up with angry, self-involved parents, but she also keenly explores the difficult childhoods of both Edward and Marcia in order to better understand them."

—Kirkus Reviews

· · · ·

"Definitely not the usual culinary memoir, this is a moving, tell-all story of survival, resilience—and the healing power of food."

— Barbara Fairchild, Editor, *Bon Appétit Magazine*

· · · ·

"A brave, delicious, and often darkly funny tale of growing up in the Hollywood of the 60's and 70's, *Rottenkid* is Brigit's story of breaking free from parental disapproval and finding herself. I loved reading this deftly crafted, insightful memoir by my childhood friend."

— Cecilia Peck, Emmy-nominated filmmaker; daughter of Gregory Peck

"Brigit Binns has written a powerful memoir of a childhood of Hollywood privilege among the offspring of other household names in competition with her father's bottle and a wicked mother right out of Disney. "Born with a silver spoon in my mouth and a knife in my back," somehow her precocious, painful, and randy youth led her to a life of sophistication as she waded through ill-fitting men and learned how to cook. She has gone on to author numerous cookbooks that I count as indispensable. What a tasty read."

—"Meathead" Goldwyn, Hedonism Evangelist and BBQ Whisperer. Author of *NY Times* bestseller *Meathead: The Science of Great Barbecue and Grilling*, and proprietor of the world's most popular BBQ and grilling website, AmazingRibs.com

. . . .

"A zippy, engaging, and sometimes infuriating story about growing up in Hollywood with neglectful parents. Binns includes dishy bits about stars and politicians, and I am still picturing a certain celebrity's toupee floating in the family swimming pool. But this memoir is also about becoming an adult, and how the author made her way by trial and error, without role models. If you're into food, you'll find plenty of mouthwatering descriptions of what the author cooked with aplomb in London and on the Spanish coast, for dinner parties and eventually as a caterer and cookbook author."

— Dianne Jacob, author of *Will Write for Food: Pursue Your Passion and Bring Home the Dough Writing Recipes, Cookbooks, Blogs, and More*

. . . .

"There's no shortage of childhood trauma on display in Brigit Binns' disarmingly honest *Rottenkid*. But with the knowledge that the author scripted, of all things, a Hollywood ending for herself, we're able to enjoy the gallows humor and novelist's eye for telling detail that enliven every page. For all its celebrity cameos (Henry Fonda! Fred Astaire!) and privileged settings (including a memorable stretch at boarding school), at its core, this is the story of a search for self amid the ruins of a lavishly dysfunctional family. You don't have to be a Coppola to relate."

— Andrew Friedman, author *The Dish: The Lives and Labor Behind One Plate of Food,* and *Chefs, Drugs, and Rock & Roll: How Food Lovers, Free Spirits, Misfits and Wanderers Created a New American Profession*

. . . .

"A brutally honest and sometimes painful look at growing up in a truly dysfunctional family that will have you crying one moment and laughing the next. Celebrated cookbook author and "rottenkid" Brigit Binns has the courage to bare her soul while conjuring up enticing recipes in a memoir peppered with Hollywood stars, politicians, boarding schools, and travel abroad that are simmered together in a pressure cooker to create a real page turner."

— Mike DeSimone and Jeff Jenssen, The World Wine Guys; Authors of *Red Wine, Gourmand International's Best Wine Book in the World*

. . . .

"Brigit's delicious, darkly humorous memoir is written with such tangible introspection and self-awareness I was swept along with her on the journey. Always fearless and accountable, my friend has manifested self-confidence in life with such grace. The notion that this "Rottenkid" would never make it is probably the biggest irony for the disapproving mother who held that opinion. Out of a wildly dysfunctional family, this memoir is a triumph of spirit, generously served."

— June Lockhart-Triolo, freelance photographer, graphic artist, daughter of June Lockhart

ROTTENKID

A succulent STORY OF survival

BRIGIT BINNS

Sibylline
PRESS

AN IMPRINT OF ALL THINGS BOOK

Sibylline Press
Copyright © 2024 by Brigit Binns
All Rights Reserved.

Published in the United States by Sibylline Press,
an imprint of All Things Book LLC, California.
Sibylline Press is dedicated to publishing the brilliant work
of women authors ages 50 and older.
www.sibyllinepress.com

Distributed to the trade by Publishers Group West.
Sibylline Press
Paperback ISBN: 978-1-960573-99-5
eBook ISBN: 978-1-960573-07-0
Library of Congress Control Number: 2023947568

Book and Cover Design: Alicia Feltman

Photo credits: Unless otherwise noted, all images come from either the
Binns Family Archives or the author's personal collection.

This is a work of non-fiction. Very occasionally, names have been changed.

For Casey, the guy who rode in on the white truck

ROTTENKID

A succulent STORY OF survival

BRIGIT BINNS

We can have all the world has to offer in terms of status, achievement, and possession, yet without a true sense of belonging, our lives feel empty and pointless. Like the tree that puts roots deep into the clay, each of us needs the anchor of belonging in order to bend with the storms and continue toward the light.

—Irish philosopher John O'Donohue

SALTING A STEAK FOR TV GUIDE

prologue

The movie *Twelve Angry Men*, in which my father, Edward Binns, was acting, was out in theaters. His father-son cop show *Brenner* had been picked up for a second season. *TV Guide* sent a camera crew to our Santa Monica house for a photo shoot; this included several patently polished set pieces by the pool. One showed my bathing-suit-clad mother leaning forward so that Dad could light her cigarette (my mother was rabidly anti-smoking all her life). Another image shows my much older half-sister Nancy Binns holding her nose and jumping into the pool while Dad looks on, oddly roaring with hysterical laughter. Meanwhile I, all of three years old, hold onto a lawn chair and glare directly into the camera—demolishing the fourth wall—as if to say, "Who the hell are you, and get out of my pool!"

But my hands-down favorite is the steak shot: I sit in front of an indoor fireplace, my grimance-smiling mother seated on my left, and vacuously grinning father perched on my right. He holds out a platter containing a great big steak. I am adorably salting the steak (at age three, was I already beginning my love affair with meat and salt?). Too bad the steak was frozen solid, a prop.

Forty-some years later, *Saveur* magazine sent a camera crew to shoot the kitchen in my almost-finished barnhouse in the Hudson Valley; I'd just signed the contract for my 21st cookbook and had appeared on *The Today Show* twice in the previous six months. We had to tie back the power cords for the nail gun and compressor so they wouldn't intrude on the overhead shot and mar the bucolic scene. Of course, the final glossy images didn't show the wires or dust, nor my puffy eyes—resulting from a contentious conversation with my mother that I'd just cut short. They showed only the ideal of a rustic and enviable "gourmet" lifestyle.

The road in between these two photo shoots was rocky, paved with embarrassing mistakes and, in earlier years, a crippling lack of self-confidence. There were dangerous pitfalls for which a glaringly privileged Hollywood childhood left me ill-prepared to cope. Many of my friends from that early era ended up as movie stars, or dead. Sometimes both. Brett Easton Ellis was a few years behind me, and we went to the same prep school—although I left after fourth grade. The Los Angeles he portrayed in *Less than Zero* and later *The Shards* is the one I escaped by going off to boarding school at age 14.

Some people had claimed to love me, but evidence seemed to prove that they didn't even like me. To manifest self-confidence in the world when you have never known unconditional love is, possibly, impossible. The simple goal has always been just to carry on, ideally with a sense of humor and a bit of style. But a few rules have always stood fast, from beginning to end:

Do not look behind the curtain. Do what you must to survive.

Photo credit: Edward Binns

My mother with trout at the Hollister Ranch

CHAPTER 1

The barbecue

CALIFORNIA, 1968

I WAS BORN WITH A SILVER SPOON in my mouth and a knife in my back.

Upstairs on the covered porch that wraps the sprawling Spanish ranch house, a screen door squeaks open. A tall, slim, tousle-haired woman emerges from the bedroom, her filmy white negligee fluttering in the California breeze. Toting a steely-eyed glare and a .22 rifle, she shades her eyes against the sun and the glittering Pacific for a moment, to better locate the screeching blue jay that had disturbed her noonday slumber. She lifts the gun to her shoulder, takes careful aim, and blows it to smithereens. The poor blue jay flutters down and hits the dirt, dead. His feathers are the same blue as the ocean. The screen door slams. My mother has gone back to bed.

In the scrubby courtyard below, I am one of a bunch of kids surrounding Uncle Clinty Hollister (one of the famed family of early—white—California settlers and landowners, for whom the town of Hollister is named). Uncle Clinty fries a few of the gleaming trout we'd "helped" catch early that morning, marveling as he pulled one flapping and wiggling from a creek nearby. I steal a glance at the upturned faces around the firepit, curious to see if this captive audience has found my mother's performance bizarre or cool. I need a cue for my own reaction, desperate to feel something other than the urge to run far, far away, as quickly as possible.

At age eleven, I don't yet know the meaning of the word *eccentric*—I am simply embarrassed to be the child of such a flamboyant person. I have long had trouble parsing some of the events that peppered my privileged childhood. Maybe they were funny? The truth was this: My mother's larger-than-life persona is so overarchingly important (to her) that my needs are justly inconsequential. It's not worth the effort it takes to stoop down to my level and look, even for a moment, through my coke-bottle glasses into my confused and needy little soul. I haven't yet learned that her star shines so piercingly bright—the razor-sharp wit and glittering repartee, the limpid brown eyes and impish flirtations—that the firmament has room only for her. I am a jagged little unfinished moon lurking hopefully in the shadows.

No one was around then to warn me that I mustn't ever allow this woman to see me as a rival. Even if some kind, intuitive person had done so, it would have been akin to telling a loopy little kitten not to compete with a leopard.

The trout are still sizzling away, their earthy-fresh perfume swirling lazily around the courtyard, like the carrots that always lured Bugs Bunny to follow their siren call slavishly and nose-first. I timidly ask Uncle Clinty if I can add some butter to the pan. *Didn't I hear someone say that butter makes everything better?*

When his eyes light up, I rush off to the kitchen and grab the plastic butter-keeper out of the fridge. It's not real butter, of course; Mom would never allow that. So it's Fleischmann's margarine. I've never had real butter. Returning with the plastic butter dish held high, I clock the somewhat surprised but admiring eyes of the other kids. Butter adds flavor, color, and crispness to the skin of the trout, I note. It also, apparently, adds a little bump-up to my position in the kid-centric pecking order.

Back then, California felt real. Grounded. It was a place of dirt roads, clean beaches, and unlimited parking. Her curves had been sculpted by millennia of shifting tectonic plates, pounding surf, and capricious winds, not a surgeon's blade. Paradise had yet to be paved. It is only in my gossamer memory now that California's rustic beauty—and the idea that my mother and father were flawless—remains intact.

I was lucky enough to spend perhaps the happiest times of my childhood on the legendary Hollister Ranch, a rare piece of the California coast that had been completely left behind—even by Sixties-era "progress."

The 18,000-acre working cattle ranch had originally been part of the famous Spanish land grant known as *Nuestra Señora del Refugio* (Our Lady of Refuge). During my mother's initial tenure with the Hollisters—as a repeat boarding-school-holiday guest in the late thirties and early forties—many members of the huge family lived on the ranch, sharing one party telephone line that was anything but private. The Mexican vaqueros and their families lived there, too, and the community was a utopian microcosm of disparate cultures and foodways—life was equally hardscrabble for all the residents, irrespective of their backgrounds. A little schoolhouse took care of all the ranch kids until they were sent to boarding school or the public high school in Santa Barbara.

After the second World War, bit by bit, the various Hollisters took their cattle money—and a little oil money—off the ranch to more glamorous digs in Montecito and elsewhere. The year-round Ranch population was reduced to ranch-hands, cowpokes, managers, and their families. And the utopian microcosm began its gradual decline. My mother remained an unofficial member of the family until her death, long after it was still possible to visit the Ranch.

By the time I arrived, a scant few Hollisters visited there regularly. I was a fortunate witness to the tail end of a precious era, but all I understood was the oak-dotted dusty canyons and mesas of the Ranch were where I always wanted to be.

For this lonely-only child, those times spent with friends, various Hollisters, and extended family at the big, Spanish ranch-house we nicknamed the "Ritz" were glimpses into an unknown world, heady with warmth and camaraderie. I reveled in being a part of a kid-gang, as we explored the thinly treed piñon forests, building forts in the rocky gullies behind the Ritz while softly lowing, brown-eyed cattle watched us with indifference. I became adept—a virtual prodigy, I thought—at imitating their low-bass, long-drawn-out moos.

Blissfully, I'd toss off a wave toward the adults as we sped past their various positions (making sandwiches, washing beach towels, or celebrating the sunset with a cocktail), hopefully too fast for us to hear any chore-related exhortations they might have shouted out. We rose together and tumbled into gritty beds at the same early hour, while the grown-ups did their unknown late-night things. The adults had little interest in us, and that felt like freedom. Later I'd come to see it as an early form of abandonment.

At dinner, always, my dad would be very, very jolly. We younger kids would giggle so hard we had to hold our tummies and gasp for air. As the evening wore on, Dad would get progressively sillier. This didn't seem odd to me: The adults drank wine, and some of them got silly; we roasted marshmallows, told ghost stories, and squealed with fright. My half-sister Judy—from my dad's first marriage—told me recently that on her infrequent visits she'd used to surreptitiously drink his wine, thinking she could stop him from getting drunk. I just thought my dad was the funniest guy on earth—the word *drunk* was not yet in my lexicon.

Perhaps the behavior that disturbed her happened after I'd gone to bed. Or maybe I just saw what I wanted to see. My Dad was subtly hilarious, sarcastic, smart, loving, and an accomplished and respected actor. My mom *seemed* to giggle along with the rest of us—for me, then, still the ultimate stamp of approval.

At the ranch, the Ritz was the center of our world. A big, functional farmhouse kitchen occupied one wing of the U-shaped, stucco-and-tile building; a huge sunken living room with a massive fireplace and several scratchy horsehair sofas punctuated the far end of the other wing. Mounted steer antlers topped every interior doorway in the house, and barefoot-unfriendly seagrass runners centered every hallway. The artwork was of the Remington school.

Downstairs, embraced by the two parallel wings, was a rough garden with scrappy roses, a threadbare lawn, and a little stone firepit where marshmallows and various denizens of field and stream were sizzled and crisped. Upstairs, a deep, covered porch wrapped the entire circumference of the courtyard. Wooden screen doors led from the porch into each of the many bedrooms that strung out around the ranch house like diamonds on a rattler's back. Inside, there was no hallway; all the bedrooms connected to one another. Every three or four bedrooms, there was a bathroom.

Our menus were classic California Rancho style, informed equally by the bounty of the coast and canyons, and a dash of Mexican influence from the families who had worked the land and the cattle for generations. Flank steak, avocados, seafood, beans, and macaroni and cheese were all constants—deer liver if the hunters were successful—but this was still the Sixties, so convenience food was rife, especially on nights when my picky mother wasn't cooking. The two or three families who often joined us at the ranch brought their own Californian foodways, and this is where I learned that other children were allowed to eat sugary cereals like Lucky Charms and drink 7-Up. These were luxuries I'd always been denied at home because they were considered "middle-class" and "lacking in imagination."

Down at empty, endless Bulito Beach, where we spent so much of our time, the high tide trapped big pockets of seawater far up on the sand, creating, at low tide, a bath-warm lagoon that we called The "Slu." (It would take me years to discover that it was spelled "Slough.") There, we small people could wade and paddle to our hearts delight, happily making popping seaweed necklaces and building dribble-castles far from the chilly, rough-and-tumble Pacific. Since The Slough was so shallow, the adults believed that we couldn't possibly harm ourselves and thus we were spared any possible, if unlikely, parental supervision. After a day at the beach, all the kids would scramble for seats on the edge of the tailgate, where we dipped our toes in the dust as the Rambler bounced over the ruts back up to the Ritz. One day a

Hollister cousin named Charlie Ramsburg shot a huge rattlesnake in the middle of the road just after we'd tucked in our dangling feet, and after the requisite amount of screaming, we grilled it up on the firepit for an hors d'oeuvre.

The other kids were squeamish about snake, but I found it to be quite tasty. My suggestion of butter, however, was shot down with disdain. *Butter is a fine debut, but clearly this pony will need more than one trick.*

The Ranch was still an out-of-time relic of the crudely practical old West, caught between the years of cattle-rearing self-sufficiency and the fast-approaching era when first surfers, then millionaires, and finally wealthy preservationists would claim the windswept terrain as their own. My mother may have suspected it could not last; I assumed that the Ranch—and my happiness, there—would go on forever. But in the early 1970s, 18,000 acres of coastal California was worth far more as real estate than for raising cattle, even if there was a bit of income from oil.

Although there were many dissenting voices, a majority of the many fractious factions of the Hollister family eventually prevailed, and they voted that the Ranch be sold off for development. I was about to lose my key to the world of old Southern California and be relegated to the budding malls, parking lots, and traffic that the rest of the population had no choice but to endure. This was the same fast-disappearing Good Life that Joan Didion mourns in her seminal (for me) book *Where I Was From*.

DURING THE SUMMER OF 1968, the group of adults collected at the Ranch was, as usual, heavily weighted with actors, my father's profession. All I cared about was the kid-quotient: There were plenty of children, and they were all safely of my age group and independent temperament. We set out to do the usual: range around as one nut-brown flock of kids, catch and eat impossibly fresh and crisp trout, prise mussels from the rocks and drown them in butter, and finally, tumble into rumpled beds at the end of each salt-crusted, sun-drenched day. In such numbers, there was a precious element of safety from the harsh pronouncements of my judgmental mother; she became almost normal at the Ranch—perhaps because she herself had once been a child in those deep canyons. *Or maybe she feared the other parents present would see her mothering style as autocratic?*

One night after the kids had gone to bed, one of the assembled adults had the bright idea of bombing on down to the beach and building a great big bonfire. In retrospect, I think it can be assumed that this was a well-lubricated inspiration. The bonfire was duly built, and a wonderful time was evidently had by all—until the moment when one of the invited but non-family actors—we'll call him Ron—was dancing naked around the fire and fell into it. The poor guy's skin actually caught fire, and quick-moving men rolled him in the sand to put out the flames. A helpful voice suggested immediately putting him in the ocean, and they'd all later learn that this action is what had saved his life. It was decided to haul ass back up to the Ritz and calculate the next step.

Although there were plenty of still crisp-minded individuals to handle the emergency action of getting Ron back to the Ritz, the story goes that my dad, now that he'd sobered up a bit, really, really wanted to help them out. My mother—no shrinking violet, certainly—was unable to dissuade him verbally, and when his fumbling but well-meant assistance threatened to slow the process of unloading Ron from the back of the Rambler, she threw a bucket of water at him. Then he punched her. And I mean *out*. And ran off into the piñon pines and scrubby arroyos above the Ritz. Since I was upstairs at the time, it was a few weeks before I found out about this incident, but I wasn't too young or self-possessed to notice that something profound had changed between my parents, beginning with that trip to the Ranch.

Meanwhile, the younger generation was snugly tucked in upstairs. Suddenly the door of my room slammed open with a rude bang, and a large, loud man stumbled in, shouting. His hulking profile was backlit by the bright light from the hallway, and I couldn't make out any features. Was he a nightmare? He seemed larger than any human being I'd ever known and loomed over me like some sort of under-the-bed ogre.

"Where's your good father, my dear?" he expounded theatrically.

Ah. It was dad's friend Judd Pratt, another actor. I'd been asleep for several hours at that point and had no idea, and sleepily told him so. The brouhaha, which, I now realized was permeating the whole of the big house, moved off downstairs.

After this unexpected awakening, we youngsters were forcefully encouraged to "Stay out of this and go back to bed!" Fat chance. We sneaked downstairs to spy on the proceedings, and although the adults were too busy to notice us, an hour or so of clever eavesdropping brought us no closer to understanding what was going on. Eventually we left them to their folly and dragged back up to bed. It never occurred to me that we were being left to fend for ourselves in the midst of a crisis; I just loved that feeling of freedom, of being with the other kids. Later I understood that a more attentive mother might have sought to protect me from the ongoing trauma.

Judd Pratt had sensed the danger that my dad, his drinking buddy, was in, and set out in his own possibly ineffectual way to rescue his old friend. I'm sure my dad would have done the same thing for Judd if their situations were reversed. Perhaps they'd been doing this dangerous dance for decades. This upstairs drama was happening at the same time as the adults downstairs were trying to decide whether to risk the long drive over dangerous roads to Route 1, and then north to the closest hospital, forty miles away in Solvang, or wait until first light.

They decided to wait, and all that long night the heat from the burn was driven further and deeper inside Ron's right arm and leg, meaning that when he did finally get to the hospital, he had third-degree burns over sixty percent of his body and would have to endure three months of painful skin grafts before he could resume his life and career. His face and other delicate parts, thank goodness, hadn't been affected. I remember visiting Ron in the Solvang hospital with my mother several times, still largely in the dark about what had put him there. Within a scant few years, my mother would start referring to the event as "The

Barbecue." I hope this term never made it back to the Barbecue-ee, who may not have found it as amusing.

My father did not come back to the Ritz until the next morning, That morning's conversation between my parents must have been like a tremor along one of California's deeply hidden fault lines, prescient of a destructive shake-up on the surface, approaching fast. I've heard it said that when you lose both of your parents, you truly grow up; that only an orphan can be an adult. Although my parents lived between them another sixty years, that last summer at the Ranch was when I had to grow up.

As soon as we returned to Los Angeles Dad joined Alcoholics Anonymous and found a sponsor. He started to attend twice- and sometimes thrice-weekly meetings and began to blossom in a whole different way; his humor was still dry, his pregnant pauses still full of promise, but the hilarity was tempered. My mother professed disdain for "The Program," which confused me to no end. If it was helpful to her husband's mental and physical state, why wouldn't she support him? I went to Al-a-Teen meetings to learn about the disease of alcoholism and how it affected the alcoholic's family. Dad developed a powerful affinity for cookies and hid them away from my mother's stern gaze and commentary. She never went to an Al-Anon meeting (supportive forums for the spouses of A.A. members to share and benefit from others' experiences with their very own drinkers). She proclaimed that A.A. was a crutch, rather than a lifesaver.

My dad told me many years later that he had been an alcoholic for a long time, hiding a bottle of vodka in the garage when I was little because it didn't make his breath smell of booze, while quaffing liters of Soave Bolla in polite company. In general, children remember most things that happen after the age of four. But the only questionable thing I could recall during this pre-1968 era was coming downstairs one morning to find handprints all over the butter. In a break from tradition, it was my normally late-rising mother who inhabited the kitchen that morning.

"What happened to the butter, Mommy?" I asked.

"Your father threw it at the ceiling last night," she responded, sugar-sweetly.

I lived with an actor for a father and was surrounded by other actors and creatives; it wasn't as if flamboyant gestures were new to me. I had no idea there was a problem, but I did know that my mother was routinely and vocally very angry with my father, and that he often seemed uncharacteristically dejected, not his beloved funny self. I was also conscious that he was never equally vocal in defending himself against her disdain, and I couldn't understand why he didn't just stand up to her. Through my thin young skin, I absorbed that she could be dangerous, and others might be helpless against her wrath.

After the Barbecue, however, everything changed. When my father stopped drinking, my mother lost the power of rightness over him. Their arguments began to take on a different tone; he seemed to be gaining some ability to stand up to her. Hangdog no more, his life gradually became the healthy and sane one he wanted to live. Within a year he had shifted his base of operations to the East Coast, leaving me behind with just his frequent, chatty but superficial letters to provide some proof of paternal love. As far as I know he never, ever took another alcoholic drink in his remaining twenty-two years of life.

After he left—some might say abandoned—his home and family in California, my mom turned her genteel venom upon the only remaining member of the household, me, now all of 13 years old. More alone than ever, I gradually developed my own powerful methods of defense—arguably, even offense—against her potent and always exquisitely reasoned vitriol. I was grateful to inherit her sharp mind, but wrapped up the sharp tongue that came with it in layers of tissue and put it away in a locked chest. But I always know it's there, and it would be wrong to say I have never taken it out for a walk.

Since the days when I lost the Ranch and my assumption that the concepts of all good and all bad would maintain their separate identities, I continue to search for my old California. Up the coast in Santa

Barbara where, by rights, it should be, the landscape is suffocating under a sticky varnish of money. So I go farther afield, and wherever I can sit among dust and scrub, or oak and piñon, and watch the setting sun turn the hills golden, then lavender, then gray, I tentatively begin to feel at home. It's happened in Sedona, west Texas, the high desert of southern California, southern Spain, and the hills outside Siena. And yet—the horizon is always too close, the hills too populated, the house too small and too empty. And there is certainly no wide-eyed, brown-haired girl playing vainly at Happy Families.

EDDIE, MARCIA, JUDY & E.G. MARSHALL ON THE TOWN IN NYC

CHAPTER 2

all that glitters

NEW YORK AND LOS ANGELES, 1963-1967

WHEN I WAS BORN, my father already had another family in Minneapolis. Some might say he'd abandoned them, too.

He'd met his first wife Katherine, known as Kaddy, performing in summer stock theatre before World War II, ranging up and down the Hudson Valley with a bunch of other kids and a few real actors. Kaddy's family in Minneapolis was quite wealthy and Dad apparently liked the feeling of class she exuded. They married just before World War II. In family legend he'd shared with her the momentous news that he'd enlisted in the army, by telephone. When Kaddy spoke again her voice was shrill, reedy, scratchy, like cats yarping their temporary love across the rooftops. Only this wasn't temporary: A condition called hysterical laryngitis dogged Kaddy for the rest of her life. A myth? All I knew for sure was that fifteen years later her voice on the phone still sounded (and felt) like fingernails on a blackboard.

When their two daughters Nancy and Judy were quite young, Kaddy was committed to a mental hospital. My rakish dad simply had zero ability to care for the young girls, so he farmed them out to various relatives until Kaddy was released. Kaddy's parents in Minneapolis arranged for her and the two girls to live a simple, quiet life in a tiny house nearby. Shortly after that, my father divorced Kaddy. A year or so later when on tour with the play *The Lark* in San Francisco—playing opposite Julie Harris—he met and not long afterward married my mother.

The two older daughters grew up in Minneapolis with their quite fragile mother but spent summers in Los Angeles with their brand-spanking-new stepmother and infant sister, me. Nancy is ten years older than me, Judy, six. Much later they told me that, at least at the beginning, their arrival in Los Angeles for the summer was by far the best moment of their year. The glamorous L.A. life was completely unlike their Minneapolis existence, and for the first week or so, everything was happy-happy. Then the anger, judgment, and unrelenting disappointment began to creep out.

On one of her last summer visits to Los Angeles, at 15, Nancy got off the plane from Minneapolis "fat," according to my mother.

"Oh dear, what's happened to you?! Well, Miss Nanny B, we're just going to fix you this summer!"

With a singular desire to help Nancy escape this "fate-worse-than-death," my mother set out on a summer-long campaign to help Nancy lose weight. The road to hell being paved with good intentions, my mother studied up on calories and weight loss, and over the course of two months, Nancy shed many pounds. But my mother could never understand why Nancy was not more grateful for her efforts. After that summer, Nancy radically distanced herself from the woman who would remain officially her stepmother for another twenty years.

When MLB related this story to me many years later—still slightly perplexed and even a bit hurt—I offered up this insight: "I think girls that age have a very hard time with self-confidence. Maybe she felt judged, and less attractive than you, her glamorous stepmom, and by drawing attention to her weight, you made her feel even more insecure."

"Well, I couldn't help it. I was evidently more attractive than Nancy."

Correspondence about the summer visits was exclusively between Kaddy and my mother; my dad did not participate.

EXCERPT FROM A LETTER FROM MARCIA BINNS TO KATHERINE (KADDY) BINNS, OCTOBER 1960:

> *About Judy, it's true that both of us have been concerned for some time. After the past two summers, we've had to admit to ourselves that there is definitely something wrong. More than just "immaturity". Whether it's a problem of low I.Q. —the easy conclusion to jump to—or whether it's something more subtle such as emotional disturbance that blocks her thought process, we are not equipped to know without proper tests."*

EXCERPT FROM A LETTER FROM KADDY BINNS TO EDWARD AND MARCIA BINNS, NOVEMBER 1960

> *I had a conference with Judy's teacher and the principal of the school. They said that Judy is an introvert, speaks quietly, is well above the national average of the Standard Achievement tests, excels in language, participates fully and is well adjusted at school. In view of these facts, she cannot be referred to the school psychiatrist, as she definitely is not a misfit.*

Years later, Judy wrote to me: "By the way, Dad and your mom never did send me to a psychiatrist at UCLA for tests. They decided they couldn't afford it. They were both so blind about my perplexing behavior. But they got a little close to the reasons when your mom said it is like I have two different personalities, one for Minneapolis and one for California. What they didn't get is that it was their fault. They treated us badly, and we felt unloved."

Soon after my mother's death, I went to meet with a psychologist we'd shared when I was a teenager, Irene G. I needed closure, understanding, some way to lay this demon to rest so that it would not sit on my shoulder stabbing me in the heart for the rest of my life. The therapist, shockingly still practicing in her UCLA office, had counseled MLB off and on, with me and without me, for decades. Perhaps she would offer me something helpful.

"I can understand your confusion, and I can tell you that your mother was the most narcissistic person I ever encountered in my career," Irene told me. "You were like an accessory to her, like a cute purse that matched her shoes. She was shocked when you turned out to have a personality of your own."

I gave myself permission to feel vindicated. I was 54 years old.

DAD HAD TO BE IN NEW YORK FREQUENTLY FOR WORK, so my mom and I flew out to join him several times a year. They rented a small, well-worn apartment on the third floor of 123 E. 62nd Street from when I was age two to about ten. My "room" was a tall but tiny closet, with a skylight set into the ceiling several miles above the crib-like bed. When we weren't there, the apartment was frequently sublet to others, so my mother took pictures of the precise positions of her kitchen gadgets on the pegboard in the kitchen alcove. The pictures were taped next to the pegboard so that all residents would hang the garlic press/measuring spoons/vegetable steamer in its precise, correct position. Kind of like the outline of bodies at a murder scene.

On one early TWA flight, I sat next to my mother while the two of us critiqued the dinner offering.

"I'm not sure this should *really* be called Peach Melba," she proclaimed, dubiously examining an assembly of canned peaches topped with a grainy swirl of whipped cream and a maraschino cherry. She'd told me such cherries were made of "cardboard and horse's hooves," so I should never, ever eat one. One of us, likely her, came up with a new name for the dish: "Peach Maybe." At the age of eight, I was thrilled to have this glamorous creature all to myself for once, and desperate to be as much fun as she was.

Our life in New York was all about the theatre. I quickly learned how to pretend to mingle during the intermission, stealthily lurking next to little clumps of chatting audience members while pretending not to eavesdrop. Later, I'd breathlessly report to one or more parents:

"They thought the second act was really engaging!"

I yearned to catch my dad, or whomever we were visiting, back-stage after the performance, before they'd fully changed out of costume and removed their makeup. When the applause died down—I always cried at curtain calls—I rushed to the stage door ahead of everyone else or, on rare occurrences when the stage manager was friendly, across the actual stage to be the very first audience member backstage. I was intrigued with that moment when the actor settled back into his or her true self and cast off the character they had played.

When I grow up, I'm going to be an actress.

On opening nights, we went to Sardi's, and I adored all the caricatures on the wall in the bar. My half-sisters were off on their own adventures by this time, so I was effectively an only child, always the sole kid around, getting dragged to places that were not traditionally kid-friendly. I loved it.

My mother took me to see a dizzying array of "important" Broadway shows in the mid-to-late sixties and early seventies, almost all of them in their early incarnations with the original cast: Richard Kiley in *Man From La Mancha*, Lauren Bacall in *Cactus Flower*, Jason Robards in *A Thousand Clowns*, Angela Lansbury in *Mame*, the original cast of *A Chorus Line*. We even saw Carol Channing in *Hello Dolly!* With my mom-mandated pixie cut, plastic headband, and horn-rimmed glasses, I was a distinctly unglamorous hanger-on, trailing down the avenues behind my whirlwind of a mother.

Now I understand what a heady time it was to be in and around the theatre in Manhattan. I might even admit that I'm grateful.

WHEN WE WERE AT HOME IN CALIFORNIA, MLB worked late into the night—often until 4 a.m.—on nebulous busy-work: obsessively re-editing her personal correspondence, transcribing recorded phone conversations, or tinkering with the book she'd sold but never finished. (Eventually, the publisher's advance had to be returned). Consequently, she did not arise daily until noonish. It fell to my often at-home father, very possibly hungover, to make breakfast for his willful little daughter. He always asked, with unsinkable hope, what I would like.

"Weenie-and-Egg!" I'd yell. Every. Single. Day. (Recipe pg. 285) This closeness was precious to me; an entire secret world existed between me and my dad in that time before she emerged and grabbed control of the day.

*　*　*

I WOULD SPEND THE REST OF HIS LIFE yearning for a return of those Weenie-and-Egg moments.

I was told that when I first learned to walk, I was full of explosive energy and a fierce desire to be snuggled in the lonely mornings of an only child. Before she went to bed late at night, my mother hung a hairbrush on the closed door of her bedroom. Right at a toddler's eye level, it was there to remind me that if I woke her up, she would use it to spank my bottom until I screamed, my face bright red and tear-streaked. *Where was my dad while this was happening?*

When I was almost three, the half-sisters were visiting for the summer and had been delegated to look after me one afternoon while my parents went out. Nancy, at twelve and a half, was as usual named as the responsible party. Escaping from my nap while the sisters' attention was elsewhere, I toddled unseen up to my mother's vanity table. Likely enticed by the aroma of Chanel No. 5, I drank the whole bottle down. When the parents returned, all assembled were treated to the sight of a falling-down-drunk two-and-a-half-year-old. Stumbling, face-planting, and slurring the few words I had, I was apparently quite an amusing sight, and much hilarity was enjoyed by all. Until someone suggested this might be dangerous. I was rushed, rather belatedly, to Santa Monica Hospital where my stomach was pumped. After the laughter died down, the recriminations began. Nancy was blamed for this crisis, and a "far more trustworthy" neighbor of exactly Nancy's age was detailed to "baby-sit" all us girls for the rest of the summer. Nancy still burns from the humiliation. Fun times.

I must have had an affinity for the smell. At the age of ten I accidentally broke another bottle in the shared bathroom at our house on

Kiel Street in Brentwood. Mom made me cover the cost of replacing it out of my allowance, which at $1 per month took me eight and a half months. Today, the smell of Chanel No. 5 makes me gag.

AS A YOUNG GIRL, I had little to do in the mornings, which stretched out like the frozen food aisle of a late nineteen-fifties supermarket, appearing ripe with colorful promise but boxed away and unavailable. Believing that television was a crutch that would rot the brain of any and all children, Mom hid the electrical cord to the TV.

After reading *A Wrinkle in Time*, *The Chronicles of Narnia* (twice), and all the Nancy Drew mysteries, I began to plumb the family bookshelves. There I discovered a book called *Candy* by the comedians Terry Southern and Mason Hoffenburg. Perhaps I was attracted by the title; at the age of 11, I still had a sweet tooth. But *Candy* the book—later a film with Brando, Burton, John Huston, John Astin, Walter Matthau, and Ringo Starr, which is so horrible it's actually wonderful—was not in any way about candy.

In fact, *Candy* was an erotic satire about a luscious but naïve young sexual being and her exceedingly graphic, naughty adventures and misadventures with various men, boys, doctors, hunchbacks, gurus, and gardeners. I read it over and over again, trying to parse the book's meaning with the brain of a solitary but precocious pre-teen. Instead of *Bugs Bunny* or *Gilligan's Island* or *Casper the Friendly Ghost*, I immersed myself in graphically depicted sex, in which lecherous and despicable characters preyed upon an innocent ingenue. The tongue-in-cheek goal of the authors, whose intention was to write a sexual farce, was completely lost on me.

I saw poor, pretty Candy as a role model, and I would play that particular role well for quite some time. I did not realize for decades that she was a manipulated and naive victim, because I was focused on what my brain perceived to be her hypnotic power over men.

Once when I was little, my mother smashed her finger, and the fingernail turned ugly and bubbled and black, then eventually fell off. My father, still a drinker at the time, played tooth fairy and replaced the fingernail she'd placed under her pillow with a bottle of gin. Much hilarity all around.

When my parents first met in San Francisco in 1956, the cocktail hour was sacrosanct. I imagine the two of them standing over their cocktails, my father still amused by her affectations. How long did this amusement last? Certainly not beyond the point, just ten years later, when he joined AA and forswore booze in perpetuity.

On a shelf in the glass-fronted bar cabinet in the home I've lived in for 12+ years sits a small glass pitcher. It has a helper-handle on one side, and a Victorian-lady shape, cinched tight toward the neck above a fulsome, rounded bottom. Above the cinch the shape widens out again, with a tiny, rounded spout to one side, opposite the handle. Viewed with no knowledge of its history, this is an organically pleasing piece. It seems to speak of ripe gourds full of promise, of water burbling over stones in a pristine mountain creek. There is a faint grayish cast to the glass, which may or may not have been blown by mouth from one lump of virgin glass; there are no seams to be found. When I was 11 years old, I was trained to stir a few ounces of gin in this pitcher, over ice, for precisely 100 turns-of-a-chopstick. Not 99. Not 101. Over time, the movement of the ice wore a belt of cloudiness into the widest point of the pitcher. This is its only imperfection. The pitcher has traveled: From Pasadena to New York to Nassau to San Francisco to West Los Angeles to Paso Robles California. For my mother, her every-other-night gin martini was a moment of repose, and escape from the vagaries and outrages of the day. Its ceremony was crucial to its enjoyment.

Soon after we unloaded the things I'd decided to save from my mother's home after her death, I made a martini—gin natch—

in the pitcher. No one has touched it since.

In this house, we shake.

THE THREE-PERSON BINNS FAMILY frequented three restaurants in nearby Westwood Village. Up at the top of the first really big office building in the then-sleepy UCLA-adjacent community, there was a brand-new penthouse restaurant, the Westwood Marquis, with stunning views. The Marquis was a special-occasions-only spot, and I *always* ordered twelve *escargots* as a main course. The server would peer at me incredulously.

"Are you sure that's what you want, little girl?" Unsaid: You know those are *snails*, right, honey?

"Yes, please, sir."

A few doors down was Le Foyer de France, a coffin-sized cafeteria-style spot with a steam table, run by actual French people. Once I discovered the seafood *vol-au-vents* I was hooked: Little towers of shatteringly crisp and golden puff pastry were filled to overflowing with a creamy concoction of various fish and shellfish, then topped with a crispy golden "hat." I never saw the point of ordering anything else. This was a go-to spot for Dad and me when my mother was "working."

Then there was Mario's, an Italian restaurant on the corner of Weyburn and Gayley. The manicotti was absolutely heavenly: soft pasta tubes stuffed with ricotta, then blanketed with tomato sauce and lots of mozzarella. The semi-circular booths fit a family of three like a glove.

For dessert, if I was very lucky: Wil Wrights Ice Cream Parlor, across from Le Foyer, all pink-and-white stripes and fancy wire-framed chairs and marble tables. The marshmallow sundae was my favorite.

Jack's at The Beach was a clubby bar and restaurant at the Santa Monica Pier. Ten-year-olds are not famous for their patience when grown-ups sit around and drink for hours. After about ten minutes, I liked to slide down the red faux-leather banquette and set up camp on the carpet under the table. Passing waiters slipped me colorful plastic mermaid drink decorations, and I played house with these drink sticks on the beer-soaked carpet.

I remember a time of innocent joy in being with my family back then, hairbrush spankings aside, but clearly my mother had already begun to find faults in my nascent character.

I was ten years old and already learning the Art of War.

EXCERPTS FROM MY SELF-IMPROVEMENTS PROJECT PAGE, AT AGE TEN (SIC):

BB: "I must be more considerate."

MLB: "Yes."

BB: "I should use my head more."

MLB: "Give examples."

BB: "I should knot act as if I know so much."

MLB: "Examples?"

BB: "I should not misenterpot my elders when they no so much more than me."

MLB: "Do you believe this?"

BB: "I should grow up."

MLB: "How?"

BB: "I should lie less and tell the truth more."

MLB: "Not good enough."

BB: "Impossible to explain."

MLB: "Not acceptable."

BB: "I shouldn't of run off like I did today, I could have been killed by the cars on Sunset:

MLB: "Write it correctly. Pretty self-centered thinking."

BB: "I have to grow up sometime, so I must look ahead to see what I can do improve myself."

MLB: "Give example."

BB: "Too bad."

MLB: "Do the whole thing over in legible writing and sincerity. [A] perfect example you don't mean a word of what you have written."

SUAVE DAD ON THE
ITALIAN COAST

MR. AND MRS. BINNS' FIRST CLASS PORTRAIT

Photo credit: Marcia Legere Binns

Photo credit: Staff photographer, *The Italian Line*

rearranging the deck chairs

ITALY, 1969

IN 1969 MY MOTHER HAD ENVISIONED and then implemented an extended family trip to Italy for the summer. In the family of an actor, this kind of planning is akin to a death wish. If you don't foresee work, you plan a trip. Bingo! You get a job, and the trip is scuttled. But hope springs eternal.

By the time I was 11, Nancy and Judy were busy with their own lives and the summer visits to L.A. had evaporated. Thus, the Italy trip. Supposedly it would cement the bonds that had frayed between my mother and her two stepdaughters. By this time, my sisters, particularly Nancy, the eldest, viscerally disliked my mother, who certainly had not yet fully realized this. In the irrational hope that some stepmothers carry around, Mom sought to fix the un-fixable.

Through a friend at the American embassy in Rome, my mother was introduced to an older English couple in the teensy village of Ansedonia, near Orbetello on the west coast about 200 kilometers north of Rome. They worked for the W.H.O. and were about to embark on a two-month sabbatical in Africa, during which time they were more than happy to rent their house to the Binns family.

But first we would have to get there. Our fearless leader selected the Italian Line, on the ship *Michelangelo*, as the method of our ocean crossing. My parents went first-class, while middle sister Judy and I were assigned to steerage. Nancy, on summer break from college at Barnard in New York City, would fly over with her boyfriend, Jimmy; there was no time nor budget for them to join in our indulgent crossing.

Just one short week before our departure, Dad got a work call. But it was the exact opposite of the call all actor's families desire/fear: A very nice producer was, yes indeed, offering Dad a really sweet acting job that summer—but in a surrealistic twist, the job was *in Italy*. In fact, just a stone's throw from Ansedonia, on the isthmus of Monte Argentario in the town of Porto Santo Stefano. Robert Wagner's show *It Takes a Thief* (an obvious imitation of Cary Grant's iconic collaboration with Grace Kelly, *To Catch a Thief*) would be filming in Italy all summer, and Dad was asked to take over the role of Wagner's character's boss (previously played by Malachi Throne). There was no audition; this was an actual offer—as rare in the world of episodic television then as a fifty-year-old leading lady. And this offer involved multiple episodes. Eureka! In retrospect, this seems less like magic and more like a smart casting director, who'd gotten wind that my father would be in Italy during the shoot, thus saving the production some money on travel.

I still have the felt-tip-marker drawings I made of our embarkation on the good ship *Michelangelo*. There were confetti and streamers; those staying behind on the shore (Nancy) held one end of the long, kinky crepe runners, while the lucky departing held the other end. Eventually, as the ponderous ship was pushed gently away from the dock by an adorable little tugboat, the streamers broke.

Another kind of rope defined our separation while onboard the ship: a velvet one. This separated the steerage folks from the denizens of first class. (See *Titanic*.) For seven days, I was blissfully free from the peering, all-seeing eyes of my main critic. This was a form of abandonment I could embrace! Judy, sixteen to my eleven, found other people her age to pal around with. I concentrated on matters of the table. For seven days, I ordered Fettucine Alfredo three times a day, debarking in Cannes sporting what appeared to be a concealed basketball under my dress.

For the trip, my parents had purchased a brand-new Super-8 movie camera. The old one, a "regular-8," was bestowed upon me with deeply serious exhortations to protect it at all costs, including with my life. One afternoon in the shipboard movie theater, while wholly entranced by *Planet of the Apes*, I stowed the camera in its plastic pouch under my seat. Several hours later I realized my error and rushed back to the theatre. It was gone. In deep and mortified fear for my life, I sought out Judy.

"What am I going to do?" I wailed, abject with bone-deep fear. "She will *kill* me! Seriously, I am not kidding: she will literally kill me." I felt like I was falling from the deck of the ship in slow motion, with piranhas boiling in the waters below, just like in the James Bond movie *You Only Live Twice*.

Judy counseled calm and insisted the camera would be recovered at Lost and Found. It was not. For the rest of the trip, I saw nothing: not the white-tipped blue waves crashing along the sides of the ship, not the fashionable Euro-teenager clothes on the other kids, not the fine spectacle of a pre-teen boy walking his two Italian greyhounds every morning and evening at the stern of the ship, visions that once might have given me such joy. I saw only the moment when I would have to confess to my mother that I had lost the camera. I held my heart in my mouth whenever it was not actually full of Fettuccine Alfredo. The only pleasant moments on the ship occurred when I awoke each morning on the top level of my rickety bunk bed and spent two minutes of bliss before I remembered The Camera.

Almost before we'd settled into the lovely little house in Ansedonia, with its verdant garden and sparkling view of the Tyrrhenian Sea, my mother announced that she was not going to get stuck cooking for the family more than one night per week. A system was put into place:

Cooking responsibilities would be on a democratic rotation, and when it rolled around to Dad's night we'd go out to dinner in nearby Orbetello.

One day we three sisters went to the butcher in town to secure a rump roast for dinner. Peering into our phrase book, we stammered out our request. A bevy of black-dressed ladies emitted outraged gasps and pulled away from us physically as if we'd emitted a trio of audible farts.

We learned later that we'd asked for a "piece of ass."

On her first night of cooking, Judy seared off all her eyebrows trying to light the gas oven. On my first night, I prepared a packet of powdered cream of mushroom soup but failed to stir the mixture thoroughly. Little pockets of undissolved powder lurked in the innocuous white soup, prompting my father to come up with an amusing taunt that he would repeat for many decades, especially after my career veered into the culinary realm.

"I know—let's have undissolved cream of mushroom soup tonight!" he'd chide me. Over, and over.

Filming for *It Takes a Thief* took place in and around Porto Santo Stefano for a couple of weeks. One location was on a motor-yacht right in the port, another at a stunning villa on a hill overlooking the port that had been rented from the head of Fiat, Gianni Agnelli. Fred Astaire, perfectly cast as Wagner's character's father Alistair in multiple episodes, was dapper and debonair and I was awed to be in his presence, as was anyone even remotely connected to the production. It was like straddling two distinct eras in Hollywood.

Astaire was treated like a king yet behaved like a true gentleman and made everyone feel like a million bucks. My mother was in her element, clad in late-sixties-era paisley mini dresses with matching *chapeaux*. She was as close as she was ever going to get to Audrey Hepburn in *Two for The Road*, an actress she liked to consider her *doppelganger* in a movie that reeked of glamorous malaise.

Tall, slim, even lithe—my mother was a sparkling, designer-dressed harridan armed with a typewriter. A social drinker only, she was a drinker with style. In her purse, always until her later years: a perfume atomizer filled with vermouth. She would order gin on the rocks with a chilled martini glass on the side. She stirred the gin until it was frigid, then decanted it into the waiting glass. For the final act, she'd mist a spritz of vermouth over the ice-flecked gin. My mother was quite taken with the theatricality of her concoction. In fact, whenever—and wherever—she overheard the "pop" of a Champagne cork, she would instantly trill "They're playing my song!" and bat her eyelashes. Some people found this fetching.

In Italy, my mother was beside herself with excitement as Dad strapped a rubber boat atop the rented Citroën and packed the inside with Nancy, Judy, me, various bathing suits, towels, and sun lotion, and a wooden oar for the boat. We headed up the coast a bit to the Wagners' resort for a day of lunch and Italian-style beach fun. Bob Wagner was still married to Marion Donen at the time and their daughter Katie was about 4. The Citroën was a strange vehicle, like a dome on the outside with its famous, proprietary hydraulic system that caused it to raise and lower at stoplights like a horny iguana. As we motored north, we girls were crammed into the back seat with our feet atop the wooden oar. Suddenly a car going south, waiting in the left-turn lane, turned directly in front of us, and we hit it head-on. Hard. Everyone in the car was thrown around like tennis shoes in a dryer, and it took several moments to discover that we were all alive and mostly well. Dad had gripped the steering wheel so hard that he dislocated his thumb, which was the most painful injury sustained, besides the scrapes and scratches bestowed on back-seat riders by the oar.

The crash had occurred just in front of a large roadside restaurant, and Good Samaritans rushed out to help, pulling Dad out of the driver's seat and immediately attempting to dose him with a good shot of brandy. Dad, barely a year into AA, waved it away forcefully. The car, which we were supposed to return to Citroën at the end of the summer, was totaled. But it had saved our lives: the hydraulic system absorbed the bulk of the impact and the heavy gauge metal that made the car drive like a tank had protected all of us from dire injury.

When the *Polizia* dropped us at the *ospedale,* we all waited in a hallway dotted with buckets of discarded, bloody rags. There was no room available, so a kind *dottore* re-located Dad's thumb in the hallway without benefit of anesthetic. Dad howled like a banshee. Our idyllic beach lunch with the Wagners was not to be; my mother's social-climbing plans were crushed. But my father had stayed true to his commitment to AA. I always wondered if she resented his strength. Perhaps she preferred the weakened version of my dad from his drinking days.

There is a photo, taken not long after the crash, when Dad's hand was in a cast. It was much smaller than the costume cast he wore in the movie *Night Moves*—the one that went from shoulder-to-waist with a metal brace holding it out from his torso—when he was trying to kill Gene Hackman with a propeller plane. In the photo from Italy, all three of his daughters are hovering over him, Nancy and Judy lathering his hair with shampoo, me standing awkwardly at his head, lamely soaping up his salt 'n' pepper beard. Always feeling like a wallflower, I was an only child with two sisters, except they weren't really my sisters. I was well aware of the significance of the label "half."

COPY FROM *THE HOLLYWOOD REPORTER*, 8/7/69:

> *Ed Binns and family are alive today, thanks only to seat belts. In Rome for "To Catch a Thief," (sic) guesting, Ed decided to take the family for a drive in the country, but cautiously settled only for a rented Citroën with seat belts front & rear. Hit by a careening truck head-on, the car folded like an accordion, but Ed suffered only a dislocated thumb, while wife and their three offspring needed treatment only for shock and minor bruises.*

Dad was a hero to us three daughters for the rest of that summer. In an attempt to live *La Dolce Vita,* he bought a fresh sea urchin from a fisherman in the marina of Porto Ercole as we strolled by the water.

"See girls, you just snip the top of this spiny globe—watch out for the sharp spikes, girls—and then you just scoop out the tasty bright orange roes and slurp 'em down. This is how the pros do it!" (*Slurp*).

We were slack-jawed. Trouble is, he didn't know how to clean an urchin and ended up with a mouthful of yuckiness. The fisherman stifled a grin below bright eyes; my mother rolled hers.

One day about two weeks before the end of the trip, my mother asked me where the old movie camera was. I could barely speak. I couldn't even breathe. There was no choice but to fess up, which I did while choking and sobbing and stuttering out the sad, lame story.

She was "very, very disappointed" in me. I had failed her, and Judy had failed her, too, by not telling on me. The entire family would suffer. I ran to the partially underground bedroom that had been assigned to me and cried so hard and so long that I almost suffocated, gulping for air like a fish pulled from the safety of the sea. Nancy came to comfort me, the only one who was blame-free since she had not been on the ship when my crime had been committed. She would not remain blame-free for long. By the end of the summer, Nancy would have committed a far more heinous offense.

Actors have a way of becoming thick as thieves during a play or filming; literally, they often think of themselves as family—then never see one another again. We socialized with Bob Wagner and family a few times back in L.A. and Palm Springs, and that was the end of it. And anyway, by that time Marion Donen was out and Natalie Wood was back in again.

It was time for everyone to leave Italy. My increasingly ill-tempered parents would motor up to Paris through northern Italy and southern France—another chance to pretend she was in *Two For the Road*, except without the mutual boozing. Oddly, it seemed that the lack of boozing on my father's part was contributing to their unhappiness. Nancy had already returned to New York, and I was to join her and stay in her shared apartment near Columbia for a few days before going up to spend a month with the daughter of renowned mystery writer Rex Stout (creator of Nero Wolfe) and her young family in Redding, Connecticut. Judy returned to Minneapolis.

I flew alone to New York. The stewardesses thought I was very brave for an eleven-year-old and plied me with Shirley Temples. Unsupervised in Nancy's apartment, I somehow managed to score a box of blond hair dye, and followed the weird instructions in her communal bathroom, gasping from the fumes. Blonde! I was suddenly a blonde! I would have more fun, I felt certain. When my mother found out that Nancy sent me on to Connecticut alone on a bus, she melted down. Nancy was, literally, never forgiven. Like *never*. But by this point, such hyperbolic rhetoric meant very little to Nancy.

And then, when my mother saw the blonde hair a month later back in Los Angeles, she grimly steered me to a Beverly Hills salon where a fancy stylist painstakingly returned my hair to its natural dark brown.

"Don't wash your hair for a day or so, sweetie" the stylist admonished.

I rushed home and washed my hair immediately. Yippee, blonde again!

Disgusted, my mother let me live with the awkward process, as the blond grew out on its own. My seventh-grade class picture shows the unfortunate result: dark brown for about four inches down from the roots, then bottle-blonde below a sharp horizontal dividing line.

I was gleefully unrepentant. At about this time, my mother had my braces removed two years before my teeth had finished their straightening process, because she "didn't want to spend any more money" on improving her "Rottenkid."

The battle lines had been drawn.

Peace, please

CHAPTER 4

a damned dirty low-down thing

LOS ANGELES, 1970-1972

I WAS 11 YEARS OLD WHEN MY MOTHER ANNOUNCED to me that my father was impotent. This, she explained in a giggly, conspiratorial tone, was why she had a "Mr. X." in her life. Perhaps there was some further reasoning, I don't recall. It didn't take long for her to break down and admit his identity,

"It's your Uncle Pat."

My godfather Uncle Pat, a.k.a "The Guv," a.k.a Edmund G. "Pat" Brown, Governor of California from 1959 to 1967 (and father of Governor Jerry Brown), had been a part of my life ever since I could remember. He was generous on my birthdays, and we had lunch together with MLB at Pepino's in Brentwood Village at least once a month. He seemed to get along with my father, though I rarely if ever saw them together. His bookish appearance—Poindexter glasses, round face, barrel chest always perfectly buttoned-up—belied a hail-fellow-well-met boisterous nature. He was a politician through and through, never forgetting a name and always with a little joke or snippet of personal encouragement on the tip of his tongue.

"Never marry a man who doesn't have a good belly-laugh," the Guv always exhorted me starting from the age of 10.

He and my mother had met when Pat was still the Attorney General of California, around 1955, not long before she was introduced to my father.

FROM THE ONLINE ARCHIVES OF CALIFORNIA; *THE EARL WARREN ORAL HISTORY PROJECT*:

> *"As a matter of fact, the Ford Foundation had retained a gal by the name of Marcia Binns (I think it was the Ford Foundation—some foundation), and she came in to see me on some of my civil rights stands and positions. She was assigned by the Ford Foundation to spotlight any place in the West, anything of a civil rights nature.*
>
> *She came into my office. I can't remember the particular case, but there was some particular case. There must have been ten or fifteen occasions in the next six years, or five years. After that she high- lighted in the media things that I did. It really was very helpful to me in my campaign for the governor. She put them on television. Later, when I became the governor, I was so appreciative of what she'd done, I put her on the board of trustees of the women's prison. As a matter of fact, she's been a friend of mine ever since."*

Uncle Pat was the kind of man who referred to women as "gals."

He was her senior by about 25 years, and at first, it appears my mother saw him as a father figure—having never had one in her life, she was always on the prowl. One has to assume that he preferred a different role for himself. It's not entirely clear when the relationship became physical, but I believe it was after 1957, absolving me from the need to doubt my paternity. Up until I was 11, he was, simply, my godfather. When I was 2, he had been elected governor of California, a role he'd serve in until 1967, when he lost to Ronald Reagan. In 1964 after stepping into a hole on the golf course and breaking his ankle, he sent me the following letter, on gubernatorial stationary:

August 21, 1964
Miss Brigit Binns
11338 Kiel Street
Los Angeles 49, California

Dear Brigit:

After I broke my ankle bone I received many letters. But the best one I received was from Brigit Binns.

I think you are the greatest painter I have ever seen, and tell your mother and father I think you should exhibit your work at the State Fair where they give prizes to little girls who paint. Whether you win one or not, your pictures made me feel much better.

I am already out of the cast and ready to nominate the president. Sincerely,

"The Guv"
Edmund G. Brown, Governor

Ever the politician.

Strangely, my estimation of Uncle Pat didn't change much after I found out that they were having an "affair," if I even knew what that meant. This was Hollywood, after all, and marriage was not exactly a sacrosanct institution. He was simply an extended family member, though one whose real family I somehow never met. He was funny and warm and loving, and he gave my mother expensive gifts that made her happy. I sensed that I shouldn't tell my friends about my mother and Uncle Pat, but this awareness didn't stop me from normalizing the arrangement. *Mom thinks it's okay, so it's okay, right? According to her, only small-minded people are uptight about such things.*

Dad often fielded phone calls from Pat—she had a visceral horror of being interrupted when she was "working." My dad seemed oddly encouraging of their affair; he may have been relieved to get her off his back. Some of the work she did at that time involved a book about capital punishment, which she was co-authoring with Uncle Pat. He'd commuted the death sentences of 23 condemned convicts, and later appointed my mother to serve on the board of parole at the women's prison in Pomona. Diane Feinstein was on the board, too, and I remember a nice playdate with her children where I learned about crossword puzzles for the first time. But the friendship didn't last. My mother's private diary entries about Feinstein were scathing.

My mother had the idea to interview inmates who had been on death row before Pat's commutations—convicts who had returned to productive lives rather than being executed. It wasn't hard to secure a book advance with "The Guv" attached ("The Guv" being his license plate until his death). The work went on sporadically over several years until the publisher got fed up with her endless delays and excuses and clawed back the advance. Pat went on to write the book with another writer, a move that caused my mother to be intermittently and caustically furious with him over the next almost two decades of their tumultuous romance. One of her main beefs with Pat was his calling at all hours of the day and night and expecting her to be available to chat on the phone. This was "wanton disrespect," she said, and showed his "utter contempt" for her work.

She had a separate phone line installed and refused to give Pat the number, at least for about a year. After that, I always knew that when it rang, it was Pat; the line was otherwise never used for incoming calls. In her safe after she passed away, I found a packet of their incendiary and passionate letters and micro-cassette tapes; it was marked "Open at Your Own Risk." She kept carbon copies of every letter she ever wrote to him, and many originals from him to her. I can't fathom why Pat continued to pursue the relationship, long after it had ceased to be physical and in view of the contemptuous criticism she heaped upon him. An old friend of hers with some connections in the world of espionage had helped her find and install a gadget that could record both sides of a phone call. She taped and saved many of her phone calls with Pat and others, including me. On one occasion, she revealed to Pat that she knew he was breaking a promise, because she'd recorded a previous call.

He went silent for a moment, and then: "Well, that's a damned dirty low-down thing to do."

Pat was the kind of man who said things like "damned dirty low-down."

In a carbon copy of a 1980s-era letter to her lifelong friend, the director Frank Perry, she related her feelings about Pat, here describing him in the past tense due to some recent battle and/or breakup, one of so very many over the years. This was also a thinly veiled nod to the fact that he was, at that moment, *dead to her*:

> *The key word is Passion. There are few men or women of true Passion abroad in the land. The artists, yes, who are indulged and tolerated for their "peculiarness" because they amuse, sometimes inspire. But the great in all fields are passionate. And he was a man of passion. In his love of life, of people, of the wonder of it all. He was Larger-Than-Life. He had that rare capacity for wonder and from-the-toes-up suffusing joy. He offended some of the more uptight types because he seemed sometimes lacking in subtlety. But few of them could match his enthusiasm. They may have only envied him his enthusiasm, his freedom to feel. He seemed "corny" to some, but again, that was a part of his openness, his need to communicate, instantly, without tarrying to find "just the right words," without stopping to consider and calculate, without caring whether this would sound sophisticated, simply needing to share what was in his heart with all who were nearby. He "let it all hang out" as the saying went. No debonair, cocktail-party sophisticate, he was a true Primitive.*

For a woman who was countless times described as the ultimate sophisticate, sparkling in any social milieu, sharp of wit and biting of word, she seems to have found her true opposite. She often described their relationship, to me and other intimates, as "The Great Love Affair."

Below, a note (again, carbon copied) she sent to Pat in the late 1970s:

> *Maybe I could have tolerated your position if I'd never been publicly insulted by your wife and if you hadn't recently opted in favor of your daughter's birthday party, one more in a long line of such options over the years. As it is, when I think about it at all it is only with anger, indeed with Rage (my sense of Fair Play is that much offended).*
>
> *Fortunately, I don't seem to be dwelling on it. The rest of the time I've been feeling alive and encouraged. That must mean it's, to use one of your favorite expressions, "For The Best." You always said it would be. Perhaps that platitude had truth in it after all.*

WHEN ONE DOOR SLAMMED SHUT, another cracked open. When my birth was imminent, she'd had me induced so she could attend an "important" party a few days later. And thus, it was for many decades. I was to be a bit-player, a lonely-only child, an inconvenience to be shunted off to camp and boarding schools to clear the decks for her social climbing, clandestine meetings, and incendiary tiffs. I had to learn to create my own private world if I was to feel that I had any importance at all.

TRANSCRIPT OF PHONE CONVERSATION BETWEEN PAT BROWN AND MARCIA BINNS, CIRCA 1971:

> *Pat: Don't you think maybe something is wrong with her? Mentally, I mean? Where does she get this hostility? I don't think it's normal, and I happen to think you are a wonderful mother. Do you think if you and I were ever to marry, you would be as patient with me as you have been with her? I worry you would lose sympathy for me and walk away.*

Marcia: *She is just full of resentment. It's very strange. I mean, I respected MY mother when I was her age. I think maybe she has been jealous of me since she was 13. Her father agrees with me.*

Pat: *What are you wearing?*

Marcia: *What I may or may not be wearing is not pertinent to this conversation. Can you have dinner this Thursday? Eddie is still out of town, and I can send Brigit to a friend's house. Or are your shallow Rotary Club friends more important than I am — again?*

AT SIX I'D BEEN INVITED TO A BIRTHDAY PARTY for Todd Fisher in Beverly Hills.

"I hate that Hollywood crap," thundered my dad.

The party was to be quintessentially Hollywood: Hedda Hopper would judge a fancy-hat competition amongst the six-year-old guests. My mother was adamant that I go. She tasked our housekeeper/cook Huguette, also an accomplished seamstress, with creating the ultimate hat for me. The hat took shape even as Dad grumbled; it was a replica of a Swiss mountain peak, complete with a castle at the top and little lederhosen-wearing figures climbing the tiny road that wound around and around the *chapeau* on their way to the castle. It was almost bigger than I was, and I looked like some sort of munchkin in this top-heavy construction. The memory of my father's anger is so deeply embedded in my psyche that I scarcely remember the party itself, meeting, presumably, the divine Hedda Hopper and Todd's older sister Carrie. My dad despised the idea of having a cook, but my mother took to having a servant as if she'd grown up with a bevy of them. This convenience allowed her to continue the tradition of rising at noon and then dithering about in her office for the rest of the daylight hours. She considered herself a "writer," but did little more than produce a few short columns for *TV Guide*. The dithering was almost entirely unproductive, though at one point she was driving out to Pomona for board meetings at the women's prison about once a week. My father, frequently unemployed as actors often are, skulked around the house avoiding Huguette. I took his anger and disappointment about the hat party as a personal judgment against me—I had failed him.

Dad was intermittently a hero to his daughters. He was aware of his sexiness, and cultivated a sort of preppy appearance before anyone called it that. His casual look consisted of white button-down cuff-and-collar shirts, open at the neck, with khaki trousers. More formally, he preferred a subtly checked sport jacket atop a V-neck sweater, with an impeccably knotted tie above. By the time his eldest daughters were approaching young adulthood, he was a still handsome hambone with a heart of gold but a list of faults and weaknesses constantly called out by his then-spouse.

In the film *Judgment at Nuremburg* when he was 45, he was still able to project a military bearing in his big jeep scene with Spencer Tracy, one of his heroes. By the time I was grown up enough to notice such things, his physique had started a gradual metamorphosis from slim to poochy; he had one of those guts that stood proud of his belt by several inches. Up until 1969, it was the booze; after that, it was cookies. His glossy, never-thinning hair was always jet black and combed back from his forehead in the style of a 1940s movie villain. At the Buckley School just off Sunset Boulevard, my classmates were just the sort of people my mother yearned for me to befriend: Cecilia Peck (Gregory), Liza Todd (Liz Taylor/Mike Todd), Timolin and Casey Cole (Nat "King"), Tracy Granger (Stewart). I stayed at Buckley from "Reading Readiness" (their term for pre-kindergarten—the motto of the school was "College Begins at Two") through fourth grade, the longest I would stay at any school. But my mother had set her sights on an experimental elementary school attached to UCLA called U.E.S. There, I spent fifth and sixth grades, an awkward and unattractive time—exacerbated by exceedingly thick glasses—during which I fell deeply in love (entirely unrequited) with my classmate Adam (son of Leonard Nimoy and Sandra Zober). But there were more schools to be sampled; she simply couldn't stop herself, and my father had no desire and no armor with which to fight on my behalf. By seventh grade, it was time to change again, this time to a boarding school. They sent me to my mother's own alma mater from the 1940s, Ojai Valley School. There, she had become fast friends with Lizzie Hollister and been unofficially adopted by the Hollister clan, thus embarking on her life-long project of self-improvement.

The school was in the idyllic town of Ojai, California, where the terrain looked like my beloved Hollister Ranch. One of my classmates was the daughter of Louis Prima and Keely Smith, Luanne Prima; years later I re-encountered her as a real estate agent in Palm Springs. Again it was clearly very important to my mother that I ingratiate myself with the children of the wealthy—although luckily I still had not realized this. To her mortification, less than two months after commencing seventh grade I was expelled for leading an anti-war student walkout on the first moratorium day. No other private school (read: *opportunity for social-climbing*) was available on such short notice, so I had to spend the rest of that year at Paul Revere High School on the border of Brentwood and the Pacific Palisades, a—gasp—*public* school.

I adored it. But it was not to last.

Another school for wealthy kids had caught my mother's eye. The French *Lycée* was known for offering the same curriculum at its schools all over the world, making it simple for titans of screen and boardroom to uproot their children according to their own travel needs, with (supposedly) no adverse effects on the kids. The idea was that one could be assigned homework in Paris and then turn it in at Los Angeles or Rome. The children of Robert Culp (Josh) and Roger Vadim (Nathalie) were in my class; Marlon Brando's son Miko was two grades below me, a then-unknown Christie Brinkley two grades above. A few years later Jodie Foster graduated valedictorian, and Molly Ringwald attended shortly after that.

When I was about six, I'd had several play dates with Christian Brando until he kicked in a door, and someone decided he was "a very disturbed little boy" and I was no longer allowed to play with him. In 1990 Christian, the only child of Marlon's marriage to troubled actress Anna Kashfi, fatally shot his pregnant half-sister Cheyenne's boyfriend, in front of her. Cheyenne died by suicide in 1995, a year before Christian would be released early from prison because she had refused to testify against him. She hanged herself at her Tahitian mother's home in Puna'auia, Tahiti. Marlon Brando later blamed his own selfish and stormy lifestyle for Christian's troubled life, and his death from substance abuse-related pneumonia at the age of 49.

From the age of 13, I chafed wildly against my mother's authority. With absolute conviction that I knew better than she what was right for me—what I could handle at my age—I resented any attempt by her to act as a controlling parent. After all, she was the secret mistress of a prominent politician and family man, who was, by the early seventies, helping his son Jerry start a presidential campaign. *Remind me again why you deserve my respect?* It was slowly becoming clear that my mother had been designing my life for her own benefit, and I'd had no authority or power to dispute her plans. As our therapist later said, I was simply an accessory, like a scarf or a brooch. When I was no longer willing to behave like her cute little Mini-Me, I was recast as an enemy.

It seemed as if my mother always had to have someone to hate, and it was my turn. *To survive, I'm gonna have to fight.*

My father preferred not to get involved between us and decamped for the East Coast theatrical community. He had given up on what he called the "shallowness and avarice" of the acting profession in Hollywood after a director had instructed him to punch an actress in a scene. This made it easier for my mother and Uncle Pat to spend time together, and when I was packed off to summer camp and/or boarding school the decks were cleared even further.

"It'll be so much easier with Brigit gone," my mother wrote to Pat at one point.

I shed no tears. For my part, I was learning to fit seamlessly into new situations and student bodies. *At home I will be feral; elsewhere, I'll be jocular and engaging.*

As an only child in the early years, I was intensely lonely and longed for a sibling to deflect my mother's venom. By the time I was ten or eleven, the brief summer visits from the Minneapolis sisters had come to an end. Switching schools so often forced me to become good at making friends, at least superficial friends. But it was hard to keep up a friendship at that age when I had to adapt to a new school every year or so. Soon, I discovered that men, or rather boys, found me attractive. I had a boyfriend at 14, and he illicitly picked me up from the French *Lycée* on his Honda 150 motorcycle. I was intoxicated by the freedom of bombing along the Santa Monica freeway with my hair streaming out behind, my arms around his chest. This is the power of a woman in the body of a child. Of course, the *Lycée* reported to my mother that I was not taking the school bus, and in the first of many such instances, I was immediately grounded. Yet another school loomed on the horizon.

MY MOTHER IN <u>HER</u> MOTHER'S PINK LAMÉ FLAPPER DRESS

mommy's got a gun

L.A. AND IDYLLWILD, 1971

I AM FOURTEEN.

Just south of the Sepulveda Pass and within view of what will later become the Getty Museum, our low-slung, split-level Spanish house, with its tile roof and thick stucco walls, hails from 1925 and boasts a 100-year-old olive tree in the front yard. My bedroom window faces the street and, although a huge, defunct wooden window box prevents my classic Los Angeles metal casement windows from opening all the way, I can squeeze my 80-pound body through the small opening, balance on the window box, and slide to the ground—*after* stuffing my bed with pillows in imitation of my sleeping form.

Outside on the beckoning streets of Brentwood twenty-plus years before O.J.'s rampage, manicured lawns are touched with dew, Mercedeses crouch low to the ground, and the streetlights simmer. Freed from the oppression of the house, I meet up with other young Brentwood denizens in the dark of a nineteen-seventies suburban L.A. night. We prowl the deserted streets together, peeking into and sometimes even entering neighboring yards, yet never once getting caught out by human nor dog. One night I return well before dawn, but my casement windows are closed and securely locked.

Uh-oh—busted!

On a lounger by the pool in those early morning hours, I ponder my options. I don't seem to have any. In my super-wide bell-bottoms, knee-length denim work-shirt, and sockless Keds, I am cold. After shivering in the morning dew for an hour, I muster the courage to venture around to the French doors of my mother's bedroom. Through the gauzy curtains I see a dim light. I know she is awake and waiting to divine an adequate punishment for the "Bad Seed," the "Rottenkid" she's somehow gotten stuck with for a daughter.

I knock tremulously. She slowly opens the doors, and I am met with the barrel of a .22 rifle, pressed against my belly, the same gun she'd used to murder a blue jay at the Hollister Ranch just a few years before. *Does that gun even work? Has she used it since she shot the blue jay?*

"I thought it was a burglar," she says. Both of us know she is lying.

Now comes the hurling of capital-letter-style pronouncements: "You Are No Daughter Of Mine." "This is Criminal Behavior." "I Have Simply *Had It*, Kiddo."

I assume my usual position: eyes narrowed to slits, chin thrust out belligerently, and mouth firmly closed. Actually, I curl my lip. *If I do not engage with this screeching witch, perhaps she will, eventually, stop.* I am scared, yes, but also very angry. I wish I could turn the tables; at that moment I'm not sure I wouldn't pull the trigger.

Mercifully, she does not. But life will never again be the same for either of us.

THE SCENE THAT PLAYED out that night during my turbulent adolescence might have taken place in any fortunate family home of that place and time (*sans* the gun, perhaps). Teenagers are historically some of the most beastly creatures on earth. Some of them truly believe, for a time, that they hate one or both of their parents, although usually it's just one. Those who grow up in relative comfort, as I did, are often the worst, and I must confess I may have been on the further end of this continuum.

But there were factors, both inside me and outside me, that led to the roles my mother and I played on that night becoming almost life-long. Until her death, I remained fixed in her mind's eye just as I had appeared that night. Eventually I came to understand that, in order to survive, I'd have to completely reject her opinion of me. And so almost all of her other opinions became suspect.

And yet, my inner child still thought that my mommy was always right. By extension, then, her opinion of me must be the truth. I would have to fight tooth and nail to emerge from my privileged childhood as a balanced, reflective, and rationally functioning adult.

I wrote everything in my Dear Diary. It was a small, faux-leather-bound book with gilt-edged pages and a wholly ineffectual lock. I wrote of my fears and frustrations, teen angst, perceived slights by girls at school.

I also detailed my shambolic adolescent experiments with kissing and touching with my "boyfriend," Kevin. Each entry was actually prefaced with "Dear Diary," and when I finished writing, I tucked the little book underneath my mattress, a ludicrously obvious place to hide such an incriminating document. After the incident in the nighttime, my mother considered it her urgent and justified right to find my diary, break the lock, and read all my secrets. Afterwards she told my father and a close family friend that I was a nymphomaniac. I overheard her saying this on the phone one night as I snuck past her open bedroom door, hoping to avoid a confrontation.

Alone on the stupid canopy bed that I had once—when I was younger—yearned for, I cried tears of shame and humiliation. A few years later, in my final year in high school in Arizona, I would approach her construct, sleeping with virtually any seriously good-looking guy who crooked a finger. In my mind, this was excellent proof that I was actually a desirable person, that my mother was wrong about me. To put this in historical context: Many people at our ultra-liberal boarding school were doing the same thing.

Some people consider boarding school to be a way of getting rid of kids, a heartless, selfish parental move. To me it was a lifesaver.

VERY SHORTLY AFTER THE INCIDENT, I was dispatched, mid-ninth grade, to another boarding school, this one in the mountains above Palm Springs in a since deforested little mountain town named Idyllwild. The school, Desert Sun—my sixth since third grade—was a catch-all for youthful Angeleno fuckups, and the students there inhabited a higher level of "bad" than I'd ever imagined.

Harmlessly sneaking around a nighttime neighborhood and riding on a petite Honda was child's play to these badass kids. We listened to The Cars and the Eagles, shared sips from a pint of Bacardi in the overgrown pasture and they showed me how to roll a joint. I spent one unhappy night in the big communal girls' dorm bathroom trying to aim my vomit into the toilet bowl. One of the girls cut her wrist but survived. It was within striking distance for a dedicated kid on a Honda 150, and I snuck out into the woods to meet Kevin every week or two, until attrition brought an end to my first great, but virtually virtuous, love affair.

When the school year finished, I was supposed to head off for my eighth summer at Gold Arrow summer camp on Huntington Lake in the High Sierra. The camp catered—surprise!—to the scions of Hollywood royalty: perfect for my mother's social aspirations. Jamie Lee Curtis (then just Jamie Curtis) had been in my cabin the previous year; she was a thin and rangy tomboy who tagged around after me wanting to be friends. *Breakfast at Tiffany's* heartthrob George Peppard's daughter Julie was in the cabin next door; her hair was as fine as gossamer, her skin glowed like pearls. We learned to sail, waterski, tie lanyards, throw pots, execute an emergency dismount from a galloping horse, and roast wicked-tasty marshmallows. Lying prone on a padded platform and firing a rifle at a tattered target, I became a "Golden Sharpshooter," with a badge to prove it. I even hit a few bullseyes with the rainbow-colored arrows in my quiver. Each cabin performed a skit on the big communal platform every Sunday; there was singing and dancing, of a sort, and a lot of really corny jokes. A substance called bug-juice was the beverage of choice. My family had driven up to inspect the camp for the first time when I was six—too young to actually attend at that point—but my parents left me there for the rest of the session anyway.

"Oh, she's old enough—she'll fit right in with the older kids!" Abandoned again—but I loved it!

After flailing a bit as a latecomer that first summer, I had adored this golden, girls-only camp for the next seven summers. But at the age of 14 I had no intention of behaving like a child. The night before camp was to start, I snuck out my window again and hitchhiked back to Idyllwild to hang out in a camper in the woods with a couple of seniors who were working there for the summer. As I sat by the on-ramp that led from Wilshire Blvd onto the San Diego Freeway south, thumb out and confidence radiating, I saw my dad driving my grandmother's old, inherited Jaguar up the onramp. By then he certainly knew that I had run away. He didn't see me. I didn't try to be seen but watching him calmly drive along made me feel like an appendix that had been sliced away from my family, if you could even call them that.

The well-used camper sat in a pine needle-strewn clearing surrounded by stunning, towering redwoods who had yet to succumb to the bark beetle. Raf inhabited the camper itself, and Feilding parked his converted van across the clearing so he could share the bathroom. "Converted" meant the entire area behind the two front seats had been turned into a bed, usually with multiple rumpled Indian bedspreads and, if you were lucky, actual sheets, though if present they were best left unexamined. Raf's rented camper itself, having seen better days, had not been improved by the presence of a bearded and long-haired, college-bound guy working a summer job in construction. I set out to clean every surface, assisted in my enthusiasm by a tablet of speed. When I finished, it shone, and I was proud—a first stab at domesticity.

Just a few short days after I arrived, my mother apparently threatened to turn me over as a ward of the court unless I was found, and an L.A. friend gave up my location. On a perfect summer-in-the-mountains evening just after Raf had returned from work, a squad car crept into the tree-lined clearing. It disgorged two uniformed officers who indicated I'd be going with them. Like, *now*. I sulked in the back seat on the 40-minute drive down to Banning, where I was stashed in the county jail overnight before a morning transfer to Riverside Juvenile Hall. I was wearing ridiculously short cut-offs cinched by a wide belt and a man's white shirt; they took my belt and wire-rimmed prescription glasses, presumably so I couldn't somehow use them to attempt suicide.

Dinner was chipped beef on toast, a.k.a Shit on a Shingle. Dad wanted to pick me up right away, but my mother insisted they leave me in "Juvy" for three days to "learn my lesson." I met some very scary girls there, and they all told me I'd be back.

"Everyone comes back."

Indeed, I did learn a lesson, but I doubt if it was the one she had in mind. *Why is she so keen to find me if she's just going to leave me locked up?*

When Dad eventually arrived and ferried me home, my mother didn't speak to me for days. A third boarding school, this time in Arizona, hovered on my horizon.

Photo credit: Yearbook staff, Verde Valley School, Sedona, AZ

AT MY "WORKJOB" (TRASH PICKUP) IN SEDONA

going deep

ARIZONA, 1972-1974

SUDDENLY, I HAD THE THIGHS OF A VALKYRIE, the stamina of a long-distance runner, and a tan that could've inspired an Eagles song. It had been eight months since my sullen and rebellious arrival in Arizona. Being away from home, this time in a far healthier atmosphere than the Idyllwild reform school, allowed me glimpses of a less cringing and fearful self. The regular, densely typewritten letters full of back-handed compliments and condescension seemed less threatening when read on a warm outcropping of red rocks.

"Thanks also for your little note. Especially the one you left upon leaving. It was sweet and thoughtful, and I appreciate the effort. I'm afraid I am sometimes too impatient for you to grow up and then disappointed when you seem not to be doing so."

I threw them away, little suspecting that forty-some years later I'd discover a trove of carbon copies that set my teeth on edge. *These words come from beyond the grave—how can they still sting?* She did warn me toward the end of her life that I would find things among her papers that would be "upsetting." Understatement of the century.

I was attending a progressive boarding school in Sedona. In the forties, an educational revolutionary named Hamilton Warren had started the school on a shoestring and a vision. For the first two decades, students in all grades spent three weeks every spring living on a nearby Native American reservation or working with the homeless in inner-city Phoenix. It was then the only high school at which anthropology was a required subject. On the one-week orientation hikes that began each academic year, youthful faculty and students often skinny-dipped together in Sedona's rocky creeks. My mother had often gone naked around the house and backyard when I was growing up. This was purportedly a sign of her lofty progressive chops, but in reality, just one more opportunity to show off the still-lithe body of which she was hyperbolically proud. Yet she seemed more focused on the supposed academic excellence than the liberal-to-a-fault social reality. Other people's nakedness was of less interest than her own.

I thrived in Sedona.

By the time I started at Verde Valley School, the culturally and geographically diverse spring field trips had been expanded with journeys into the natural world. A group went sailing in two-man skiffs in the Sea of Cortez; several of the students almost drowned. I signed up to hike 150 miles in the Grand Canyon. My motivation is still buried in the sands of adolescence. On the trip were five boys, one other girl, and the school's tennis coach. I was fifteen years old, weighed 90 pounds, and had never owned a pair of hiking boots, but I had read all of Carlos Castañeda.

I don't think any breathless description of the Grand Canyon can possibly prepare one for that first glimpse over the rim. The eye has trouble comprehending the vastness, the redness, the layers, the ancient history, trying to place it in some previously known context that as of this moment no longer exists in your brain. It almost literally blew my mind.

We started off for a break-in hike at the south rim, away from which most tourists never stray. We hiked down the Kaibab Trail to the bottom of the canyon where the temperature is always twenty degrees hotter than at the rim. A lodging called the Ghost Ranch is nestled in the cradle of the canyon floor; most people who visit arrive on mule-back, which may be slightly more comfortable than walking. May be. Slightly.

The Grand Canyon is Very Deep. After walking at a precipitous downward slope for 10 miles in my new hiking boots, I had two heel-sized blisters. The trapped seas of saline squooshed painfully inside my cool new boots at every step, as though I were walking on water balloons.

At the Ghost Ranch, we spent the night in a dorm-like structure. I was tucked up in my fresh new sleeping bag on top of a crinkly new foam pad. There was a shared KYBO (this stood for Keep Your Bowels Open; it's now known as a Porta-potty). My little Brentwood-raised body had never been subjected to such intense physical exertion and registered profound shock: I spent much of the night in the KYBO, gushing from both ends. The next day, we shouldered our packs and hiked straight back uphill to the rim again, this time on the Bright Angel Trail. The school van then drove us 100 miles up-river to our trailhead, where we loaded our packs with enough supplies to last 15 days and then set out to walk back down to the Bright Angel Trail on the Tonto Platform. This is a spectacular plateau that snakes in and out of the ancillary canyons about halfway between the rim and the Colorado River.

I punctured and drained all the blisters, hoisted up my 60-pound pack (two thirds of my body weight—but who's counting?), and set off behind the others.

The other girl in the troupe was six feet tall and all ebony muscle, a statuesque modern dancer and choreographer. Teresa also carried a 60-pound pack, as did the five guys who rounded out the team, wiry urban cowboys with boots that had seen a lot of action and sleeping bags that told tales I didn't want to hear. Or smell. It was all about equality. It never occurred to me that I was totally out of my depth and heading into the middle of nowhere with one 24-year-old tennis teacher as the sole "responsible" adult.

Each day we walked between 10 and 12 miles, dropping down to the Colorado River occasionally to collect water for our canteens—and for reconstituting the highly anticipated "chicken-flavored a-la-king" dinners from their shiny foil packets. Granola was the breakfast and lunch of choice. Occasionally, we washed our bodies and hair in the river with biodegradable Dr. Bronner's soap. Sometimes a raft-full of tourists would bobble by on the rapids and we'd wave and hoot, naked, at the wimpy river-riders who didn't know the true way to shoot down the Colorado River: on foot. One hundred and fifty miles. Not as the crow flies—as the trucker trucks.

I wanted to be the dusty desperado, the nut-brown scrabbling desert rat, but my little body couldn't cut it and I had to rest more often, so I slowed the others down; they quietly but pointedly didn't like it. Unsaid: It was me, not just the doughy raft-riders, who was a wimp. Most nights during the first week I cried myself to sleep.

Halfway along the Tonto Platform, we stopped for a "Solo," *a la* Outward Bound. Each kid was assigned 150 feet of creek and supplied with a journal, pen, sleeping bag, and tarp, then left alone for three nights with a bag of granola. Even if you spied your creek-side neighbor at one end or the other, there was to be strictly *No Talking* for the duration. This sort of "find yourself" time-out was ubiquitous in the late seventies. Crouched under the red rock overhang, the front edge of my tarp dripping with rain, I tried very, very hard to Go Deep. I gazed at the stars and the spectacular rock formations limned against the velvet-blue sky and tried to ponder the big things: Destiny... Meaning... Humanity.

Instead, I wondered what Ian might be doing up at the top edge of my domain, or Eric at the bottom end. Had everyone else managed to keep their sleeping bags completely dry? How many packets of chicken-flavored a la king remained? Was our faculty leader sneaking food from the group cache? Although my mother and I had waved goodbye before my departure with a palpably false sense of mutual camaraderie, grins pasted on like disturbing clown-faces, the most meaningful piece of reflection to come out of those three days was a long letter extolling her excellent lamb stew. A rare show of affection, and later I even mailed it.

With time, I grew stronger. There were good days when the truckers just trucked, silently and purposefully without complaint, into and out of the serpentine little side canyons and back to the glory of the open plateau with the river sparkling far below. The main topic of conversation around the Bleuet stoves at night was the menu at the Fred Harvey restaurant at journey's end.

"What are you gonna have when we get to Fred's? Grilled cheese? A patty melt?"

"I'm thinking the full breakfast with bacon, eggs, biscuits 'n' cream gravy, and hotcakes with maple-flavored syrup."

Each voice, in turn, waxed lyrical in the star-lit darkness. Maybe we'd just have it all. The world would be our oyster; we would have earned it and we planned to eat it.

I've lost track of the picture someone took of me the moment we finally hit the Bright Angel Trail, fifteen days after we'd set out. I'm caught in the act of placing one booted foot over the rocks onto the main trail, with the other foot still officially out in the wild. My boots are massive, especially plopped at the ends of my spindly little-girl calves. But my thighs are cut and muscular, the fringed cut-offs above them as short as shorts can get. My hair is long and blond and messy, and my brown face is upturned to the sun, wearing a wide and victorious smile.

In the end, I *had* gone deep. I'd climbed down into myself and seen my limitations—hey, *everyone* had seen my limitations. But at the bottom of the canyon, a hundred miles from a telephone or a car or an airplane, there was no running away and no shortcut to easy street. There was only the road ahead and the necessity of putting one boot in front of the other. Over and over and over again. And now I held in my heart the reward for that persistence: a thing of true and everlasting glory, all mine.

Just up the trail was a real bathroom, the first we'd seen in two weeks. Teresa and I made a beeline for the ladies' side, falling-down eager to see what we looked like after those mirrorless days on the trail.

The image that truly endures from that journey is captured only in my memory: the single cracked mirror reflecting both our faces, Teresa's round Black one directly above my dirty white one, great big shit-eating grins on both.

I made it through high school, graduating a year earlier than usual, at 16. Because of the accelerated learning program at the French *Lycée* in L.A., I'd arrived with enough credits to skip a grade. In other words, I could have stayed in Sedona for three blissful years, but instead elected to cram 10th, 11th, and 12th grades into two years by writing a long essay on one of the most stultifyingly dull books in the literary pantheon: Thomas Hardy's *Tess of the D'Urbervilles*. Why was I in such a hurry to grow up? Ask any 16-year-old.

It was made clear that I was not wanted at home that summer, as my mother was involved in a "writing project." Dad was doing the play *A Touch of the Poet* in Toronto, so no paternal care option was offered, but he did send occasional chatty letters. I stayed behind in Sedona for six weeks and got a job as the busgirl at a white-tablecloth restaurant called The Owl: dark, polished wood and brass, sparkling glasses, and bottles of Blue Nun anointing the bar. The menu was jam-packed with standard special-occasion fare for the mid-seventies: prime rib with horseradish sauce, far-from-the-sea sole *meuniere*, rice-stuffed Cornish hen, iceberg salad, French Silk Pie, and Schnebly Hill Road ice cream—a local version of rocky road.

A girlfriend from school joined me after the first week, and for $100 we rented a lockless, abandoned, and unfurnished cottage in the middle of uptown Sedona, from an absentee landlord whom we tracked down in New Jersey by phone. There was no electricity or gas—or perhaps I should say we never figured out how to get them hooked up. Candles and a camp stove, plus a couple of mattresses salvaged from the dorm, were our only furnishings. Minimum wage at The Owl didn't go far, so we hitchhiked up Oak Creek Canyon to Flagstaff and applied for food stamps. There were several high points of this heady, first-ever summer away from all authority: spectacular thunderstorms seen across the canyon from the crumbling back patio. And the canned crab we bought with our food stamps, then warmed up right in the can over the Bleuet and doused with butter, savoring each little bite on forks pilfered from The Owl. It was unutterably delicious: The taste of freedom.

Two weeks before my freshman year at Lewis & Clark College in Portland, Oregon, was to start, I left Sedona with tears in my eyes and landed at "home" in Brentwood to gear up for my college career. I was still just sixteen. It would be the longest stretch of time I'd spend in the same house with my mother since being sent off to the reform school;

it would be many decades before I stayed so long again. She instituted strict parameters for our brief cohabitation.

THE RULES, SUMMER 1974 *(after high-school graduation)*

BB Kitchen Privilege Hours:	MLB Kitchen Hours (Private):
8:30-10:30 a.m.	10:30 a.m. – 12:30 p.m.
1:00-3:00 p.m.	3:00-5:00 p.m.
5:00-6:00 p.m.	6:00-8:00 p.m.
After 8:00 p.m. by mutual	Any other hours not
agreement or as K.P. requires	listed to left

OTHER HOUSE RULES:

❑ BB room inspected daily at 12:00 noon. Requirements:
❑ Bed made, clothes away, floor cleared, bathroom and shower clean
❑ Written List of accomplishments at the end of each day to include:
  (a) chores performed
  (b) steps taken toward plan-making for the future, of any kind **
  (c) any questions or requests
** examples of (b): appointments made, job inquiries, letters out, etc. etc.
❑ Conversations by appointment only, please, for a while at least (written request in advance). All other communication by note.

Every effort should be made to comply with this program exactly as laid out. Exceptions should always be explained by note, which will be judged as fairly as possible as acceptable or unacceptable.

I will be trying to follow a routine of my own which will take priority over any domestic responsibilities. It will include 2-3 hours in "studio" which you respected beautifully before.

Thank you for your cooperation.

—Mom

What I did sense by this point was that soon I was going to be completely on my own. *I can't wait.*

WITH MY TAMIL HOST MOTHER IN PENANG

CHAPTER 7

Travels with my appetite

PORTLAND AND PENANG, 1975-1978

MY FIRST TWO YEARS AT LEWIS & CLARK COLLEGE were marked by a spectacularly un-academic approach to life. Not quite 17, I was about two years younger than the other freshmen and unexpectedly unprepared for the relative freedoms on offer. My mother agreed to send me an allowance of $100 a month, but only if I wrote and sent her two actual letters every month. At long last, in my freshman year the Coke-bottle glasses were consigned to history.

Contact lenses were a game changer: Inside I was still a gawky kid, beset by self-doubt, but suddenly people started to treat me like I was pretty. At the tail end of boarding school I had become sexually active, but in college serial monogamy was my saving grace. It allowed me to believe I was wanted—desirable, *worthy*—without having to wake up every day and prove it by adding more notches to my belt. I accidentally began the system on day one of my freshman term at a dorm orientation meeting in the common room.

"That's gonna be my guy," I said to my assigned roommate, a comically inappropriate (for me) person with whom I had about as much in common as a waitress and a snake; we just didn't inhabit the same biosphere. She wore frosted pink lipstick and horizontally striped double-knits. I wore vintage lace blouses atop flowing patchwork skirts and John Lennon sunglasses.

Ned, a sophomore, was attending the freshman's meeting just for fun; he was seated in the corner of the large stained-sofa-filled room, which had been painted in indifferent pastels to attempt a feeling of lightness totally cancelled by the low ceiling, rabbit-eared TV, and a collection of magazines that appeared to have been savaged by dogs. Ned had luxurious, shoulder-length blondish hair, blue eyes, bushy eyebrows, and a body that was all muscle. He also had a liquid-honey accent from his native Mississippi. I had never met a Southern boy before.

Within a month I had abandoned my assigned dorm room and roommate and moved briefly into his miniscule single dorm room. Within six weeks we had struck out into a cheap one-bedroom apartment, far from campus, with rust-red shag wall-to-wall carpet (freshmen were not officially allowed to do this). Ned and I were inseparable for three and a half years. At age 17 I lived with him as if we were husband and wife, paying rent, parenting puppies, and planning weekly menus to save on funds. I rented a sewing machine and made curtains out of cheap, patterned sheets. It was the first of about a hundred nests I would do my best to feather, only to move on almost before the amateur paint job was dry. Soon we tired of paying all the rent alone and merged into a communal living situation in the small suburb of Lake Oswego, where my ability to maintain any possible cleanliness became nonexistent.

Scant attention was paid to coursework. I even failed ceramics.

I was already taking on the cooking duties; this was the debut of "Binns' Breasts." (Recipe pg. 286)

"YOU WILL NOT RECEIVE YOUR ALLOWANCE unless you write and mail two letters home per month, each to include at least 100 words. The letters must be received by the 21ˢᵗ of each month in order to trigger the issuing of your check, which will be sent by Dorothy [the accountant] only upon my approval." Had I lived in the dorm like every other freshman, the $100 per month might have gone further, but the need to escape authority ASAP had urged me off campus into an oddly domestic life. Covering rent, utilities, food, Almaden wine, and gas for my Moped was deeply challenging, and yet each month I avoided writing those two letters as if I was being dragged through the ninth circle of Hell while having my fingernails pulled out.

I had begun as a drama major, but abandoned the pursuit after a professor repeatedly called me on the carpet in front of the entire class for not "giving enough of myself" to the text. My actor dad had always said I had many talents, but "acting is not one of them."

Disapproval didn't sit well with me; I got enough of it at home. I decamped to an English Lit major, the safe haven of all directionless American liberal arts college kids. My youthful ambition to be an actress evaporated without a whimper.

Lewis & Clark was famous for its ambitious overseas programs, hauling five different groups of 22 students plus a faculty member off for six months of study abroad every year. In my sophomore year, I set my sights on the South Pacific trip purely because it sounded like a great place to drink gin and tonics on the beach. When the trip filled up too fast, I lowered my sights to Malaysia, envisioning myself as a pith-helmeted Cary Grant, ordering (once again) gin and tonics amidst charmingly seedy colonial architecture and grinning islanders. I'm not sure I even looked at a map of Southeast Asia.

And so, in the fall term of my sophomore year at Lewis and Clark, Ned and I set out with 20 other college students and one out-of-her depth humanities professor. Heading off for my encounter with Southeast Asia, I had little if any idea what to expect other than a great adventure. On the flight from Portland to Hong Kong, the plane overflew the coast of Vietnam and the pilot let us know we could glimpse the country that had occupied such a huge place in all of our still-short lives via the infamous Vietnam War, still actively festering in everyone's consciousness. In a scene out of *I Love Lucy*, everyone rushed to the right side of the plane to gaze out at the iridescent green, curving coastline, as if just by looking we could somehow parse a deeper understanding of America's disastrous attempt to forestall the dreaded "domino effect."

I was surrounded by kids whose parents had the financial resources to fund an extra twenty percent above the usual annual tuition/room/board fees but had no clue how fortunate I was to be able to engage in such exotic travel. In hindsight, I've come to understand that my mother would have done almost anything to get me as far out of the way as possible, so she could pursue her "Work" and her "Great Affair." I was the very lucky beneficiary of her lack of maternal instinct—just starting to understand that the wages of her sin could provide me with some great adventures. After Verde Valley School, I'd become convinced that the only responsible adult I needed in life was me.

On the flight we were alternately raucous and sleepy, each of us experiencing a packed, long-distance flight to a developing country for the very first time. We'd had all kinds of weird vaccinations, but to label us *mentally* unprepared would be an understatement. Our faculty advisor had all the people skills of a troglodyte. First, we were to have separate month-long homestays on the lovely northern island of Penang, then a four-month academic program in Kuala Lumpur, and finally a one-month project period where we could scatter to the winds either alone or in small groups before returning to the U.S.A. as seasoned "Old Asia Hands."

We were left mostly to ourselves, and a great deal of seasoning was clearly needed. Although I am not a parent, I think the concept of sending twenty-two 18-year-olds to a developing country with questionable supervision and no financial safety net ranks right down there with paying off the Watergate burglars with a suitcase full of cash (something that one of my school friend's father, as a member of the

Nixon administration, had actually gone to prison for). I was the only kid on the trip who didn't have a credit card for emergencies.

I had pleaded for one. "What if there's a war? A coup? And I get stranded somewhere?"

But my mother and—by attrition, my dad—both felt that I was "too immature to handle the responsibility." *Do these people have any idea at all who I am?*

Passing briefly through Bangkok on the way to Malaysia, reminders of American G.I.s on R&R from Vietnam were everywhere, mostly in the form of hotel staff who offered us "very cheap Thai-stick!"

After planes, trains, and trishaws, we finally arrived on the small island of Penang, a.k.a the Pearl of the Orient. Colonial Brits developed Penang as a tourist destination and, as a result, prices were much higher than in Bangkok. The architecture was colonial, but cleaner and less crumbly than we would see later in Kuala Lumpur. During our stay we often played darts at a little pub.

In every spot the Brits ever colonized, either in actual colonial times (Malaysia, Hong Kong, India, Australia, New Zealand, South Africa) or in the modern day (Spain, Majorca, Madeira, the Canary Islands, amongst many others), you will always find "pubs." Some are more authentic than others, but they always seem to have a contingent of red-faced, gap-toothed rowdy-types in residence, and a particular smell I'd be happy never to encounter again.

In Georgetown, the capital of Penang, colonial influence on culture, food, and beer were on full display. The E&O (Eastern & Oriental) Hotel stood right where Hermann Hesse, Rudyard Kipling, and W. Somerset Maugham had first encountered it. As a college sophomore on a blisteringly tight budget, I couldn't afford to be drawn to its airy white terrace, in spite of the literary chops. But alongside the open markets—where wrinkled ladies in coolie hats and baggy black trousers squatted for hours over rattan trays full of mysterious, alluring vegetables—stood small open-air cafes where a tall Singha beer was dirt cheap and a fine excuse to linger all afternoon before returning to my homestay with a Tamil Indian family. The guidebook *Southeast Asia on a Shoestring* was my bible.

I was creating and starring in my own tropical tale.

The homestay was my first foray out of an upper-middle-class American comfort zone. I shared a bed with the eldest daughter of the family, and the mom dressed me up in a sari, even painting an authentic *bhindi* on my forehead. Once a week, we all polished the family collection of brass. Mealtimes were a challenge for me for two reasons: I absolutely hated curry and had a hard time learning to scoop up food with my right hand (for God's sake, *always* the right!). In the end my host mother kindly fed me simple white rice doused with soy sauce and butter at every dinner; she even found me a fork. This must have seemed like a cultural rejection at the time, but I was too wrapped up in my own wants and needs to care; I gained four pounds in a month.

Sometimes on weekends some of the students would gather for a foray out to the tourist beach Batu Ferringhi ("Foreigner's Beach") where the Golden Sands hotel offered a Sunday brunch buffet that was so culturally rich and varied and colorful that I wanted to grab handfuls of deliciousness and rub it all over my face.

Just before the gang was due to finish up our time in Penang and move down to Kuala Lumpur for our academic stay, we planned a party to honor and thank our hosts. Twenty-two different families and twenty-two students, plus our professor. In an early sign of things to come, I conceived the menu and insisted on cleaning the necessary twenty-five pounds of shell-on shrimp all by myself. The resulting shrimp and rice dish likely seemed insipid to our host families, lacking in flavor like a watered-down vanilla milkshake, but no one said a negative word.

Malaysia was a bit too far for R&R from Vietnam and so had not been overrun with American soldiers. The western influence there was still 100 percent British. This was clear in the architecture, idioms, and accents, and surprisingly best of all, in the food. At the monumental train station in Kuala Lumpur, a small dark restaurant tucked away in the depths of a cavernous waiting area offered *"Chateaubriand* for Two" for just $7. This was a dish I'd never heard of but quickly became enamored with. With its wood paneling, the place could have seemed clubby if the mysterious and inviting booths hadn't been grimed with the sweat and dirt of generations of travelers, the plates cracked and chipped, and the plastic water tumblers cloudy from decades of dishwashing. This out-of-the-way place became my little piece of heaven, a W. Somerset Maugham moment quickly added to my fast-developing inner narrative.

They served lamb with mint sauce; carrots and potatoes were "turned," a wasteful practice that renders all vegetables into identical tiny barrels. Later, at cooking school in England, I was given a special knife for turning veggies; it looked like a diminutive scimitar. Today's "baby" carrots look very similar to turned veggies but bear no relationship or texture to any sort of baby vegetable (they're extruded from huge woody carrot specimens). In the mornings at our hostel an Indian chef twirled ethereal, many-layered *rotis* (Indian bread) in the air, then slapped them onto plates for our waiting bellies. I slathered mine with butter.

At the Kuala Lumpur Hilton, Sunday brunch was to-die-for and absurdly cheap: a huge buffet that mixed curries, *mee goreng* (fried noodles), and *pukkah* English trifle. Directly across from this shiny new multi-story hotel was a shantytown where multitudes of brown people shared plastic and tin lean-tos precariously teetering above muddy, sewage-lined lanes. I was learning about the world that existed outside my Hollywood bubble.

I made many marvelous memories during those six months of adventure, some responsible and some not so much. I learned to love Malaysian, Chinese, and Indonesian food, sampled plenty of interesting beers, and even tried smoking a cigarette laced with heroin on Batu Ferringhi beach—not a success, if instantly vomiting is any sign.

And a funny thing happened to me in Malaysia. I became fascinated by something other than having fun. It was as if my carefree, world-explorer identity had a half-life and I'd reached it. I'd never felt the pressure to excel academically, in fact, had always skated by with the minimum of attention to studies and requirements.

Later I would learn from her old diaries that my mother didn't want to inflict upon me the same pressure to excel academically that she'd been subjected to, and for this small mercy I am grateful. My adherence to *her* moral and ethical rules was paramount; in her view, academic requirements took second place. The truth is that I had a deep and visceral dislike of being told what to do, a knee-jerk response that made navigating young adulthood into a minefield. This hangover from my struggles with and against my mother would last for many decades. But despite my best intentions to exist as a party-girl, my heart and mind looked around Malaysia and saw compelling once-and-future history. I had to investigate.

Needing an official project in order to receive full academic credit for the trip, I settled on a photographic study to capture the zeitgeist of this post-colonial Southeast Asian outpost. As I recorded the faces, cultures, and history of the three intermingling populations—Malay, Chinese, and Tamil Indian—I was repeatedly struck by the plucky persistence of the Chinese people against often overwhelming odds. In some odd way, they reminded me of me. Four thousand years of civilization had yielded a complex and poetic history with soupçons of riotous humor, self-deprecation, and a strong superiority complex. While my original intention for this college overseas trip had been to party down on a beach, I had accidentally fallen in love with the Chinese culture and people.

WHEN THE SIX-MONTH ACADEMIC STINT in Asia was over, I was Los Angeles-bound for a brief visit "home" before returning to Portland to resume junior-year studies at Lewis & Clark. The flight landed at 9 o'clock in the morning, an hour with which my mother was unfamiliar.

Her response, communicated in a brief and costly phone call: "Good grief! That's way too early for me to drive to the airport! You'll have to figure out something else."

Gee, thanks. Am I really surprised? By this time, I should know this woman does not have my best interests at heart.

I was eighteen years old and knew it all, so I hitchhiked from LAX to Brentwood.

The Crown Vic that slowed to a crawl, then stopped to pick me up, was inhabited by a sole male driver wearing double-knit trousers and a shirt with too many buttons undone.

"Sure, I'll drive you to Brentwood sweetie, no problem."

That was the end of the conversation, because he then pulled a pressed and folded white hanky from his pocket, unfolded it on his lap, and calmly masturbated underneath it as we headed north on the San Diego freeway toward my childhood home. I was bulletproof on the outside, scared shitless on the inside.

I fumbled with the car door handle (mercifully, unlocked) and tumbled out onto the leafy, sidewalk-less Brentwood street just a block from Sunset Boulevard and three blocks from the San Diego freeway, looking like Casper the Friendly Ghost. It took only a moment to shrug back into my usual *sang-froid*.

Dad would have picked me up if he were here. Of course, he was not. Dad was doing *Long Day's Journey Into Night* at the Indianapolis Rep, opposite the actress Elizabeth Franz. It was the first time they'd met or worked together. After one early performance, they shared an elevator up to their respective, rented and soul-less flats.

"I hope the angel of peaceful repose perches on your pillow tonight," Liz said to dad companionably.

"I'd rather *you* perch on my pillow tonight."

Some years later Liz became Dad's third-and-final wife, and my stepmother (I often referred to her as my "preferred mother").

I'd written my mother with my travel plans. In addition to about ten sarongs, I was bringing home two very personal souvenirs of my time in South-East Asia: a bikini-area tattoo of a sunburst and a cheap, emerald-chip nose-ring. I had proudly—okay, provocatively—described these additions to her in a letter, but she'd been disappointingly quiet in response. Not long after I rang the bell of a home that felt like a fortress barred against intruders, specifically me, my mother opened the Spanish-inquisition-esque peephole and surveyed me. The heavy door then creaked open to reveal her, in a diaphanous bathrobe at 1pm.

"Ah, Brigit! How nice to see you. It looks like you have a piece of snot on your nose."

I lasted an entire week at "home" before making my escape; she and I both pretended to be sad at the so-soon parting. She never saw the tattoo.

Upon returning to Portland, I set out to change my major once again, this time to Chinese Studies. The experience in Malaysia had opened a fascinating world to me. I was learning to look outside of my own shallow little concerns. Lewis & Clark College didn't offer such a major, so I had to assemble and convince a team of faculty members to approve and monitor my self-designed major, cherry-picking classes from Portland State University, Lewis & Clark, the Monterey Institute of International Studies, and later, Georgetown University's language school in Washington D.C. This pursuit claimed my energy for the next two plus years, and as the final coup, I engineered another overseas trip to Asia, this time to Hong Kong and Taiwan. I may have been the only Lewis & Clark student to participate in *two* overseas trips.

My parents, likely equally thrilled to be rid of me and relieved that I had experienced an academic epiphany, were only too happy to approve and fund this second trip. My B.A. in Chinese Studies was awarded at the tail end of a six-month stay in the ultimate City-by-the-Bay. But during my final year at Lewis & Clark before leaving for Hong Kong, I accidentally fell in love—to the unfortunate distress of Ned.

Baird was tall and lanky, a golden-maned intellectual from Oklahoma City, and he was as taken with me as I was with him. *What the heck did I do to deserve* this *guy?* His accent was smooth, with hints of sweetened iced tea, his broad chest—right at my eye level—was upholstered with a welcoming furry carpet perfect for finger-twining, a lifeline in moments of passion. Almost painfully intelligent, he was my first truly grown-up boyfriend, and yet boasted a wicked-smart sense of humor and an ill-concealed love of college-style partying. Smart *and* fun. His well-traveled cast of good friends was way ahead of my previous posse in talent and street savvy. Baird's friends were the kind of people who would drive out to the Malheur National Wildlife Reserve in Eastern Oregon to do some serious birdwatching, and then have a dinner of straight bourbon and canned beans around the campfire at night.

"That's gotta be a grebe," said one.

"How can you be so sure, man?"

Reading aloud from the *Field Guide to the Birds of North America*: "Grebes. Habitat: Ponds, lakes, marshes. Voice: *Kuk-kuk-cow-cow-cow-cowp-cowp*."

A short silence ensued. Doubtful glances were exchanged. And then, loud and clear from the marsh: "*Kuk-kuk-cow-cow-cow-cowp-cowp.*"

"Totally a grebe."

My mother thought Baird was quite a catch, which she expressed with her customary éclat.

"Whatever happens to the two of you, I would think he's made an important contribution to your life already if it was he who turned you around from being a rather trivial, non-motivated hedonist into the real human being with depth whose potential had never been explored before. Perhaps it might have happened to you anyway, but I certainly never saw any evidence of it before you started hanging out with Baird, so I have to give him at least some of the credit. This is not to suggest you didn't have the intelligence or even some of the frame of reference for it already. I think you had much more than you realized. Hard to say. Maybe you're just a chameleon and will always take on the colors of your companions, good or bad."

A YEAR AHEAD OF ME, Baird graduated a few months before I was set to fly off to Hong Kong. We spent the summer in Washington D.C., where he'd been awarded a juicy internship at the Congressional Budget Office. We drove across the country in his beat-up blue Scirocco with Singha the Siamese cat—named after the Thai beer—and set up housekeeping in a tiny sublet at 25th and L. I enrolled in a Mandarin immersion class at Georgetown University, speaking nothing but Mandarin five hours a day for eight weeks. There was a funky kitchenette in the sublet where I attempted to make brown rice and vegetables exciting, and a balcony perfect for Singha's cat box. It was an intoxicating age and time to be in D.C., and we sought out the many low-cost dining, drinking, and entertainment options that catered to the smart and motivated young people who flocked to the city in summer.

We forged a mature, intellectual relationship, something with which I was unfamiliar. He was at the beginning of a glittering career that would likely take him all over the world, and we assumed we would ride the waves of life together. At the end of the summer, leaving him to fly to Hong Kong was wrenching. But for the first time, I had a purpose beyond my own personal desires. Baird had eight months to kill before the start of his master's program in International Studies (he was hoping for Yale), and six months until I was finished with my trip and bachelor's degree.

He set off alone to circumnavigate the entire African continent on the cheap. It was a brave and likely somewhat risky plan, but he was eager to become a true man of the world, a global citizen with high ideals and an impeccable education. I knew we would have a glorious and triumphant reunion when my trip was over, my own diploma firmly in hand.

EXCERPT FROM ESTATE PLANNING FILE OF MARCIA BINNS, 1977 (I was twenty, and a junior at Lewis & Clark College):

> **DECISIONS OF 12/29-30/77:** *I am not disposed to participate financially in any graduate school program for my daughter Brigit for a minimum of five years from this date. This is not to suggest that I will necessarily wish to participate even after four years have passed following her graduation from college. I have no idea what changes may occur between now and then – in my financial situation or in her worthiness. But if my financial situation has not deteriorated to the point where it is impossible for me to help even should I want to, and if she has demonstrated by developing skills and standards presently absent that she is a worthy candidate for advanced study – i.e. should she prove*

capable of "pulling her own weight" in society and perhaps even qualify for a scholarship – than I might contribute to 50% of whatever total her two parents agree to carry. Or, I might not if I don't like her for some reason, new or old, at that time.

That can be determined in December of 1982 & and should be so indicated in my will so that the trustees can consider her qualifications at that time if I am not present to do so – i.e. can she win any kind of scholarship? If so, they should be instructed to flesh it out. If not, they should continue holding the trust as originally set forth, until she has reached age 35. This is prompted by a realization that the last thing she needs is further subsidization. After 20 years of virtually total subsidy (with none of the usual vacation earning periods or of supplemental earning during schooling, only token and very brief "pretend" experiences, too abortive to achieve substance), she is still in danger of developing along the unfortunate lines of her adolescence. Both potentials have been tapped now – the earlier one of being a lazy, self-indulgent, self-consumed & not very fine person, frivolous and trivial, and a newer one of being a resourceful, capable, responsible, and strong, lovely & independent young woman. The latter is there now but remains less dominant than the former, still. In short, she is still a "pain-in-the-ass" human being, as even her own friends have pointed out. Her willingness to exploit others is alarming, & her success at it with people she wishes she could respect must fuel her own self-hatred. (As well it should!)... I love her for her charm and wit and growing strengths. But I don't really like her very much. I'm afraid she's just not a very nice person. Yet....I still have hopes she may one day become one. The day has just not arrived.

* * *

Observation: Last time I determined I didn't like my daughter (September 1975) it took 2 full years before I could actually look forward to being in her company again.

My Mother and The Guv

orient excess

HONG KONG AND TAIWAN, 1979

HONG KONG THEN WAS A PLACE of Vietnamese refugees, spoiled South African baby-businessman, tacky topless bars, and visible history. It was 1979 and the place had reinvented itself more times than Madonna. At that point still to come in Hong Kong's future was their ultimate reinvention—as a province of Mainland China. The exodus had already begun and even with twenty years to go, the prospect of Chinese rule hung over every single citizen's head like a sickening black cloud.

Yet for a visitor it was a wonderful time to be there, before the big airport, before the subway; the Star Ferry was still the easiest mode of transport from Central to the teeming streets of Kowloon. For another twenty cents, you could go first class. Junks, both beautiful and ratty, shared the bay with the ferry.

Tacked onto a group of twenty-one younger students from Lewis & Clark, I shared some of their studies and all their travel arrangements but was there to accomplish different academic goals. I would study intensive Mandarin and research, and then write, my senior thesis. I'd also take part in the group's planned excursions into Mainland China, and at the end of the trip, to Taiwan.

In order to fulfill the graduation requirements imposed by my advisory board, I was required to write a thesis—an effort not necessary for students matriculating with a standard major. This was during the time of the Vietnamese diaspora, when Boat People were streaming out of the country to escape communist rule. We were witnessing a profound shift in the population of Southeast Asia and the ramifications for western countries fascinated me. Some of these refugees had very recently been "enemies" of America; many others had worked for or somehow been associated with the occupying forces.

I entitled my thesis, *The Behavior of Nations Regarding Vietnamese Refugees*. In pursuit of facts and understanding, I interviewed consular staff from Canada, the U.K., Germany, Australia, Japan, and the U.S.A. Contacts supplied by my Uncle Pat allowed me entrée to these embassy staff and most were happy to reveal their motivations and actions when it came to resettling such large numbers of civilians who were in dire need. The most surprising revelation from all that research was this: Japan was happy to send plenty of aid money to the process, but absolutely refused to take in any refugees. Not one.

Under the auspices of the American Women's Association of Hong Kong, I worked in a refugee camp two days a week as part of research for the thesis. I imagined this as a sort of mini-Peace Corps experience, but in fact it was mostly distributing the contents of care packages and donations to proud but traumatized people who were living in a precarious state of limbo while watching their culture recede into the past. It was impossible to disassociate my experiences in the camp, and talking to the people there, from my conversations with consular officials about the "Vietnamese problem." The reality was that here was an entire population who had lived alongside American GIs for many years and were now reduced to begging for settlement in some unknown corner of a mostly unwelcoming world. *I am ashamed of my life of extreme privilege.*

I also frequented some interesting bars, and often took my meals at a small, open-fronted restaurant up the hill from Central. The group's digs were halfway up The Peak in an old monastery with tiny cells and a large, shared bathroom at the end of a long hallway.

I had the luxury of a private Mandarin tutor while the younger members of the team studied Cantonese. I adored the alleyways and vistas, the incredible excitement of communicating with non-English-speakers, and the life-altering diversity of food on offer at little stalls and hole-in-the-wall eateries. My favorite was the birdcage-bedecked dim sum halls where ancient Chinese men sampled diminutive delicacies while petite and pampered songbirds perched and serenaded just above their heads. Although it ate up nearly half of my walking-around-money, I bought a full set of blue-and-white china, with all the western plate sizes, plus Chinese soup bowls, variously sized saucers, Chinese teacups, and serving pieces appropriate to both cultures.

At the time, my Kelty backpack was the only home in sight, but I was certainly anticipating some future, fully independent nest. My "home," i.e., the place where I grew up, never felt like a place of refuge, but rather a jousting tournament in which I was constantly on a smaller horse with a broken spear. *In order to have a true home, I'll have to make one for myself.*

One of the girls on the trip was a vegetarian. Since my Chinese was better than anyone else's, I was nominated to convey to all the restaurants we frequented that she could not eat any meat. The fact that I was studying Mandarin and everyone in Hong Kong spoke Cantonese didn't seem to register with my fellow students.

"No pork, no beef, no meat—okay? Just vegetables."

Our server's smile was luminous and toothy with perfect understanding. Then he'd proudly carry out a steaming, glistening-green platter of vegetables—draped with lots of saucy pork. This happened quite a few times. I began to lose faith in my language prowess, and so did everyone else. We often ate in large groups, and our favorite entertainment was to pass one single pea from chopsticks to chopsticks all the way around a table of twelve or fifteen, thus demonstrating our superior chopstick prowess. Later we graduated to passing ice cubes. This was rarely as successful.

For me, however, pork was prime nourishment even then. In Cantonese, the words for pork and dog are very similar (pork is *gau-yuk*, dog is *ngau-yuk*). We had heard about—but happily never saw any sign of—the rumored Asian penchant for eating dog, and we were all quite sensitive on the subject.

Our favorite server was aware of this discomfort, and several times a week just as I came up the steps, he used to sing out to me in Cantonese, "Brigit want special *dog* platter tonight?" It was always good for some cross-cultural protestations and feigned misunderstandings, and neither of us ever tired of the game.

The school group was scheduled to spend a week at a Buddhist monastery on the island of Lantau in Hong Kong bay. I tagged along. Apart from the food, I remember little about the experience. Perhaps I was off practicing my Chinese characters in a peaceful garden surrounded by circular gates. At the table, three times a day, we ate tofu. It was shockingly delicious, but I had to be convinced that it was indeed tofu. The Chinese do some magical things with bean curd—layered, pressed, in leaves, in sticks, deep-fried—the curd does such a good job of imitating meat that it's hard to tell the difference. We had, or so it seemed, chicken, pork, and fish with various tasty sauces and vegetables, and aside from the lack of Singha beer at the tables, the week was festive and enjoyable when it came to matters of the stomach.

There was another important benefit of the week at the monastery on Lantau: From then on, I would tell our favorite waiter in Cantonese, "My friend here eats like a monk." (*Wǒ péngyǒu chī de xiàng héshàng.*) She was never again presented with a plate of meat.

I've never been a lover of sweets. I almost never order dessert (or make it, to the chagrin of some of my dinner guests over the years). Chocolate, although it is certainly very nice, has never been as important to me as it seems to be to many people—except when I was in Hong Kong. The whole time, I absolutely craved Toblerone chocolate bars.

As I write this there is one on the counter behind me; I received it as a Christmas gift and it's now the end of August. But in Hong Kong, I needed chocolate. What was the dietary imbalance that caused my system to require something it could normally do quite happily without? News Flash: Chocolate cravings can be caused by a lack of magnesium in the diet, i.e., all those the leafy greens that were either not present or always cooked to death in Cantonese cuisine.

In 1979 no one thought of Hong Kong as part of China. Visiting the mainland at that time was another story entirely. It was only a year or so after the first Western visitors had been allowed in, and in some of the areas we visited, people had never seen a non-Asian face. Once in Changsha, our ancient school bus was literally mobbed—every window a kaleidoscope of faces smashed up against the window and each other, desperate for a look at us.

Our little group was assigned several "guides." These were young people who would have been just as happy quoting Mao to us from their Little Red Books. In fact, the true goal of our guides was not to show us around but to keep us away from the people on the street. I think it was equally to protect us from learning something inappropriate from the regular folks, and to protect those folks from seeing something objectionable in us.

When we ate, always in government restaurants, large screens were erected between our tables and the other diners. I was told that this was so they wouldn't have to watch us eat—evidently being quite disgusted by the whole fork thing. I chafed under the constant supervision of our guides and was eager to try out my hard-won Mandarin on some real Chinese people. When we arrived in Guilin and were given a strict thirty minutes to shower, I was right out the back door with a new Mandarin-studying friend. We were semi-mobbed in an instant but did get to practice both our own Mandarin and our new friends' English for a few minutes, before the breathless guides caught up and gently admonished us to hightail it back to the hotel.

Before we were forced to leave, our new friends asked us to dance. Western-style dancing, in particular the waltz, was all the rage in Guilin that year, and actual Westerners to dance with were thin on the ground.

We all waltzed briefly in the barren streets of Guilin, that strange vertical village so woefully unprepared to be blasted straight from the early nineteenth century into the last third of the 20th. Concrete alone does not a community make.

One night there was a gala banquet to celebrate the meeting of two cultures. You know, peoples of two countries that are destined to be "great partners in the rosy economic future we would all share," now that China had begun to open its borders? At the prospect of a room full of Americans, the local—what? Chamber of Commerce, I suppose—really pulled out all the stops. I guess they didn't care that most of us were under 25, not usually a respect-worthy age in Chinese culture.

In China, the rarer a foodstuff, the more honor is paid to the guest to whom it is served—thus the unfortunate delicacy of the bear paw. Yes, the paw of a bear. Then, there's the monkey-brain thing, but I'd rather not go into it. We were really and truly honored that night in Guilin. On the menu, along with about ninety-'leven other things, were bobcat and fruit fox.

Fruit fox? What's a fruit fox? A gay game of guess-the-animal ensued, and we eventually discovered it was a possum. Then there were the toasts. Toasting in China is like a game of one-upmanship; only it's not that much fun after you've matched your host toe-to-toe through fourteen exclamations of "*Gan bei*!!" Literally "dry cup"; i.e., you must drain your cup in order to show respect for your host. Now I'd like to think I can keep up with some serious drinkers, but I was way out of my league on this occasion. Mostly, it was because of what we were drinking. Sorghum liquor. Here's what it tastes like: chewing on a concrete block.

RIDING A TRAIN IN MAINLAND CHINA at that time felt like going back to a pre-revolutionary era of grand journeys, steamer trunks, paneled wood compartments and beveled-glass windows with discreetly close-able blinds. Every seat had a pretty lace doily-type thing draped on the top called an antimacassar; this looked lovely but was a functional repellent for men's hair oil, a relic of the mid-nineteenth century—likely the last time these coaches had been updated.

I was seduced by the rickety ambience of the train we all took from Guilin to Guangzhou (Canton), and imagined myself an Old China Hand, traveling through the pre-war China I had studied so much about, like Rita Hayworth in *The Lady From Shanghai*—this despite my constant attire of jeans, Wallabees, and a wool sweater. Although there were no white-gloved cabin boys or glittering glassware, there *was* a tall young man with sparkling blue eyes, jet-black hair, long eyelashes, and an infectious smile—the twinkling embodiment of Ireland's most attractive genes in one long, lean, Pendleton-shirted package.

Our little fling was a welcome salve for my need for physical contact after so many months away from Baird. I clearly functioned in the same way for Mr. Pendleton, who had a serious girlfriend patiently waiting back in Portland. The excitement was no less profound for being ephemeral and naughty; in fact, I suspect it was even more intense. My imaginary personal cinematographer was very happy on that train in China, although the costume department threw up their hands in horror. The newsy, lonely letters that arrived from Baird weekly were precious to me, yet entirely removed from my relationship with Mr. Pendleton. I had become adept at setting my morals aside, clearly an inherited talent. I answered his letters with upbeat stories and passionate plans for our future together, mailing off flimsy airmails to Senegal, Mali, Gabon, Chad, and Cote d'Ivoire, all according to the schedule we'd mapped out before parting. Later I would come to learn that while in the embrace of deepest darkest Africa, Baird, too, had strayed.

The final stop for the group was a month in Taiwan, where I was finally able to use my Mandarin everywhere. I couldn't resist the urge to over-share, telling everyone my life story and inquiring about theirs. We lived and took classes at Soochow University, right across the street from the legendary National Palace Museum. The collections of this museum are so huge—700,000 pieces—that only a fraction can be displayed at any given time.

All the antiquities were hijacked when Chiang Kai-shek, his wife the scary Madame Chiang, and the rest of the Nationalists fled Mainland China in 1949 to escape the incoming post-war communist administration of Mao Tse Tung. My favorite was an intricately carved ivory ball made up of seemingly hundreds of concentric globes. Reading the description informed me that three generations of artists from the same family had labored to produce it.

"What are you going to do when you grow up?"

"I'm gonna work on the ball."

MY COLLEGE CAREER WAS DRAWING TO AN END. The only thing left was to write the thesis I'd spent almost six months researching. There was no way I could write it in the communal living accommodations at Soochow U. I needed the privacy of a hotel room but had virtually no funds. A creative solution emerged. Not too far northeast of Taipei was a famous, generations-old red-light district known as Peitou. "Hotels" there were dirt-cheap. I secured a small room at the end of a hall, and after the management—with great amusement—located a table lamp, I sat down at my little manual Olivetti typewriter, surrounded myself with scribbled, categorized index cards, and started to write. Mr. Pendleton brought in spring rolls for sustenance and read drafts of the thesis. Our time was in countdown mode. Three days later, it was all over.

I look back at that senior thesis now in light of the Afghan diaspora, and the many multi-generational, naturalized Vietnamese folks in all of our lives, and wonder at my brutal honesty and non-judgmental analysis of a heartbreakingly complex situation. It's not an easy read, but I'm kinda proud.

When I slid the thick thesis into a manila envelope and sent it back Portland, it was my last act as a college student. I bid goodbye to the group and—choosing to skip my college graduation—headed off alone to Bangkok, and then a side trip by train to Penang and back. At the far end of the entire Indo-European continent, I had a long-arranged rendezvous with Baird, who would be coming up from Africa. We were to meet on June 1 at a café in Constitution (*Syntagma*) Square in Athens.

We hadn't spoken on the phone for six months—except for the two-minute conversation when he'd called me in Hong Kong from Gabon to tell me he'd been accepted for the master's program in International Studies at Yale. Even then it had sounded like fifty other people were on the line with us. They may well have been. There was still no such thing as e-mail.

The Dress

CHAPTER 9

The dress

SOUTHEAST ASIA AND GREECE, 1979

HUNDREDS OF LETTERS WITH EXOTIC STAMPS and postmarks from all over Africa had flown thousands of miles before landing in my mailbox in Hong Kong, and the latest of these (about a month old) confirmed that the meeting was set, for June 1 at a café in the southeast corner of Constitution Square in Athens. Until then, I was free and twenty-one, and there were a few places I wanted to go first: The world was my very plump oyster. Traveling light would be crucial. Into a box and back to Portland went my jeans and corduroys, fawn-colored Wallabees, and the Olivetti. I pondered my fresh new image: My academic wardrobe was officially history—it was time to let out the feminine, authentic me. Yet I'd need to feel confident traveling alone, so I passed on anything too risqué. After two weeks of solo travel, I'd be meeting with the main man in my life; he would certainly have become more worldly after his solo hegira. How would I measure up? Although my budget was virtually non-existent, it was clear that a new garment was called for.

At a street market just a few yards from the old Hong Kong airport, I bought The Dress from a woman long deaf from the roar of jet engines. She completely ignored the sudden, shocking sound as I looked up, cowering, suddenly able to identify each and every rusted bolt on the underbelly of a China Airlines jet.

There it was: The Dress. It was cheap, a throwaway for many, but for me, it was something far more. The neckline was collar-and-placket, the short sleeves slightly puffed, the rich reddish, floral-patterned fabric cut straight down from armpit to just below the knee; a thin, matching belt cinched the featherweight garment at the waist. It cost me less than five Hong Kong dollars. It was practical and appropriately conservative for solo travel, but just by undoing a few extra buttons at the neckline I could transform it into something that approached alluring. Later on, I would find that it was truly wash-and-wear: the cotton seemed slightly polished, and after handwashing, dried in ten minutes, when it would miraculously appear to have just been ironed. But it was not, at first glance, a significant dress.

Before going on to my reunion in Athens, I'd planned a little detour down the Malay Peninsula to revisit the stunning island of Penang, almost four years after my month-long homestay there. On the eve of my departure from Taipei, I had a ticket to Bangkok, but no further. According to *Southeast Asia on a Shoestring*—my tattered bible—it was *far* cheaper to buy the Bangkok-to-Athens leg in person from a funky travel agent on one of Bangkok's many backpacker-jammed streets.

I was ready to become a fully independent creature for the first time in my life, but there was a humiliating glitch: my very last—*ever*—allowance check had failed to arrive in time. Both my parents had let me know that there would be no more free ride; they'd done enough. The private schools, allowance, college, multiple overseas trips were history.

"You're on your own now, kiddo, the checkbook is closed."

I waited by the mailboxes at Soochow University in vain hope until literally the last possible moment. I had no cash, no credit card, and a next-day departure. In the morning while I was packing all my possessions into my threadbare Kelty backpack and fretting about my options, one of the remaining students rushed in with a much-traveled envelope from my dad. The check had arrived!

Perhaps predictably, in Bangkok no airport moneychanger, no bank, and no hotel would *touch* a personal check from another country. I didn't even have enough to cover the one night I'd already spent at the misnamed Royal Hotel. And thus, in the initial heady moments of my full-and-proud adulthood, I had no other choice but to call home.

"Mom? Hi, um, I'm in Bangkok, I can't cash Dad's last check here, and I don't have enough money to buy my plane ticket to Athens."

As I yelled these words into the humming transcontinental line, my hands clutched the telephone in such a way that, had it been a human neck, it would have snapped. *My humiliation is now complete.*

Fate and privilege grinned. Uncle Pat—who was on the board of Indonesia's national oil company, Pertamina—just "happened" to be at the house when I called. One hour later a sleek black limo pulled up to the hotel. A uniformed chauffeur got out, handed me an envelope containing four thousand Thai baht in cash (about $200), and then sped back into the snarled traffic. *Thanks, Guv.*

Down at the discount travel agency on Khao San Road, my ticket to Athens was indeed far cheaper than it would have been in Taipei. The universe had provided. *Okay, enough already with this adolescence thing.* As they say in England, remember the "Six P's": Prior Planning Prevents Piss-Poor Performance. Never again did I ask Uncle Pat for financial help, nor did he offer it. I paid back the $200 dollars within a month of my return stateside. But I was becoming aware that I was a very fortunate girl indeed.

THE RATTLETRAP POST-COLONIAL TRAIN that plied its way from Bangkok to Singapore and back ferried locals and overland travelers alike. In those days, you could travel "over land" from London to Southeast Asia, because Iran and Afghanistan were a lot more friendly. It was another chance for me to channel Marlene Dietrich in *Shanghai Express*, but this time there was no illicit love interest and, instead of jeans, I was wearing The Dress. When we debarked at the Thai-Malay border to show our passports, scary rifle-toting guards wanted to refuse me entry, since I didn't have a credit card, bank letter, or much in the way of cash after buying my ticket to Athens. But in The Dress—and my new, coolly capable mode—I produced my Bangkok-Athens ticket and had no trouble explaining to the guards my brief stay in Malaysia and onward-to-Europe plans.

By the time dusk fell on the rice paddies outside, the last-century paneled-wood dining car was filled with travelers of every nationality, all sharing tall tales and Singha beers while gleefully bemoaning the incendiary heat of the little chilies that garnished every roti and bowl of rice. In The Dress, I finally felt like the Old Asia Hand I'd so long aspired to be, trading stories and beers with the train's other dusty, twenty-something nomads deep into the clattering night.

Traveling second-class meant the sleepers were *Some Like it Hot* style: short, swinging curtains were all that separated each little upper and lower bunk from the aisle. For security, my backpack was my bunk-mate. Outside in the passing night, there were no electric lights, but once in a while a little cooking fire would zip past the window.

Deep in the loud dark night I awoke suddenly to a heavy male body forcing itself on top of me, and in an unheard but frantic struggle I attempted to push it away. Boozy breath and a German accent clued me to the identity of the intruder: one of the dusty travelers from the dining car. Materializing from the upper bunk like a silent, saving angel, a bearded merchant seaman from Scotland, Derek, also from the Singha circle, made short shrift of packing the drunk German off to his own bunk. Derek and I returned to our separate slumbers none the worse for wear.

When dawn peeked gently under my eyelashes, I could see that we were approaching the Penang/Butterworth station. The usual cluster of trishaws waited outside, and I splurged on one to take me to the hostel. The bike-assisted ride was not long, but in a newly effortless, solitary assurance I imagined myself straight out of the pages of Maugham or Anthony Burgess. Sitting back with crossed legs, I let the warm wind play through my long hair; The Dress was so perfect for the tropical tableau that my imaginary Hollywood costumer would have chosen nothing else.

In Penang, the beach out at Batu Ferringhi was as pristine as I recalled from my first visit, and the street markets still rich with colors, sarongs, food, and smells. Penang felt just a little like home, and I lingered a while to taste some flavors and gossip with my former host family before training back to Bangkok for the onward flight to Athens and the much-anticipated meeting with Baird. I prayed his plans hadn't changed, because after buying the plane ticket and then going down to Penang, I had only about two dollars left from the Governor's bailout package. I had resolved to never again ask for help from my family.

After the all-night flight to Athens—we touched down briefly in Dubai, where the runway appeared to be scattered with hundreds of small fires—we landed in Athens in the middle of a rosy sunrise. I changed my handful of coins into drachmas, brushed my teeth and hair, smoothed The Dress, and took a bus to Constitution Square. I was able to convince a small hotel to hold my backpack for (I hoped) a few hours while I went to American Express to check for a message. *Yes! It's here! He's here! I'm saved! Of course, there is no worried message from my mother. I've graduated and thus she's washed her hands of me. Cool.*

Baird had gone down to Nafplio on the Peloponnese peninsula for a few days, the message informed me. Not good news. But wait—the note was written a few days ago—he'd arrived early from Africa. The meeting was on, then, for noon. It was still just 10 a.m. I walked back to the little hotel, and hand washed The Dress in the public bathroom. In ten minutes, as always, it was dry.

As I waited there under the bare, dangling light bulb, I wondered how six months alone in Africa would have changed Baird. Certainly, I was a different girl—in fact, a woman. Would we still feel that same alchemical pull toward one another? The answer lay just down the street and across the ancient, sunbaked stones, and it was time to find out. I didn't spend even a moment worrying about how I looked, because by now The Dress had become my passport to an honest and easy self-confidence. (Okay, I undid a few buttons.)

Baird seemed taller than I remembered. His hair was shorter, blonder, his reddish beard trimmed close. His blue eyes—that had seen so many places since they had last seen me—sparkled as they looked me over, slowly up and down, and then up again.

"Hi."

"Hey."

A century of longing in two little words.

There were a few awkward initial moments—in all perhaps thirty seconds. It soon became clear that in our times apart, the easy confidence I'd gained made me more comfortable sharing what I truly felt, while the quiet self-esteem he'd embraced allowed him to listen. We both had wild tales of our own, and suddenly I knew we'd spend the next two months—at the very least—sharing them. Our adventure together as a team of two was just beginning.

After that meeting in Constitution Square on June 1, 1979, I wore The Dress virtually every day for two months—unless I was wearing a bathing suit or nothing at all. Baird and I ferried from Piraeus to Chania, then chose the small town of Paleohora at random on the map of Crete.

"It's right on the coast," I trumpeted, "and there's only one tiny road leading to it!"

This was long before the Michelin became my guide to adventure, and Googling was not even a gleam in anyone's eye. Paleohora beckoned, and we followed the siren's call. There, in that tiny golden village, the daily routine was simple. At the local taverna, we perched on blue-washed wooden chairs at an unstable table, where morning coffee extended into lunchtime as our salt-crusted heads met over the crossword puzzle from the *International Herald Tribune*—plenty of intellectual challenge for the day. At lunch, we consumed grilled octopus or *pasticcio,* and celebrated the constant but welcome color and crisp simplicity of cucumbers, tomatoes, red onions, feta cheese, and black olives, married by smooth Greek olive oil and pungent red wine vinegar.

Later, when the retsina had made our heads too groggy to focus on the puzzle, we dove from the rocks just next to our chosen taverna and swam through the crystalline water to a nearby beach. After that it was nap time. This was my first introduction to a restrained sort of hedonism: A long, lazy lunch. Preferably with a view. Local wine. Luxury not required. My view from Paleohora was a long one—it stretched out into the future and what I saw was full, almost pregnant, with promise.

When the stooped old landlady of our open-air cottage offered us peaches in return for the labor of harvesting them, we climbed the tree in her garden and split the pickings. On the island of Skyros, I laughed with the husband-and-wife proprietors in the tiny kitchen of a sidewalk restaurant, where they explained the elemental pairing of ingredients in a true Greek salad—although we had no language in common. "Cucumbers always star," they gestured/explained; "tomatoes—the kind that actually taste like themselves—play a supporting role. Slivered red onions, Kalamata olives, and feta make crucial cameo appearances. No lettuce, *please,* no!"

When it came to matters of the mouth and stomach, a common language was never necessary for me. From Hong Kong to Guilin to Skyros, grins, gestures, and happy taste buds were always communication enough. Way too soon we were climbing onto the Magic Bus for the four-day ride from Athens to London, where eventually a Freddie Laker flight would ferry us back to the USA. Even in the staid English countryside at the tail end of the summer, The Dress somehow allowed me to fit right in. Sitting among a riot of flowers outside a thatched pub that looked out over the Sussex Downs, I traded jokes and stories with a whole new set of friends. I sensed there would be many more. The allure of sharing food, stories, and smiles with people wholly unlike myself had grasped me, and it would never let me go.

Hollywood and Los Angeles were part of a past I had no need to re-visit.

My tan had deepened and my hair burnished blonde. The Dress became symbolic of the rich promise of the rest of my life, lying in wait there, just out of sight at the end of six months in Southeast Asia, two months wandering the Greek islands and Europe and, oh, yeah, getting that college degree.

BAD CUT IN NEW HAVEN

CHAPTER 10

falling far from the tree

OKLAHOMA, NEW HAVEN, NEW YORK, 1982

MY MOTHER ALWAYS SAID THAT EVERYONE must live in New York City for three years in order to become a fully rounded individual. After graduating from the University of Wisconsin at Madison, she had won a coveted internship with *Mademoiselle* magazine. She made her way to New York and took up residence with a very kind family friend. The future shined bright for such interns, and indeed after the gig ended, she landed a job at CBS, working alongside such leading lights of that era as Eric Sevareid and Edward R. Murrow. The CBS job, however, didn't last long.

Editor: "Marcia, I need that piece by Thursday."

Marcia: "Do you want it fast, or do you want it good?"

Buh-bye.

But New York City was never part of my own plan.

In my Hollywood-centric family, creativity was prized head-

and-shoulders above all else. As the only child of an actor and a sometime-writer, I grew up around people who made a difference because they created content that moved, inspired, and mattered in the universe far more than money. At least in their own minds.

According to my mother, the game of golf was "boring, middle-class." In much the same way that sailboats were prized above motorboats, a.k.a "stink-pots," she saw the business of banking and speculating for money as repugnant. Though she was fond of the benefits money could bring—she berated Pat Brown for not providing her with more generous birthday and holiday gifts—she herself was far above the money-grubbing ways that allowed him and, by extension, her, to take exotic vacations and buy designer clothes. The fur coat Uncle Pat gave her, constructed of literally hundreds of the small, cute animals known as "fitch" in the fur trade, but actually a common polecat, even had a detachable-by-zipper addition that could instantly transform it into a full-length cocoon of classism. It summered in the fur vault at Nieman Marcus in Beverly Hills and wintered in the cedar closet she'd had installed in a hallway closet.

It was a class thing, as was almost everything in her small and exclusive world. Like a mid-century Nancy Mitford, she celebrated PLU (People Like Us) and denigrated those who didn't meet her expectations for creative excellence. Her contempt was visceral, assured, and on full display to anyone who was not, to their embarrassment, PLH (People Like Her). My contempt for her had blossomed as I matured beyond the restrictions of childhood. When I graduated from college—in absentia—and found my feet as a woman, I almost instantly gained the freedom to despise her hypocrisy. *Almost.*

Upon our triumphal return to the USA, Baird and I made brief visits to parents in Oklahoma and California to gather possessions for our impending East Coast lives—this included the blue-and-white china I'd shipped on a slow boat from Hong Kong—and then drove to New Haven. I planned to work at something or other while awaiting word from Cornell on my application to the master's program in East Asian Studies.

The little rented house on Wooster Square was sparsely furnished. I set about nesting, once again sewing cute curtains out of patterned bargain sheets and refurbishing junk-shop furniture until it gleamed with Scott's Liquid Gold. I found a job at a local photography store catering to professional and amateur photographers, and made friends with a co-worker, Lorelei, who was a local. She and I bummed around the town while Baird concentrated on his studies. I learned, and then quickly un-learned, about a drink called Long Island Iced Tea. Most of a year passed.

Soon after our first landing in New Haven, Baird and I visited my mother at her converted barn in New Milford, Connecticut. This structure was an old theatrical summer-stock barn that the actor Fredric March had had transported to his property, first as a sort of party-house, and later as a playhouse for his daughter Penny and her tennis-playing friends. When Penny moved to Italy to marry an Italian, Freddy and Florence March had decided to legally split off the barn, and a sliver of land, from their main property and sell it. But due to its proximity to the main house, they didn't want to sell to just to any old stranger. They sold it to my mother, a friend of a friend and (much later) alum of Freddy's school, the University of Wisconsin at Madison. There, she had briefly assisted the playwright Thornton Wilder, according to her with a large dollop of flirtation on the side. (After Wilder's death, it was discreetly but widely acknowledged that he had been a closeted homosexual). Freddy had premiered Wilder's play *The Skin of Our Teeth* with Tallulah Bankhead in New York in 1942; my father later played George Antrobus in the same play at the Goodman Theatre in Chicago—circles within circles.

Every year my mother spent the month of May at the Barn, preparing it for the summer renters. Then in October she returned to close it down for the winter. Freddy and Florence March became another of her extended families, and mine, joining the Hollisters and the Rex Stout family. Since my mother had grown up with no father and a distant, constantly working mother, she was always in search of a family she could feel part of.

So it was that in October of Baird's first year at Yale that he and I drove up to spend the weekend with her. It was my first in-person meeting with her post-college-graduation, and it did not go well. It's impossible to recall what the issues were; there had been so many to choose from over the 22 years she and I had (arguably) known one another. She was a serial hater; there was always someone in her cross-hairs: my dad, Uncle Pat, my sister Nancy, and for a long time now, me. When we drove away, I in a silent huff, she standing in the gravel driveway screaming out invective, the face that so many found alluring all twisted and red, I swore to Baird that I would never speak to her again. *He doubts me.*

My father and older sister Nancy lived nearby in Warren, and now all three of us refused to speak to my mother. Nancy had stopped speaking to her evil stepmom a decade earlier. This was just fine with me. I cherished these rekindled relationships, and orchestrated some ambitious Thanksgiving menus, one of which—involving two rather fatty geese—resulted in Dad having to replace both of his ovens. My mother wrote reams of hypercritical letters accusing my father and Nancy of hijacking my affections. They made great kindling.

On the horizon, always, was my pending application to the master's program in East Asian studies at Cornell. The wait was excruciating. And after more than a year, life in New Haven had soured. I had developed a noticeable chip on my shoulder: Baird was a "Yalie," and I was heading toward becoming a "Townie." In New Haven, that divide was deep. Although we were not in contact, my mother's elitist gremlins were still at work deep inside my brain, and they taunted, "You do *not* want to be a Townie."

As he sharpened his prodigious intellect in the superb academic program offered by Yale, I cooked lackluster stir-fries starring limp, sun-starved East Coast vegetables, and floundered around within the non-academic population. My newfound self-confidence, always perched precariously above a precipitous drop, tiptoed closer to the edge. The application to Cornell became my guiding light, my purpose.

I didn't study and travel and grow into myself as a woman just to be a cook and bedmate for Baird. I decided it was time for some changes, starting with my long, straight hair. Walking into a small hair salon/barbershop, I told the lone, gum-chewing stylist that I wanted a permanent in the form of a style then known as a "natural." I envisioned tumbling, luxurious curls, and a sort of lush Carly Simon look. The stylist apparently thought I wanted an Afro, not my intent in the slightest. Without washing my hair, without discussing my mane and its future, she grabbed a hunk of my hair and cut it off just an inch from my outraged scalp.

I screamed. She screamed. I fled.

Many hours and dollars later, after throwing myself on the mercy of another, glossier stylist, I sported a football-helmet-shaped head of tightly curled hair. It may have been the least flattering hairstyle in the large pantheon of such aberrations. If I have not already burned all images of this horror, I've been remiss. This look did very little for my self-esteem.

A few months later a letter from Cornell admissions arrived at Wooster Square. I sat in the rode-hard Scirocco with Baird outside the little house, trembling with anticipation. He opened it. I squeezed my eyes closed and prayed.

"They've accepted you for the master's program!"

The relief was visceral, the jubilation complete. I knew this was my destiny, finally within reach. We hugged in gratified amazement. It would require us to live apart, sure, but just temporarily. *Been there, done that: no problem.*

Typed below the happy acceptance was a more ominous message: Financial Aid forms must be in by June. It was April. The message had a sub-text, visible only to me: I would have to contact my mother. *I will have to beg and plead and apologize and generally revert back to the emotional age and behavior of a 13-year-old. She'll be thrilled.*

It had been almost a year since the conflagration in the Barn driveway, and the lack of drama and criticism had been immensely liberating. But now I needed her. I swallowed my pride and crafted a letter describing the program, my exciting acceptance into it, and the necessity of filling out financial forms. I asked for no help with housing or living expenses, and hoped she might be proud of my academic prowess and motivation. I even called Los Angeles several times, with the intention of eating some crow, but she never returned my calls. Once I called twice in a day, and the outgoing message on her machine had been slightly changed, so I knew she had been home. *She is listening to me plead and ignoring me.*

A month later her secretary Dorothy called me. *Why does someone need a secretary when someone doesn't have a profession?*

"Your mother doesn't have time to fill out these complicated forms," Dorothy said, "She has too many more important things on her desk at the moment." To my next question, she responded "No, she's not willing to let you see her tax returns so that you can fill it out yourself."

My mother had two secretary/assistants during her life, both spectacularly well qualified to help her do nothing. The first, Allison Caine, was the ex-helper to Sonny & Cher; I had all of their records when I was very small. The second, Dorothy, was also a secretary to Uncle Pat and his wife Bernice. She knew all about the affair between Pat and Marcia but was somehow able to compartmentalize the knowledge and continue to interact with Bernice Brown for many years.

Bernice also knew about my mother—as did, or so it seemed, the entire Democratic Party in California and, arguably, Jerry Brown—but to the best of my knowledge this was never openly discussed in the family or in the Party. Years later I met with the author of a book about Pat and Jerry and shared some of the letters and recordings of Pat and my mother arguing and canoodling. She was grateful she hadn't known about the "Great Affair" when she'd been writing her book.

Nevertheless, I saw two choices in how to process this development: I could rest assured that my estimation of my mother's character was correct, my hostility and contempt justified. Or I could decide that her apparently spiteful and complete de-railing of my academic and future life plans was in some incomprehensible way *my own fault*. I chose Door Number One.

And that was the end of my plan to earn a master's degree in East Asian Studies. The tuition was totally unaffordable without financial aid. *Anyway, all the wind has been fucking sucked out of my sails.*

Hanging around New Haven waiting for Baird to get his M.A. suddenly felt like a dead end; his career was coming into focus while I worked the counter at a camera store. I hatched a plan to move into New York City with the local friend-of-a-friend. I carted my Mao Tse Tung posters, backpack, Chinese language books, bits of furniture, and a few records down to a five-floor walk-up on Mulberry Street in Little Italy. Baird was supportive; we would commute on weekends. I took a job as the receptionist for a temping agency and used their word processor to send out resumes to anyone who might be interested in my Bachelor of Arts degree in Chinese Studies. One night the phone rang very late, and the roommate answered. "No, this is Katie," she said. In my sleepy state I assumed the call was for me and reached across the three feet between our single beds to grab the phone.

"No way!" she screamed into the phone in instant and visceral hysteria. "How did he die?!"

The world screeched to a stomach-churning halt, and then proceeded in extreme slow-motion as my sleeping brain deduced that, obviously, since the call had been for me, *Baird had died.* It took a few minutes to pierce the veil of tears and discover that, no, it was not Baird who was dead, it was John Lennon. He had been shot outside the Dakota just a few miles from where we slept. Losing John Lennon from our world in such an unimaginably senseless way felt like the last nail in the coffin of my youth. Optimism took a sabbatical, and I didn't go along.

Chinatown was just a block or two away and provided familiar smells, sounds, and flavors for my Hong Kong-starved psyche. Mahogany-brown ducks hung in rows, and my new best friends at the market hacked them into pieces that were easily stir-fried with broccoli in my trusty traveling wok. At Thanksgiving, instead of an expensive turkey, I scared up a goat couscous. I went on innumerable interviews, choosing either the blue suit or the brown suit, both Burlington Coat

Factory special sales. During the festival of San Gennaro, I navigated my way to the subway carefully through a gauntlet of immense and overflowing sausage and pepper sandwiches, hoping no stains would mar one of my two interviewing costumes.

This was 1981, and business with China was still in its early nascency. Coca-Cola, The U.N., the World Council of Churches; I tried every company and agency that was beginning to expand into China, but all wanted applicants with an advanced degree. For a year, Baird and I commuted back and forth on weekends and talked on the phone nightly; as his horizons expanded, mine seemed once again to be rapidly shrinking. Months of sitting in the little front office of the temp agency left me fearful of ever finding a career and a calling. Despite railing against my mother's lofty expectations, I knew I wanted to Make A Difference, to make a positive contribution. When I was 12, she'd told friends I'd be the first woman president. *Of course, that was before I'd turned into the Bad Seed, the Rottenkid.* I was now 25, and in my estimation going nowhere at a rapid clip.

After sending a squad of temps out to fill in for sick or vacationing sales assistants at Morgan Stanley, I decided to take one of the temporary spots myself. It would be an experience, something new, something perhaps a bit glamorous. Within two weeks of ascending to the 32nd floor of the Exxon Building on Avenue of the Americas, I was offered a permanent job as the sales assistant to what was known as a "dance-floor broker." A nattily dressed social climber who trolled for clients in the Hamptons and canyons of Park Avenue, Richard D was something of a joke on the retail sales floor.

"Richard D. should write a book called *Everything I Know About the Stock Market*," said one wag, "Only it'll be a blank book!" My first exposure to investment banking humor.

But at that precise moment I received another job offer. After many months of sniffing futilely around the seemingly impenetrable China-related job market, my fortunes were beginning to look rosier. The World Council of Churches wanted to send me to Hong Kong, they said, where I would supervise Vietnamese refugees taking shelter in a collection of seedy military barracks while awaiting resettlement elsewhere in the world. Apparently, these stateless families wanted to cook over private fires in their assigned, individual living quarters. This was a truly dire fire hazard in those old buildings; "management" wanted all cooking to take place on a large central parade ground. Having spent time with families like these a few years earlier, I completely understood the problem; the parade ground was impersonal, de-humanizing. The individual spaces, although grim, allowed each family to maintain their dignity. I would have done the same. Many of the refugees had by then spent years waiting for a break, and dignity was a fast-disappearing commodity.

The Council of Churches was offering a salary of $4,000 a year. Morgan Stanley offered $14,000. This was clearly a huge fork in my path to a full and productive adulthood, and a vexing quandary. I wrote pages and pages in my journal examining each of the two options in great—perhaps, obsessive—detail. Going back to China had been my heartfelt goal. And yet I hesitated. In the end it was not the money that swayed me. I just couldn't envision all 95 pounds of Brigit having any sway with adults bent upon saving their family's dignity amid such profound upheaval. I never even considered reaching out to my mother for advice about how to proceed with this life-changing choice.

I took the job with Morgan Stanley. I had pivoted from the possibility of giving back and of nurturing my creativity, as family tradition required. Although I did not perceive this, I was effectively flushing away the three years I'd spent learning Mandarin, including my proudly won four thousand Chinese characters. As if to truly pound a nail into the coffin of my youthful expectations, I also severed my relationship with Baird. After a time, his sharp and sparkling intellect had become a hard shell, one I was not smart enough to penetrate. I was relegated to the ranks of the normal, the less-than, the also-ran. There was no room for my nascent ego in the construct he'd created. I already had one sharp-tongued and condescending critic, and I was trying hard to break up with her.

The once-deep love affair had run its course for both of us, although he didn't quite appreciate this at the time. And to be honest, the lure of being single in New York City was a potent one. I had discovered that I was every bit as good at flirting as my glamorous mother, possibly better. And I had gotten a glimpse of a glittering world that she abhorred. Perhaps I loved it so much because I knew she would hate it.

Edmund G. Brown
450 North Roxbury Drive
Beverly Hills California 90210

November 6, 1979

Dear Brigit,

Enclosed find check. Happy Birthday!

I do hope that you are doing well, and if there is anything I can do to assist, please let me know. It seems to me that you have to determine your own future and then let me know what you would like to do. I will then see if I can help you. Old governors can sometimes help, and you can rest assured I will do my level best.

I see your mother from time to time and she looks well, but whenever she hears from you on the phone or by letter, she is a different person. You have no idea how much she loves you, although I know that sometimes she has a funny way of showing it.

When you come to Los Angeles to see her, please let me know so that we can have lunch and meet some people from the Far East.

Love,

The Guv

GIRLS OF MORGAN STANLEY

CHAPTER 11

The concrete canyons

NEW YORK, 1983

NEWLY SINGLE IN THE BIG APPLE, I took big bites, which made navigating around the worms difficult. I was promoted from Richard D.'s Sales Assistant to an "odd-lot trader," every day sitting right on Morgan Stanley's trading floor at a mini-trading desk with five guys named Vinnie. After Little Italy, my next, now-solo apartment was a five-floor walk-up at 94th Street and Third Avenue. Across the street was a miraculously still-vacant lot populated by well-tended vegetable patches as it waited for approval as future home to the Rupert Towers. Out my front window I could see a sliver of the Triborough Bridge. A classic NY railroad flat, the apartment contained one tiny bedroom, one tiny bathroom, and an amazingly small kitchen boasting a rare pass-through window to the "dining corner" of the main room. The front door opened into a tiny hall, which strung these rooms together, except it never opened all the way because the hallway was too narrow. The apartment's most fabulous feature was an entire wall of exposed bricks.

There was an air-conditioner up front, which exerted zero influence on the temperature of the bedroom at the back, which looked out onto an air shaft. In the main room, where I slept on the floor on hot summer nights, the furniture and Mao posters I'd hauled from California to New Haven to the studio in Little Italy now felt right at home. For a while after the departure of Baird, I had a flight attendant sleeping on the foldout Jennifer Convertibles sofa for a night or two every week to help out with rent, but I soon tired of this lack of privacy. I decided to dive into solo living, spending fully fifty percent of my take-home pay from Morgan on rent.

According to various young men, I was the only date-able woman in New York City who had ever cooked for them at home. With my keen and perhaps overly exacting attention to the idea of fairness, re-ciprocation was key; if I were taken out to dinner, it was then my turn to cook. Many Manhattan women used their ovens as shoe storage and would blanch as white as a dish of plain pasta if asked to entertain a guy to dinner. My stressed-out, rent-heavy budget dictated careful attention to detail, but nevertheless my second-date menu included filet mignon topped with a smoosh of canned foie gras wrapped with a slice of prosciutto to hold it all in. This was napped with a "light" brandy cream sauce. It was my kitchen, my menu, and my very own exciting life as a self-supporting Wall Street career girl, and this was a giddy existence. On the subway, my eyes glanced away from the tired, lined faces of women I imagined had been just like me 20 years ago. *That will not be my fate.*

One weekend in July during my second year of Wall Street life, I set out to orchestrate a dinner party on the roof of my building, con-veniently just one floor above me and the site of much sunbathing and spraying of Sun-In onto hair—my own private tar beach. Four precious college friends were in town. *These guys are old friends of Baird's, so I'll need to totally slay the evening to prove that I'm fine on my own.* The sum-mer menu reeked of my characteristic overkill: A crown roast of pork stuffed with wild rice, sautéed potatoes, green beans with almonds, and chocolate mousse—most recipes straight out of my then-bible, the original *Silver Palate* cookbook.

I hired a waiter from an agency for the evening, and my little kitchen and I went into overdrive. On the night, my dining table and some chairs were hauled up the stairway and through the trap door. The blue-and-white china I'd shipped back from Hong Kong all matched. My boom box blasted Hall & Oates, Stevie Wonder, and Jefferson Starship. I had a date for the event, who shall remain nameless because I don't remember his name, nor him. The festivities commenced and the roof at 94th and Third morphed into a fairy-tale tableau of twinkly lights, clinking glasses, and the flickering lights of the city on the horizon. I had a breathless sense of excitement at this proof that I had truly grown up, this clear evidence of an ability to please people with my food. I still have the thank-you cards tucked into my travel-worn copy of the *Silver Palate*.

My job at Morgan Stanley required constant communication with the then-only-two international offices, London and Tokyo. I frequently received late-night calls from Tokyo; often a salesperson trying to track down a stock or bond settlement that had gone astray. At 7:30 a.m. when I arrived at my desk toting a half-gallon of iced grapefruit juice, the London line would already be ringing.

"*Hallo* Brigit, this is *Nigel*!"

My friends enjoyed my braying rendition of this ritual conversation enormously. I'd made a few good girlfriends in the company; Margaret, the stunning, well-endowed girl from Queens who fielded near-constant invasive, obscene comments from the wolfish traders and salesmen with consummate grace and an accent thicker than the crust on a Lindy's cheesecake. And then there was Kris, my bestie. She helped me navigate not only the world of investment banking but also the jungle rules of New York City dating in the mid-eighties. After my four years of 98 percent fidelity to Baird, it was a whole new world. At that time, to show any interest in a languidly circling date-able guy was widely seen as pointless.

"Are you stopping?"

This was the question on the lips of my inner circle most nights at closing time. Most nights, we stopped. My stopping involved one or two large Greyhounds of the non-canine variety. This made for a poetic counterpoint to my standard morning quart of grapefruit juice but after a year of this citric acid overload I was left with an ulcer.

The trading floor at Morgan was far from a diverse melting pot; virtually everyone was white. The salespeople and traders—old and young—had money, often a great deal of it; the sales assistants and other support staff like me lived hand-to-mouth. One night a few of the girls were invited to join in a small party that involved a stretch limo and much stopping, debarking, drinking, and then re-embarking. Inside the limo, I asked jokingly "Will there be porn films on the little tv?" *I am the picture of slightly saucy innocence.* There were indeed. My girlfriend had to lift my chin up with a crane as I sat transfixed at the sweaty exertions emanating from the tiny black-and-white screen. In retrospect, I consider myself very lucky not to have run across Donald Trump, but there were many just like him braying along the avenues.

My boss on the trading floor was an American married to an Englishwoman who was rumored to be something of an entitled harridan. Morgan Stanley seemed to have a plethora of such cross-Atlantic relationships. When I sought to overhaul the international settlements process for fixed-income securities, he opined that I was "too ambitious." This while he had me typing up an exhaustive inventory of his and his wife's personal possessions for an upcoming move to London.

"Forty jardinieres," *I typed. What's a* jardiniere? *Oh right, it's a fancy name for a flowerpot.*

So, um, why does anyone need forty of them?

IN THE INTERESTS OF FRATERNIZATION, my counterpart in the London office was dispatched to New York for a month, to "see how they do things over the pond." English Sally—a true peach—would become a life-long friend to both Kris and me; we taught her to pronounce lasagna correctly—she said la-*sssah*-nya, we said la-*zah*-nya—and took her out for multiple instances of girls-only, dance-around-the-purses nightlife. The boys at Morgan Stanley were too dangerous for us. Most of the time.

A conservative *looking* girl, Sally sported a wicked wit, sparkling eyes, and an impish grin. After Sally's month in New York, management asked if I'd like to travel back over the pond with her and spend a week seeing how they did things over there. On our way to London for my very first visit there, we traveled business class on Mother Morgan's dime, both wearing pearls, shoulder-pads, and high heels. On our days off, we tended to look like a Laura Ashley ad.

Sally filled me in on London office gossip. "It'll be interesting to see if you think Joffrey is attractive. He's the only guy on the trading floor who'll get your knickers in a twist." *Is that like getting your undies in a bundle?* Joffrey was a bond trader, she added, and his then-long-time girlfriend, Carole, was a secretary on the trading floor. Morgan's London office was beginning to sound like one big frat party.

When we landed, Sally took me home to her parents' house in Surrey, where they both welcomed me with genuine warmth. Having supped at my Upper East Side table on several occasions, Sally was eager to cook for me, and in the process show off her country's best. My welcome dinner consisted of poached chicken with béchamel sauce and steamed cauliflower with cheese sauce. Bless her cotton socks; every single thing on the plate was white. I adored her, and her parents, and Surrey, but harbored a few doubts about the English diet. And then Monday morning rolled around, and we were off to the office.

Well, I would have had to be dead not to find Joffrey attractive: he was a cross between a young Hugh Grant and a young Paul McCartney, with a tousled head of longish curly brown locks garnishing a fetching widow's peak, sparkling blue eyes, and a dimple that could take your breath away. It was rare to see him without a flirty grin on his face—as though there was an inside joke understood only by the two of you—the laugh lines already forming on this 27-year-old Brit served only to make him look like loads of fun. And the accent—oh my, that sexy accent. *I've always been a pushover for an accent.*

But with his stylish blonde girlfriend lurking about the trading desk, I wasn't going to do anything about it. Unlike me, however, he *was*. A month later, who should turn up in the New York office on a Monday morning? Mr. Bedroom Eyes himself. On the very first night, he insisted that we have dinner together. *Who am I to say no?*

At midnight, the Gold Room Bar at the Helmsley Palace was far too cavernous to be intimate. Housed in the historically important Villard Mansion, the bar anchored the ostentatious lobby, with its mosaic ceilings, stained-glass windows, and marble staircase. A glitzy 51-story tower housing hotel rooms had recently been tacked up behind it, but the iconic bar remained as testament to New York's gilded age. I perched on a bar stool, wearing my best Loehmann's striped silk sailor dress and black stiletto heels, trying desperately to look as though I belonged. *What if hotel security thinks I'm a prostitute?* Festooned with glittering lights, sparkly glasses, and disposable income; the only beverage one could possibly order here was a classic Champagne cocktail. Narrow-beam jewelry-store lights illuminated the sugar cube in the base of my champagne flute; tinted blood-red with Angostura bitters and shooting out tiny, fast-rising bubbles like a Perseid meteor shower. On the surface of the limpid, golden liquid the rising bubbles erupted gently but relentlessly, a flower that must bloom or stay closed and bashful forever.

Joffrey's eyes were hypnotic, quietly speaking volumes over the rims of the flutes. In the elevator up to his suite, we were glued together like two survivors of a nuclear holocaust, oblivious to any sort of world outside our tiny, exultant bubble. There was simply no other universe but the one inhabited by Joffrey and Brigit. And it was a universe to which I truly, madly, deeply wanted to belong.

Carole-in-London and my own then-boyfriend seemed quite unimportant when I woke up the next morning with a huge grin on my face and the feeling that something Very Big had just happened. And I wasn't thinking about dual infidelities.

For the rest of that heady, whirlwind week, I was a regular at the Palace, swanning in and out of the massive doors as if I were Leona

Helmsley herself, exchanging pleasantries with the uniformed door-men and practicing my "model strut"—the languorous strides, hips leading, arms jauntily swinging that my mother had taught me when I was ten. On Saturday morning, I was due to fly off to a wedding in Washington D.C. with the still-in-the-dark guy I'd been dating on and off for six months. Joffrey closed all the curtains tight and turned off the alarm, but I made it to the flight on time. I endured the wedding events, pretending to be the Best Man's dutiful date, but feeling enor-mously out of place amongst the braying, plaid-jacketed preppies. The idea of Joffrey seemed so exotic, so elevated, so worldly, so much more sophisticated than this mid-coast white-shoe scene.

By Sunday night when I returned, I was starved for Joffrey; my stomach and heart literally felt concave. I couldn't believe I had sac-rificed 36 hours of possible togetherness rather than let down a man who cared more about his fraternity buddies than about me. On the flight back, I thanked the date and told him we were done. He seemed unsurprised. *Okay, perhaps just a tad put out.*

On Monday, Joffrey went back to London. We clung to each oth-er at Kennedy airport; a bomb could have gone off and we wouldn't have noticed. After two short visits to London and many expensive, hours-long phone calls, he sent me a ticket to Greece. I slept all the way from Kennedy to Athens, dreaming of an exotic, cared-for future and envisioning myself as a sort of Jackie Onassis figure, protected from the cruel world by an armor of money. *You will not be one of those sad, forty-something women on the subway.*

On our third night on the island of Paros, we sat in a waterside taverna drinking retsina and gazing deeply into each other's eyes.

"I guess you'll have to come live with me in London then, won't you?" he teased in best Dudley Moore accent.

"But, what *as?*" was my coquettish reply, never thinking for a moment that he would *propose*. I was simply searching for some eight-ies-style *Cosmopolitan* magazine-inspired ideal of "commitment." In 1980s New York City twenty-something single-girl terms, this guy was truly a catch, one I'd never expected to come within reach of my inadequate hook.

But he did propose.

Joffrey said all the right things and I said all the right things—mostly "Yes." To celebrate, we went out into a dark, Greek field and made love under the stars. Having grown up firmly in England's middle-class, he was empowered by the heady certainty that simply because he made a comfortable living as a bond trader, we could sculpt our entire lives exactly as we pleased.

I couldn't wait to start living my glamorous new life: No more peering in at other people's marriages as if I were starving, pressed up against the window outside a smoky Parisian brasserie, maybe even no more *financial worries*. I wanted so badly to belong to a winning team of two, and to have the kind of control that is not really about money but comes so much more easily when you have a comfortable chunk of it. I was ready to be loved unconditionally, and to be taken care of for a change. The world seemed to be our very own lobster.

"GUESS WHAT, DAD?" I said into the phone.

"You're pregnant," came the deadpan response. We were both in New York City, but I hadn't seen him since the opening night of *Ghosts*, in which he was appearing on Broadway with Liv Ullman and a young Kevin Spacey.

"Daaaad. No! I'm getting married!"

"Geez, I always thought you'd be the first of my three girls to get pregnant," he quipped.

At the time, I thought this was just Dad joking; at some later point I realized that it was more likely a nasty jab at my rather early sexual awakening. *Thanks, Dad.*

Joffrey promised to break the news to still-in-the-dark Carole "soon." The word seemed to have a somewhat different meaning in England.

Over the next several months, as I navigated my way toward permanently leaving the USA, Joffrey flew to New York almost every weekend.

He'd pull his Jag into the covered car park at London Heathrow, wave at his newfound buddies at British Airways, and by 10 p.m. Friday be climbing five flights to my Spanish Harlem-adjacent nest. We shared our hopes and plans for the future, laughing hysterically at all the conversational pitfalls. We were the epitome of "Two countries separated by a common language," as George Bernard Shaw put it.

"What do you mean, you'll call me on the 'dog-and-bone?'"

"Why shouldn't I say, 'I'll squirt you off with a hose?'"

"My 'fanny' is my bottom, right?"

On one of my few trips to London during that time, he showed me his surprisingly modest duplex in Purley, an unassuming suburb not far from the blue-collar hub of Croydon.

"Don't worry, we'll buy a lovely, grand flat in Hampstead as soon as you get here," he promised.

Ooooh. Really?

I was champing at the bit to embrace every middle-class value my mother found so abhorrent. This was my big chance for a fairy-tale marriage, to break the family cycle of infidelity and mistrust.

On my last day at Morgan Stanley New York, my workmates asked the kitchen to create a farewell cake. On the top was written "Pip Pip, Cherio." I didn't bother to mention the spelling error because I felt like I'd won the lottery. Door Number One was open, and I was heading through it to a shiny new world. A world safely far away from my mother. Back in my fifth-floor walkup, soon to be emptied and bequeathed to Kris, I danced madly to Warren Zevon's "American Werewolf in London."

WHENEVER MY MOTHER DANCED, I cringed. Silly pitiful little look on her face, twirling her long strand of crystal beads like a flapper. This was probably cute, maybe even sexy, once. I don't twirl any stupid beads. I flip my hair back and forth and it is awesome.

Note to self: Let's remember to act our age. Eventually.

THE WEDDING IN NEW MILFORD

CHAPTER 12

much ado about everything

CONNECTICUT, 1984

I COME FROM A LONG LINE OF SOCIALISTS.

My maternal grandfather Ben Legere was a famous labor activist in the late 1920s, organizer of multiple strikes and even violence at U.S. and Canadian coal mines and textile factories. My maternal grandmother wrote for socialist newspapers before suddenly becoming a single mother, and then embracing lucrative work as the couture buyer at a waspy department store. My dad flirted with communism in Mexico City just before WWII; my mother considered herself a rabid progressive even though she owned two fur coats.

In other words, I was raised to be a good little bleeding-heart liberal. Imagine my parents' surprise, when I announced that I wanted a White Wedding to my English Knight, whose shining armor was a three-piece suit. Their surprise turned quickly to dismay when I asked them to pay for it. This was exacerbated by the fact that they were in year four of a ruinous and acrimonious divorce. The civil behavior that had characterized the early years of their separation evaporated when my dad came into his own with his new love, Liz. This request may have been one of the most selfish and self-centered moves of my life—thus feeding right into my mother's expectations. Liz told me later about a day when my dad drove over to my mother's Barn in New Milford to discuss plans for the wedding, and most importantly how the costs would be shared. Upon his return to their home in Warren, Liz said, he was shaking and white as a sheet, so angry that he was incapable of forming words. She was convinced that he'd killed my mother.

So not a great daughterly move.

But I had bought into the Morgan Stanley/Wall Street investment bank lifestyle and wanted to live it right. My friends expected a big traditional wedding, and certainly so did Joffrey's family and friends, some of whom would make the trip across the pond to attend.

My bestie Kris was my maid of honor, and since she was far more familiar with East Coast codes than I, her taste was a big influence on the planning. Food? A full sit-down dinner, of course. Music? A DJ would be great. Now we'll need a tent and a dance floor, natch. Cake? Let's go large! How many people? Well, 100 seems about right, dontcha think? Let's make sure we get a good professional photographer.

Both my parents were horrified. In our family, weddings were casual, intimate, unfancy, heartfelt. I was deaf to the rumblings. This was to be *my* day.

Since most of my new banker friends were in New York and Joffrey's people were coming from London, we settled on the lawn behind my mother's Barn in New Milford for a location, on a date just before it would be rented out for the summer season. I was already living in London, so most of the planning was done by telephone and through the kindness of Kris. My three-year-old niece Lily would be the flower girl, and Dad would walk me down the grassy aisle between the cemetery-like assembly of white metal chairs.

The dogwood tree planted to safeguard Freddy March's ashes would serve as backdrop for the non-denominational minister. I flirted with a simple tiered cotton dress, but at the last minute abandoned it for an ecru, silk-and-lace confection that was totally wrong for an outdoor wedding. I found matching fingerless lace gloves. I mailed a picture of a cake from the cover of *Gourmet* magazine to the little bakery in town. The *Gourmet* cake was palest smooth baby pink, three layers with no supports, and looked as though someone had casually scattered delicate, pale violets over the top. Violets made of finely worked frosting. Joffrey and his father would wear full morning suit regalia, i.e. top hats and tails, like concert pianists or the ringmaster at a circus. Two countries separated by a common language. That wasn't all that separated us.

New owners of the next-door house that had originally belonged to Freddy and Florence March had painted the pretty little bridge across the shared creek a sort of Chinese red. My mother had it painted back to its original white just for the wedding, then back to red again afterwards. This was uncharacteristically kind of her. I would later learn that she was possibly more invested in the optics of the wedding than I. Many of her East Coast coterie would attend. So, conspicuous middle-class consumption in the form of a White Wedding was okay with her, as long as it was on her terms. Got it.

When Joffrey and I arrived from London to begin preparations five days before the wedding, my mother immediately put us to work. Take out the trash, sweep the tennis court, pull the cobwebs off the pergola, run into town to pick up her corn pads; as always, her lists were prodigious. My father was nowhere to be seen, avoiding the drama by hunkering down at his own house a few miles away. After having spent the previous six months in London, I was consumed with my own rushed agenda—D.J., get dress pressed, flowers, photographer, yikes!

Joffrey felt he was being treated like a servant. Welcome to the family, I told him. Not an auspicious start to anything. If I rose at 7 a.m. I could get a big chunk of my own list accomplished before my mother awoke at noon as usual and started directing her team.

Kris drove to JFK to collect the English contingent; Auntie Eileen, who had never been to America, spent the whole drive back reading roadside signs out loud. Kris also revealed to me a little secret between her and my mother that she was not supposed to tell: My mother was surreptitiously carrying around a cute little oxygen tank, because of a recent bout of bronchitis. I absolutely was *not* to know, she told Kris, because I would "resent her for ruining my special day."

Of course, Kris told me. I examined my mother with a critical eye; she appeared the picture of health, so I chose to ignore this Machiavellian manipulation. *Outta sight, outta mind was my self-protective mantra.* Poor Kris, caught in the middle.

Although it rained the night before, the day of the wedding, May 19, 1984, was bright and sunny. The meadow looked luminous, everything green in a way that only a Connecticut spring could be. The dogwood—my grandmother Barbara's favorite tree—was in bloom.

Kris and I picked up the cake in the morning, after my hair had been fashioned into a horrible Shirley Temple-like mass of stiff little ringlets by the small-town hairdresser. It reminded me of the disastrous hair-crisis in New Haven only four years before. While Kris drove I ducked down onto the floor of the car, hyperventilating and trying to avoid seeing myself in the mirror. Or hearing her polite protestations that the hair wasn't really *that* bad.

And then, the cake: There it was inside its box. It couldn't possibly have been *less* like the picture from *Gourmet*. Instead of smooth, pale, and baby pink, the base frosting was neon pink and viciously combed. Instead of delicate little frosting violets in muted colors, the "flowers" were as big as walnuts, colored zit-yellow and snot-green. Rather than appearing to have been scattered with abandon, they were plopped evenly across the combed frosting like a really bad case of acne.

The tent and the dance floor and the chairs were in place; soon enough the chairs were filled with wet-behind-the-ears investment bankers, many family friends, a few college buddies, Joffrey's little family, and Jeremy, his English best man. Plus the Binns family—all from my father's side, since my mother had no other (acknowledged) family.

Dad, wearing a white jacket, and my mother, wearing a white and grey linen dress, eyed each other warily but were never seen to speak. My stepmother Liz had chosen not to attend, which made me sad but was the correct thing to do. I had already started calling Liz my "preferred mother." My mother had had a boyfriend in California for several years at this point, a Russian lit professor at UCLA whom she dubbed "The Professor." I liked him; in his presence she tended to relax into a human being. I'd suggested inviting him. Her response: "I don't want him to get an inflated idea of his importance in my life."

When Lily was handed her little bouquet of flowers and gently shoved out into the aisle, she erupted in tears.

"Just walk with her and hold her hand," I whispered to her mother, my sister Nancy. And she did, and they did, and other than that slight change, I thought the ceremony went off beautifully.

The white chairs were moved into the shelter of the tent, circling the round tables. There was good, small-town nineteen-eighties food, second-label California sparkling wine in tulip flutes, and speeches. There is even a picture of my mother and me sharing a giggle-laugh together that seems quite festive.

The best man gave a dry and hilarious toast about Joffrey and the rapprochement between our two countries represented by our multi-national partnership, blah blah blah. In another cross-pond partnership, Kris was having a *thing* with Jeremy. All the Binns girls danced with Uncle Johnny Binns, since my dad was not feeling in the family mood. His characteristic puns were uncharacteristically absent, and his was a rather somber table. Kris and I kicked up our heels on the dance floor, which had been a great idea. My mother danced with Jeremy, and I didn't even cringe as she took off her shoes so she could "boogie down." Joffrey's mother, dressed hat-to-toe in matching pastel just like the Queen, was radiant with happiness. Lily changed into green overalls and danced with Uncle Johnny while in her mother's arms. Despite my dad's dour countenance, it truly felt like a real family, a marginally normal celebration featuring regular people, not merely a microcosm of Hollywood excess weighted with famous folks.

I threw my blue garter, and Kris caught it. We were doing things by the book, damnit! I even changed into a "going-away" suit (grey with white pinstripes) before we drove off—amid much fanfare—to a little Inn halfway between New Milford and JFK. The next day, Joffrey and I were headed to Heathrow, where we would collect a suitcase of resort clothes from the left-luggage counter and then fly on to Sardinia for a honeymoon.

In the morning I called my mother from the hotel phone, waking her up at 11 a.m.

"Thank you so much, Mom! It was an incredible wedding and I'm so very grateful for everything you did, painting the bridge, lending your lovely home, I couldn't be happier! How did everything go after we left? Did anyone behave badly?"

My mother, however, was *not* happy.

"I never knew your sister *Nancy* was going to be in the wedding!"

"It was a last-minute thing, Mom, Lily was scared to—"

"Everyone in your family except me was in your wedding! How is that fair?"

"I'm sorry, I didn't realize it would be a prob—"

"Some of the guests asked if they could take home the floral centerpieces from the table!"

"I think that's kind of a tradition; maybe it's an East Coast thing..."

"It was *unspeakably* rude! And the caterer packed up all the leftover food, and I had friends spending the evening and there was nothing for us to eat!"

"The caterer was your cleaning lady Agnes, Mom, couldn't you have asked her to leave the—"

"I can see you have absolutely no sympathy or time for your poor old mother who went to such lengths to make your wedding a special day for you! Why am I not surprised? You've always been a selfish little bitch."

As I dissolved into tears, Joffrey was standing in front of me tapping on his watch.

"It's a toll call," he hissed. "It's going to cost a *fortune!*"

I waved him away. I had to at least try to talk her down off the ledge, but the hiccups and sobbing were stopping me from making any kind of cogent response. Her grievances were legion, and she simply was not getting off the phone any time soon. Joffrey stalked off to load up the rental car with wrapped gifts.

We were off to a great start.

At Heathrow, Joffrey collected the resort-wear suitcase and we rejiggered everything, then returned a different bag to Left Luggage, this one supposedly filled with porcelain candlesticks, silver stuff, and various traditional gifts. No one had thought of actually sending this stuff back to London, and in any event, there was no time.

Except that in the confusion, the suitcase of warm-weather clothing was left standing, alone, at the Meeting Point at Heathrow, where it was promptly inspected by bomb-sniffing dogs and sent to Lost and Found. We arrived in sunny Sardinia with a lot of wedding gifts, but only the clothes on our backs.

Another bride might have called her mom to commiserate, and maybe have a little giggle about the absurdity of being at a fancy resort in Sardinia with lots of bling but no clothes. I did not. For one thing, she'd made it clear she didn't want to hear from me for "a long, long time." For another, Joffrey had decreed there would be no more long-distance calls.

I'm a European now, and a wife. But I'm all on my own.

THE CAKE

CHAPTER 13

another country, not my own

HAMPSTEAD, LONDON, 1984

A FEW MONTHS AFTER OUR WEDDING, Joffrey made good on his promise. We—the Anglo-American newlyweds—were firmly ensconced in a blindingly white flat in Swiss Cottage, next-door-adjacent to north London's tony neighborhood of Hampstead. I was already starting to feel divorced from my American heritage. I saw American tourists on the tube with their out-of-place backpacks, Birkenstocks, brand-new travel guides and of course, the voices were always way too loud. It took no time at all to become over-sensitized to this ugly-American tendency.

Um, guys? Your polite English cousins are laughing at you.

But rather than judging harshly, I simply love them, or at least the idea of them, although these were people I'd likely never have known at home. A little part of me wanted to walk up to them and say, "Hi, I'm an American, too. Can we be friends?" This reminded me unpleasantly of my lonely early childhood, tagging along behind the glamour-puss that was my mother. Vacationing in Puerta

Vallarta, Acapulco, Hawaii—I was a bump on a log, lurking around my parents with a hangdog look.

"Look, Brigit," my mother would say while slathering on her special recipe sunning lotion and positioning her chair for optimum sun exposure. "There are some *children.*"

What was I supposed to do? I wondered then and even now. Walk up to the group of kids playing and say "Hi, I'm Brigit. I'm a child, too, so can I play with you?" I don't think I ever did, thus adding another barely perceptible layer to the stack of my mother's disappointment.

In the white flat, sheer white curtains billowed dreamily, if the weather was fine enough to open the huge casement windows that stretched almost from ceiling to floor. Two pale peach chintz sofas faced each other adjacent to an all-white open-plan kitchen, and the *piéce de resistance,* wall-to-wall white wool carpeting extended throughout. I had cooked in my tiny New York apartment so I figured I could cook anywhere. It was time for me to come out; to bite the bullet, invite people into our white place, and truly cook for them. Roast beef, being the paragon of all English paradigms, was hardly a safe bet, but apparently it was one I was willing to make.

The open-plan kitchen was daring for London in those days; there were no doors to hide behind. The calm, consuming whiteness fooled the eye into believing this was a perfect place, housing a perfect couple that had entertained hundreds of times.

I cut hearts and rounds from slices of dark pumpernickel bread, then spread them with a green-herb butter, so the perfectly matched shapes cut from smoked salmon and Parma ham would stick to the bread. Then I crammed the remaining herb butter into a piping bag fitted with a tiny star tip. I piped exquisite little rosettes cheek-by-jowl around the edges of each little canapé. On top of each one I placed a little gherkin, sliced and fanned. That night's guests, banker Dave and his wife Claire, would be bringing their two children, who were between the ages of 8 and 11. *This isn't really kid food.* In case the canapés were not enough on the appetizer front, I steamed baby new potatoes until they were just tender, then scooped off the tops with a melon-baller. Sour cream and then domestic caviar were dolloped into the resulting depressions. After the hors d'oeuvres, we would move on to the real starter: a *mousseline* of chicken wrapped in blanched spinach leaves. I unmolded the little timbales onto plates flooded with a simple tomato vinaigrette. The spinach was bright green against the red on the plate, and I piped a circle of basil mayonnaise around the timbales, then pulled a skewer through it back and forth at 1-inch intervals to create a fashionable zigzag effect.

And of course, *Le Dessert*. I had cut long, thin rectangles of puff pastry, knocked up the edges with a sharp knife and baked them to puffy, golden fragility. I spread the layers with *crème patissiére* and made a *coulis* of fresh blackcurrants with which to flood the platter. *Coulis* was very "in."

The timer went off; I gloved-up and took the gloriously crusty piece of beef from the hot oven. Proudly standing upright, my first roast appeared perfect.

"I'll just take a peek," said Joffrey, smiling.

He sharpened the carving knife with great pride and ceremony, then cut gingerly into the center of the roast. He turned to me slowly; I was ready for a rave review. But he was no longer smiling.

"It's raw," he hissed palely, with barely restrained malevolence. I fled to the bathroom in tears. The doorbell rang.

Later that evening: the snow peas had overcooked to an odd, gray-ish color while I nuked the roast at 500 degrees, during which time the open-plan kitchen filled with smoke. I was clearly struggling to present the finished meal. In English tradition, guests simply do not offer to help at a dinner party. But being American, Claire asked if she could give me a hand. I must have looked like a deer in the headlights, as I shook my head and shout-whispered, "No!"

At the table, the tension was thick enough to cut with a butter knife. Although they had certainly sipped good wines and dined rea-sonably well, the guests were somewhat somber, a little guarded. The children had gone oddly quiet, perhaps sensing that blood was in the air. I had just served dessert. Across from me, the first fork met my puff pastry...and stopped. The pastry was tough because, of course, I had overworked it. The fork, persevering, bore down hard, and a chain reaction was set in motion that ended with a piece of Blackcurrant-Cassis Napoleon, dripping with blood-red purée, sailing through the air. It easily cleared the edge of the table and came juicily to rest in the center of the new white wool carpet. I peered at the shell-shocked faces sitting deathly still around the oval mahogany table.

No one was smiling.

WITH JOFFREY AND YOUNG BOSS

out of the frying pan

ENGLAND AND FRANCE, 1985

"YOU DON'T HAVE TO WORK ANYMORE," said my brand-new husband, sometime early in my transformation from lip-sticked, high-heeled, Manhattan-prowling career girl to prim-and-proper, suburban English housewife.

"Um, okay," I ventured. I could hear my friends on both sides of the Atlantic in the background: "No work, free time; you're *so* lucky!" I was 26. What did I know? Possibly one of the worst decisions I ever made. At that time in England, a sort of precursor to the meme was floating around: "It starts when you sink in his arms; it ends with your arms in his sink." *Haha. Yuck.*

Although neither one of my parents ever went out to a daily job, I'd been raised with a strong work ethic and an imperative to give something back to society in some way, whether it was a paid position or to create art. It felt somehow *wrong* not to work.

Except—except I knew I'd always dreamed of going to professional cooking school. From my very first taste of my mother's cheese soufflé, I'd glimpsed my ideal future: a tasty journey of curiosity, discovery, and adventure. There were very few gifts from my mother that I considered precious; her love of cooking and her wanderlust were likely the two that saved me from becoming a sad and bitter person.

At this stage, the road had only been partially revealed, and I was eager to keep exploring it. I longed to refine my clumsy skills among true professionals. And miraculously, here I was in Europe, my new forever home, with a very nice young man offering to pay my way. I enrolled in the next session at a respected cooking school.

One of the best things about England is that it's so close to France. Amazingly—at least for a newly arrived American—you can go for the weekend, or even for lunch. When Kris came to visit from New York, I delighted her by tuning in a French radio station while we were still in the car, driving down to Dover to take the ferry to Boulogne for a day of cheese and ham shopping, Chablis-sipping, and escargot-slurping. We were home by dinnertime. But it was my very first trip over the Channel after moving from New York that was the true eye-opener, and palate-developer, and mind-expander.

I'd been to France briefly as a pre-teen, on the way to Italy with my family. But it was that first trip as a married woman that showed me not just another country, but a spiritual place I wanted to inhabit, one where the pleasures of the table could be taken very, very seriously. Yes, *truly* enjoyed, without that sense of embarrassment and guilt that Puritan-descended Americans still seem to feel at the prospect of such reckless self-indulgence.

It was as if I had never been to the real France before. Joffrey was eager to show me what lay just across the Channel, and even before cooking school had started, we set off for a weekend in Beuzeville, a village in Normandy just a brief drive from the ferry. Our hotel, Le Petit Castel—selected from the Michelin—was right on the town square. It was simple and spare, and the bathroom was down the hall.

On this trip, I learned The Rules:

The red *Guide Michelin* is The Bible.

The hotel is *not* where the money is spent.

Although Joffrey earned a generous salary for his age, I was just now discovering that at heart he was still a schoolboy from Twickenham, wowed by the trappings of wealth and possibly as uncomfortable in his own skin as I was in mine. When confronted with a situation in which he didn't feel he belonged, he had a habit of clasping his hands behind his back, maybe to prove he was not out to steal something.

We walked across the square to our chosen restaurant, *Auberge du Cochon d'Or*. Rated with two knives-and-forks in the Michelin, it was not a particularly high-end establishment, yet it was candle-lit and furnished with heavy antiques and dark tapestries. The huge faux-leather-bound menu was presented to me with a flourish and a whiff of hair pomade. Gentleman Joffrey, having once dabbled as a wine merchant, of course handled the wine selections.

Reasonably proud of my French, I ordered with confidence. First, I would have *paté de foie gras mi-cuit*. I had already developed a love of seared foie gras, and erroneously thought that *"mi-cuit"* meant it was lightly cooked. Well, it *was* a little bit cooked, but not right before it came to the table. This was the version made in a ceramic terrine, where a whole duck liver is packed, then ever-so-briefly poached before it is chilled, sliced thickly, and presented with tiny, quivering cubes of delicately-perfumed Sauternes aspic—i.e., wine Jell-O. It's almost always served with a tiny glass of Sauternes on the side, no matter what you might be drinking for your first wine of the evening. It was silky-smooth and yet zaftig; the contrast of cool aspic and rich liver astounded my naïve taste buds. The *mi-cuit* had been a fortuitous misorder.

And then came the main course. *Oh. My. God.*

It was *pintade*, a.k.a guinea hen, and being that we were in Normandy came with a luscious, creamy, buttery sauce. A sauce that was chock-a-block with whole fresh morels, which I'd never tasted before. This marriage of poultry that truly tasted of the farm with mushrooms that spoke of heaven *and* earth opened a door for me, a door to the future. The flavors and joys of that table, with all the right wines and the casual reverence for ceremony with which the evening unfolded, all these things brought on an epiphany which decided my onward path in life.

Later, I would learn to balance the rich with the light; fresher flavors with those weightier. But at this particular dinner I was bullet-proof. I went back to London a changed woman, no longer a girl in the ways of the table. *It is time to go to cooking school and learn to prepare the kind of food I ate in* Beuzeville.

At the time, Tante Marie was the only accredited cooking school in England. Since this was 1985 and England had a long way to go before it could lay claim to its current gastronomic crown, I might have preferred the *Cordon Bleu* in Paris. But I could hardly rush off to France for six months so early in the marriage. So, it was Tante Marie for me, and I was thrilled at the prospect.

On the first day of school in chilly January, I was sent outside to wash 40 pounds of gritty, cold, spinach at the garden sink. With cold water. *Okay, I'm game.* Then, the teacher cheerfully announced, we were going to learn to make steak and kidney pudding—with suet pastry. *Suet? What's suet? Oh, the fat that coddles the kidneys? Got it.*

I had a quick word with the headmistress Beryl about the Brit-centric start to the program. She explained that steak and kidney "pud" was a very important dish at company director's lunches, which many of my fellow students were training to cater. She assured me that the bulk of the program would consist of established French classics, the Cordon Bleu repertoire of Escoffier and his cohorts, the Mother-Daughter sauces, blah, blah, blah.

The next day, we made lemon meringue pie.

Over the next six months, I cooked everything from boiled tongue to *boeuf à la mode*, from *gougères* to *babas au rhum*, from choux pastry to *chou farcie*. We were graded on our chopped parsley: It must scatter off the palm "like delicate snowflakes at the touch of a breath." We plumbed the depths of bourgeois French cuisine and believe me, we went waaaay down.

Consider for a moment, the platter of *Chaud-froid* (literal translation: hot-cold): Boneless, skinless chicken breasts (white) are poached, cooled, and chilled. A béchamel sauce (white) is made; a copious amount of gelatin is added to it. A clear aspic (more gelatin) is prepared and chilled. Pretty little shapes—hearts, diamonds, spades—are cut from slivers of olives, carrots, and green beans with tiny aspic cutters. Leaves of tarragon and sprigs of dill are blanched and patted dry. First, the chicken breasts are coated with a thick layer of the gelatinous white sauce and chilled until set. Then the garnishes—vegetable and herbal—are dipped in clear aspic and artistically draped and studded all over the white-coated breasts. Finally, with extreme care, a last layer of the aspic is applied over the decorations, to give them what seemed to me a rather un-natural gloss. This goes off to set again.

Finally, a wine jelly—aspic, really, and yes, you *could* call it Jell-O—is made and left in a shallow tray to set. The aspic cutters are used again, to cut little diamonds and hearts out of the wine jelly; these serve as glittering, quivering garnish on the platter alongside the thickly en-robed breasts, that is, if anyone could ever bring themselves to eat such an over-handled, rubbery piece of protein. I certainly couldn't.

One of our biggest projects of the year was a Christmas fruitcake: The English kind, that lasts for decades once doused with booze and encased in an airtight jacket of royal icing. These cakes are traditionally made the April before Christmas, so the booze and dried fruit could have a chance to mature. Usually such cakes are decorated with festive, colorful scenes sculpted from piped royal icing. Everyone in my class made their own cake and decorated it to their personal drummer. Mine featured my mother water-skiing behind a speedboat, as well as multiple sailboats around the edges, i.e., all of her favorite things. *Here I am, still trying to earn my judgmental mother's approval at the age of 27.*

After packing minced dried fruits into the mold and saturating it with brandy, the cake weighed a ton. Joffrey convinced me that sending it to California for Christmas would be way too expensive and likely end in tears, so I took multiple photos and proudly, excitedly snail-mailed them to my mother.

Her response: "How odd."

At the end of the program, I weighed less than I did in junior high school. After cooking and touching all that rich food all day, I just didn't feel like eating any. But I did learn new skills, some of which still serve me well today.

One thing I learned: I'm not a pastry person: My hands are too hot and cause the butter to melt before it is supposed to. Puff pastry is my worst nightmare—my *bête-noire* if you will. Every time we were assigned pastry, I'd finagle my daily partner into making it by offering to wash all the dishes. It wasn't so bad; after the spinach incident, I never again traveled without my rubber gloves. Ever.

One of the school's staff convinced me that a box of 500 sheets of leaf gelatin—at the school's professional discount—was a great invest-ment. I may be forgiven for believing, at that particular time, that good French cooking required a lot of gelatin. And good French food was what I wanted to cook. Little did I know. That was 1985. I still have 357 sheets left, and I've given a lot away. I even pitched a cookbook called *Gelée*—hoping to find some gainful use for all my gelatin, but it didn't gel with publishers. I have moved that box from England to Spain to Venice Beach to the Hudson Valley to Paso Robles. I am open to suggestions, as long as they don't involve filling a swimming pool with Jell-O. This scenario has been discussed *ad nauseum* and I think everyone now agrees that a person who fell into such a pool would in fact drown. I know what you're thinking, and I will not make *Chaud-froid*. Nothing is that desperate.

The day of our final exams dawned and, as luck would have it, my menu included puff pastry. Hyper-ventilating while running my wrists under the coldest-possible water in order to super-cool my hot hands, I began the preparations—my *mise-en-place*. Stumbling through the pas-try, which I'd successfully avoided making during the entire school year, I was flying blind. I eventually finished my *Bouchées aux Champignons Sauvages*. *Dinde a L'Indienne* (creamed turkey curry) was a breeze—give me protein any day. The dessert, *Crème Asphodel*, was a cold, retro-confection hybrid of lemon mousse and soufflé. After squeezing the lemons and making the custard base, you were supposed to measure out three-quarters of a cup of the lemon custard and carefully fold it into your ethereally airy egg whites. Measure? What measure? I was too nervous, and just dumped all the custard in, then started folding. As a result, my *Crème Asphodel* was an inch higher in the bowl than everyone else's.

"Oooooh, Brigit, you *do* have a gentle touch with egg whites, don't you, love?" said one of the teachers. My lofty lemon dessert took center place while the puff pastry bouchées—crooked, flattish, and a bit oily—were overlooked.

I passed with flying colors. *I will never make puff pastry again. Pinky swear.*

The Mail
APRIL 24, 1988
ON SUNDAY

Your Money

A DREAM HOME IN
THE COUNTRY . . .
BUT DO YOU KNOW
WHAT IT COSTS
TO RUN?

Staff photographer, The London Daily Mail

ON THE COVER OF THE MAIL ON SUNDAY

cut and roll for five hundred years

LONDON AND HAMPSHIRE, 1986

IN THE U.K. A MAGAZINE CALLED *Country Life*—"The Voice of the Countryside"—presents a bucolic ideal which is, in brutally unfair reality, really only available to those who were born into it. The magazine exists in a sort of Downton Abbey-esque timewarp. For generations, this deceptively glossy and quintessentially British rag has purported to show the real home lives of well-heeled Hooray Henrys and Carolines. In truth an unapologetic vehicle for selling high-end rural real estate, it excels by creating the desire, then stepping in to fulfill the fantasy.

All the "articles" are heavily geared toward making mud-crusted Wellington boots and mud-splattered dogs seem glamorous. In urban centers all across the British Isles people coo over the photographs and fawning descriptions of estates abandoned by their generations-old owners because they were far too expensive to run. They pool their pennies dreaming of the day when they, too, can stroll the grounds of their historic pile, admiring the perfectly flat, rolling lawns.

In England, creating such a lawn is no small feat. After the land is cleared of trees, brush, saplings, stones, and roots, it is made as level as possible and seeded. Then a huge, perfectly smooth-sided metal drum—some of them are six feet in diameter—is filled with water for maximum heft. The drum is then pulled along the lawn in the damp season—every season is the damp season—when the earth is malleable. At first draft horses pulled the roller, then tractors did the work. Over time, a flat-as-a-golf course effect was achieved. You never get to stop doing this, because the vagaries of the English weather would return the lawn to craggy moor-like messiness in, oh, just a generation or two.

"Such a lovely lawn, darling."

"Thank you, darling. Eck-tually, it's very simple—you just cut and roll for five hundred years."

Both of us bought into the *Country Life* fantasy, lock, stock, and barrel. I realized quite early on that Joffrey was both awed by and uncomfortable with the trappings of wealth—even as he longed to have it for himself. Whenever I saw the tell-tale hands-clasped-behind-back, I knew he felt out-classed. He did this standing outside car showrooms, reading fancy menus in the lanes of London, and when trying to finagle an airline upgrade. And now, suddenly, he saw a chance to become the lord of his own manor.

As an American in late nineteen-eighties England trying desperately to fit in, I was too naïve to see through the gauzy veil and envisioned my very own destiny in *Country Life's* aspirational pages. And so it was that not long after cooking school I found myself living in a massive beamed, partially faux Tudor house in the Hampshire countryside. The house was embraced by a rustic bridge, a babbling brook, and softly rolling meadow as far as the eye could see. Of course, we tried to turn the meadow into a faultless lawn, but, as neophytes, ended up with two things: a spiky meadow, and a £400 per month gardener's bill.

Newly ensconced in "the cottage," we were eager to patronize the local pub and insinuate ourselves into the charming rural culture. With my Barbour jacket and Wellies, I was nevertheless revealed as a *poseur* the minute I opened my mouth. Every Brit pegs the class of the speaker within two seconds of hearing them speak. They can't help it. It's bred into them the same way Californians get excited whenever avocados go on sale. Americans were supposed to be class-free in the U.K., but in reality, I got shoehorned into the same box as Joffrey, whose accent placed him firmly in the middle-class suburbs south of London.

All I want is to be accepted for the truest version of me—the one my mother doesn't even know exists. Perhaps I have come to the wrong country?

Married to an Englishperson, the American is a hybrid who can either be instantly absorbed into the current zeitgeist or become a permanent outcast. My brand-new mother-in-law Marjorie bestowed her highest praise upon me when she gushed to her friends: "Brigit's not *really* like an American *at all!"*

In Hampshire, the prevailing accent is a sort of burr, which sounds a bit like you are speaking with your mouth full of haggis. On one of the first forays to our local pub, we elbowed up to the bar right next to a Wellie-wearing guy with a smooth, honey-colored Rhodesian Ridgeback lying placidly at his feet. Ridgebacks are in my blood because my mother had owned several when I was living with or visiting her. Of course, we started to chat.

As it happened, Peter was not just a Ridgeback owner, he and his wife Cilla were Ridgeback *breeders*. The one thing missing from our idyllic country existence was a dog, and this chance meeting seemed a fortuitous sign that a Ridgeback of our very own was an absolute must. As always, however, we were in a mad rush for instant gratification, and rather than wait for Peter and Cilla to find us a puppy from a respected breeder or wait a year or so for their next litter, we found a puppy in the pages of the London *Times*. We powered up to North London to secure him from a breeder unknown to our new friends. *I want a puppy. Now.* The desire for instant gratification had once again trumped making informed decisions, a.k.a. the Six Ps: Prior Planning Prevents Piss-Poor Performance.

There he was: a gangly, dark-muzzled, toasty-colored boy with soulful brown eyes and perky, alert ears signifying an innate intelligence. We named him Boss. He also had a perfect ridge (important to Ridgeback geeks), and by the time Boss was six months old Peter had agreed to show him. At an oh-so-quaint village dog show when he was 8 months old, Boss won the prize for "Most Appealing Eyes."

We were in love.

By this time, Cilla and Peter had become our great friends. Peter had been a fireman until one of Britain's many strikes put an end to that career. Now he sold frozen food out of a refrigerated van and showed his Ridgebacks. Cilla ran a kennelful of hunting hounds for a wealthy local landowner. The couple and their 8-year-old son Matthew lived in a cottage on the estate of the hounds' owner. Their cottage was cramped, crumbling, and antiquated, but it had a coal-burning Rayburn stove stuffed into the closet-sized kitchen and we spent virtually all our time at their cottage rather than at our much larger but far less cozy Tudor pile.

Boss was a joyful and cherished member of our little family, at least when we were alone with him. When guests visited, however, he reared up to his extended five-foot height and 90-pound weight, and basically attacked them. As he matured, he got more and more difficult to control, and even Peter had to admit defeat when Boss was banned from the show ring after growling at a judge. Peter diplomatically allowed that perhaps his breeding stock had not been carefully managed. Our friendship with Peter and Cilla flourished, despite our difficulties with Boss.

Joffrey felt more at home with Peter than many of the other locals because Peter had an East-End accent, almost Cockney. Joffrey's Twickenham tone was a step up from Peter's Cockney, while at the same time being a definitive step down from the toffy tones of the local landed gentry. This I realized only in retrospect, as I became more and more familiar with the not-so-subtle class distinctions in my adopted country.

Cilla—a true country girl—and I bonded over dogs, cooking, and intense, almost debilitating laughter. The four of us, plus Matthew and all the various dogs, became a tribe. Ours was a friendship that hugely mitigated the emerging trauma of moving from a vibrant European capital to the backwoods of Hampshire. Sundays were invariably spent at one of the many pubs within striking distance, always with as many dogs as we could possibly cram into my ridiculously shiny Range Rover and Cilla's ancient but beloved Land Rover. Bless her heart, Cilla never let me feel like a *poseur*; she accepted me as a true friend even though we'd had drastically different upbringings. Laughter is a universal language and can help dedicated laughers to survive cruel vicissitudes and blissful moments alike. I could scarcely have imagined then that I would share healing laughter with Cilla for many decades to come— through a great deal of *sick and sin*, as they say.

We adopted a friend for Boss, a small, awkward Ridgeback female named Chloe. She was supposed to absorb some of his excess energy, but he mauled her constantly. Boss suffered from near-daily diarrhea, and the vet guessed that he might be in constant pain, which could explain his aggression toward anyone not a part of his inner circle. Medications didn't help our boy, and he wasn't a happy puppy. One afternoon he cornered a black-clad motorcycle delivery man by the front door, barking, snarling, and slavering.

He attempted to attack a working combine harvester in the field across from the house, rushing and snapping at the whirling blades just inches away from his soft black muzzle. I chased and screamed and tried to shoo him away while the farmer looked on with derision, declining to stop his machine for this useless citified *American* and her unruly dog. When Boss rounded up the cattle in the pasture next door, shepherding them unhelpfully up to the barn in the middle of the day when they were supposed to keep grazing until sundown, the same farmer threatened to shoot him.

There were a couple of other things *Country Life* didn't mention. One, the commute to Joffrey's job in The City—London's version of Wall Street—was an hour each way, leaving me alone with the dogs five days a week, out in the middle of nowhere during all the daylight and some of the dark hours. And in the pretty pictures, those adorable damp dogs didn't smell. Since there was no fence around the property, the dogs had to be walked on leashes several times a day. In all weather. And this involved substantial effort because they were very large dogs.

We *could* have gotten something small and British, like the Queen's corgis, but no. I had the Wellington boots and the picturesque country life, but no husband, no restaurants or theatres nearby, and before long, a bit of homesickness for the urban life.

There was, however, a great butcher in the village. It was during this period that the original recipe for my evolving specialty, Mr. Beef (Recipe pg. 286), was born. And the pubs, festooned across the countryside like ancient amber beads, were undeniably charming.

RIGHT ABOUT THEN I APPEARED on the cover of *The Mail on Sunday* magazine, posed in front of the sunny Tudor and sporting the two sleek Ridgebacks, a fat leather headband, and my favorite Banana Republic leather-trimmed khaki swing skirt. Of course, Wellies. The headline: "A Dream Home in the Country—But Do You Know What It Costs To Run?" An English friend called to let me know he'd spit his breakfast cereal all over the table when he picked up the magazine and spied me on the cover.

Indeed, I was living the dream of many urban wage-slaves, but it hadn't turned out quite the way I'd imagined. It would have been churlish to complain to American friends still ensconced in Wall Street cubicles, so I kept mum, carried on, and made some forever friends. I drove for almost an hour once a week to patronize a simpatico supermarket over in Farnham, because the local market had no radicchio, prosciutto, or fresh basil. Sundays in Britain, whether in the city or country, required a substantial lunch, and this could be prepared at home or consumed in a picturesque pub.

Of course, no matter where it was consumed, there was drinking involved. After a Sunday post-pub DUI stop led to a one and a half-year driving ban, I took to sitting at home staring at my Range Rover, waiting for Joffrey to get home from The City, and scanning London real estate ads. After a year or two it seemed clear that the move to the countryside had been a youthful miscalculation. We put the house on the market. It stayed there.

While we waited (and waited) for the house to sell, there were undeniable consolations to this version of *Country Life*. Many of them occurred in the kitchen, and for a time, weekend party-planning became the highlight of my life. I enjoyed the voluptuous intercourse between shellfish and rich dairy products. For a little party on an approaching Sunday, I imagined a billowing crayfish soufflé, but my growing cookbook library did not reveal a recipe. I started thinking about a creamy gratin of wine-braised crayfish and planned to just add a lot of beaten egg whites. I modeled the planned dish loosely on the foolproof cheese soufflé from Julia Child's *Mastering the Art of French Cooking*, which had been my very first solo soufflé.

Since this was England, one didn't have dinner on Sundays, one had lunch. In high summer, the possibility for bucolic perfection existed—if it didn't rain. I always tried to create the long Mediterranean-style, wine-hazy afternoons of dappled sunlight, full bellies, and languorous discourse that we all dreamed of. In my seven years there, the weather permitted perhaps two.

It is much easier to create such afternoons *outside* of England, much to the dismay of the residents, who spend 95 percent of their time and disposable income thinking, talking, reading about, and buying accessories for such a sun-kissed afternoon. The Spanish are also well suited to this activity, but Americans, at least in those days, were not. Such afternoons spoke of indolence and hedonism and thus, of selfishness—which was felt to be un-American. We have now become much better at indulging our desires. Perhaps to a fault.

On the Friday afternoon before the lunch, I drove up to Kennet Valley Fisheries, near the city of Reading. Learning of this freshwater crayfish farm, virtually in my backyard, had inspired the menu. After trundling down a short dirt road, I suddenly came upon a small lake surrounded by vibrant green water reeds. On the left shore of the lake was a little shack, now glowing gold in the setting afternoon sun. As it was the only sign of habitation or otherwise, I presumed it to be the point of sale and knocked on the door. The man with the classic Hampshire burr was hardly expecting a retail customer.

"I was hoping to buy some fresh crayfish?" I stuttered, peering around the dingy room that was, I saw now, the fishery office.

"Mfff."

With all of his stock trucked off to local restaurants, we were obliged to put oar to limpid water and visit a few traps around the lake to make up my order. "Are you sure these are really *fresh*?" I wanted to jibe the gruff fisherman, but I didn't. *American humor not welcome here*, the flashing sign in my brain explained.

I brought the crustaceans home and set them up in the sink overnight. The sink was covered with a cutting board, but several still managed to escape. They staggered around the kitchen, seemingly unaffected by the unwavering gazes of the dogs, who in the end never acted on their implied aggression. *Isn't this just so Annie Hall?*

My approach to the dish was classically French: I extracted the crayfish from their shells, sautéed the shells, then flambéed, pounded, and simmered said shells with cream before finally discarding them, spent, all possible flavor given up. Happily, all this work was finished *the day before* the lunch. I reduced the resulting sauce until it was thick enough to be folded into the egg whites with no undue deflation. It went into the fridge to chill until the next day.

Then, I beat many egg whites to unheard-of heights—I really *did* learn some crucial skills in English cooking school!—and folded them gently together with the rosy sauce, a touch of Gruyere, and the tiny crayfish themselves, which had been turned briefly in good butter with a splash of Cognac. I half-filled the six mid-sized ramekins and let the heat of the oven perform its alchemy. The result was airy, briny, a little cheesy, and not as rich as the same thing made with lobster. Without a doubt: Excellent. It was a two-day project. My notes from the day recount "Hard work, but worth it."

For the main course, boneless duck breasts appeared alongside an early incarnation of my once-beloved cassis-shallot-red wine reduction sauce. I am indebted to Nico Ladenis, opinionated then-master-chef of London, for the first version, and his treatment of duck breasts in general: fat-side down for ten minutes, meat-side down for three. The fat that comes off is prolific, and the dish really shouldn't be attempted without a strong extractor hood.

After their rest, I sliced the breasts about 3/8-inch thick and one could see the yielding, rosy-pink interior giving way to the sinfully rich and crispy crackling-skin. "Rewardingly toothsome," say my notes. The sauce was wine-dark, slightly acidic, shallot-y, and lusciously sweet without being cloying. Duck with fruit sounds so old-fashioned, and I veered away from aberrations in the Duck à L'Orange vein, but a *little* fruit is still good—if it's complex, like cassis. *Mangetout* (a.k.a snow peas) were like luminous jade-green eyebrows against the glossy sauce. And this time, at least, I hadn't forgotten to cook them.

For starch, I'd planned a *paillasson*. In the safety of retrospect, I can see that I had not yet come to understand the potato. How do I know this? The dish involves grating the potatoes in close proximity to the time you will cook them—in this case, three pounds of potatoes. *Because everyone needs half a pound of potatoes with their duck breast.* This dish was less successful than the others, because I opted to grate the potatoes ahead of time, plus cook them all together in the same—albeit large—skillet. The result was deceptively golden on the outside, gummy and grey in the center.

A light dessert was called for after running the gauntlet of crayfish, cream, cheese, duck, cassis, and sautéed potatoes. I perched a selection of England's finest strawberries on a tower of ice. Each person received a ramekin of melted chocolate and a metal skewer, for dipping. I just love the concept of this dish. However, was it in *any* way light? *Note to self: not compatible with good linens.*

The four guests were all English—I, the only American—but this was Standard Operating Procedure. By this time in my English adventure, I didn't think of myself as American anymore, just worldly. I might have eaten a similar lunch in any one of these people's homes, and occasionally did. The assembled group was all gracious and ambitious hosts, especially when it came to the beloved Sunday lunch.

In those days at least, it was important that everything match: the china, crystal, flatware, linens, and wines—and it simply *wasn't done* to allow any kerfuffle—*hiccup*, in America-speak—to extend beyond the kitchen door. The upper lip must never, ever be seen to tremble. Perhaps you might imagine this reticence would lend a rather stilted air to a potentially festive get-together. Indeed, such a meal was likely to resemble a church service. Unless an excess of wine was consumed, which instantly releases the inner, dry-humored party animal in even the most staid Englishman or woman.

The memory of that soufflé will last forever; I congratulated myself on the fact that most of the work was done the day before. I *was* learning, if slowly, but now, the menu as a whole seems like evidence of temporary insanity.

A FEW YEARS AFTER MOVING down to the countryside, I had called Dad and Liz from England in a torrent of tears. No longer could I keep to myself the embarrassing fact that, after just four years of marriage, Joffrey no longer had any physical desire for me. This is not a particularly comfortable subject for a daughter to discuss with her father. But there was no one else in whom I could confide: My mother would have blamed me. It didn't occur to me for even a moment that I could confide in her. It was too humiliating to share with American friends, who thought I was living a perfect life in a perfect marriage. My English friends would look at us differently. The façade must be maintained at all costs; cracks were not allowed.

Obviously, I had done something horribly wrong, but my obsessive mental calisthenics had brought me no closer to discovering what it was. I sat on the floor in the guest room of our half-timbered Tudor house in the Hampshire countryside with the telephone clutched in a sweaty hand, my back up against the guest bed, hiding from the rooms I usually inhabited in the rambling house. I told Dad and Liz of waking up in silent tears, going to bed stifling a sob, always hoping that his hand would stray to my side of the bed, only to find that it didn't. Waiting, rigid as a statue, petrified at the thought of one more humiliating rebuff. They suggested a marriage counselor, but this was England: to ask for counseling would have been so, so *bloody American.* Upper lips may have been stiff but nothing else was.

THE HOUSE, DUBBED *Kingfisher Cottage,* was in fact a bit more faux than true Tudor and did not find an immediate, similarly blinkered buyer. Chloe, the smaller, younger Ridgeback had to be re-homed into a household with no other, possibly aggressive, dogs. I had quickly tired of scraping the mud off of my Wellies and the enforced solitude-with-psychotic-Ridgeback felt like the ultimate betrayal of my youthful delusions. Attempting to fit in, I finally embraced the British diet and watched the pounds pile on. Ploughman's lunch with plenty of rustic bread? Roasted potatoes? Steamed pudding? Bring 'em on. Self-indulgence crept in, while that newly gained self-confidence took a holiday.

Eventually, after much impatient—and I'll confess possibly cranky—waiting, the house was sold. We were free and easy and— Bob's your uncle! as they say in England—suddenly the owners of a beautiful row-house on Daisy Lane in Fulham, West London. The little white house was just a stone's throw from another fabulous butcher shop, plus world-class restaurants, movie theatres, and a gym.

I joined the gym, put the finishing touches on the pretty home with its yellow Smallbone kitchen, then made a list of all the restaurants we had to try. I rambled along Beauchamp Place and lunched with girlfriends at one of Princess Di's favorite spots, Menage a Trois. I interviewed with Sotheby's to help compile their upcoming wine encyclopedia—perhaps my perfect job. My still-dashing husband squired me to The Ivy, Le Caprice, and Bibendum. My 30th birthday was celebrated with friends at Langan's Brasserie just under the caricature of owner Michael Caine. Afterwards, our gang danced at

Annabel's. I was home. Life had never looked so full of promise. I began to pluck the fruits that London offered.

Boss, however, did not find London life to be so charming. The pretty, postage-stamp backyard didn't offer him the same diversions as a huge meadow. Since Joffrey was in The City every day, walking Boss at least twice daily was my job. Boss's idea of interacting with other dogs and humans was one of constant confrontation. Walking him through the urban distractions and challenges was like water-skiing, except without any skis. Luckily there was a sweet little park just a half block away, but when Boss snarled and nipped at a child, we had to evaluate our options. The vet had no suggestions to offer us. Rehoming in a rural area was not an option because of his aggression toward farm machinery, livestock, and other dogs. Rehoming with a family wasn't an option either. He was far too powerful and unpredictable. The vet recommended that we have him put down. Peter and Cilla regretfully concurred. Difficult conversations followed. *I cannot wish this away.* In an alternate reality I would have called my mother to cry on her shoulder, she who was also an avid lover of Ridgebacks. But that was not my reality. Writing this brings tears to my eyes.

Boss went to a kennel while we spent a weekend in northern France to try to come to terms with our failure as parents. Upon our return, Peter went to the kennel to retrieve Boss and then took him to the vet to be euthanized. This must have been excruciating for Peter, a lifelong dog-lover. Neither of us could bring ourselves to do it. At least our Bossy had a friendly face with him at the end. While the procedure was taking place, Joffrey and I were alone in the house on Daisy Lane. *Profoundly* alone, and as far apart as it was possible to be in the corners of the empty, too-quiet house. Boss had always been okay with just the two of us, and this step felt like murdering a family member. There was no finger-pointing, but we did not cling together to mourn.

The family I had so hopefully put together with all my frustrated maternal instincts worn like exposed organs: Boss, Chloe, Joffrey, and me, had been ripped apart.

A MID-CAREER HEADSHOT

bringing up daddy

LONDON, MIAMI, NEW YORK, 1986
AND MEXICO CITY, 1930s

GROWING UP AS THE CHILD OF AN ACTOR inured me to the knowledge that everything was mutable. There was no commitment, no
special occasion, no birthday nor graduation that could not be cancelled in favor of The Work. It was a combination of commitment to
professionalism and the freelancer's constant conviction that every job
may be their last. Bachelor actors are no less affected than those supporting a family. It is simply the way of the profession. As a spouse or a
child, you must accept this. To signal disappointment is a moral failing.

Who am I kidding? There were many times I felt completely inconse-
quential. If one bothered to look, the stiff upper lip could be seen trembling.
My high school graduation in Arizona comes to mind.

THIS UNPREDICTABLE HOLLYWOOD LIFESTYLE also came with
some memorable episodes. Like the time, after the filming of *Judgment
at Nuremberg,* that William Shatner's toupee fell off while he was
swimming in our pool during a lunch visit (in familial lore, it looked

like a drowned rat). The prolific actor E.G. Marshall was Dad's best friend and my guardian. I was desperate to know what his initials stood for. After I'd pleaded with him an "exhausting" (his word) number of times, he told me they stood for "Egregious Gregarious." I believed him for way too many years.

When my dad "drowned" on an episode of *Voyage to The Bottom of the Sea* I cried even though he was sitting right next to me on the sofa. Gregory Peck picked me up, while holding his daughter Cecilia on the other side, and showed me around his garden, when she and I were about five. Edward R. Murrow engaged me in deep conversation at a wedding when I was six. *I guess there was no one else more interesting to talk to?*

Among many other stars of the era, I got to meet Fred Astaire, Robert Wagner, Hume Cronyn, Jessica Tandy, and Henry Fonda. Dad made two pictures with "Fonda"—as my mother liked to call him—*Failsafe* and *Twelve Angry Men,* and was later directed by him in the *The Caine Mutiny* at the Mark Taper Forum in Los Angeles. Dad was a favorite of the director Sidney Lumet, who, in addition to *Twelve Angry Men* and *Failsafe,* cast him in *Lovin' Molly* with Blythe Danner and *The Verdict* with Paul Newman and Charlotte Rampling. I was a regular backstage at the Guthrie Theater in Minneapolis during Sir Tyrone Guthrie's exalted second season, scurrying around where I shouldn't be and falling madly in love at age 10 with leading man Robin Gammell.

At the huge water tank on the Paramount lot, where the waters parted in *The Ten Commandments,* I got to be present as Dad sank, slowly and dramatically, in his "crashed" airplane after buzzing Gene Hackman's boat in *Night Moves.* I was completely entranced with the precocious young, first-time actress who co-starred with Dad and Hackman: Melanie Griffith. *OMG, I want to be her when I grow up!*

When I was 14, my father was filming an episode of *Hawaii Five-O,* and my mother and I joined him at the end of the shoot for a longed-for glimpse of America's most exotic state. *What new world is this? Porpoises in the pool, orchids on the pillows?* After a couple of days, we were to all fly back together. In reality, my parents were confirmed in first class, and I was to fly standby. I didn't make it onto their flight and spent five and a half hours alone in the Honolulu airport. *I guess this is what normal parents do?* I re-read *A Wrinkle in Time* from cover to cover on the hard vinyl bench. Childhood experiences like this would later give me the fearlessness to travel to all corners of the world, but I'd never forget that I was, essentially and always, alone.

I WAS 29 AND LIVING IN ENGLAND when my father decided to go to the Pritikin Institute in Miami for some much-needed weight loss. Recovered alcoholics often find they crave the sugar that's lost from their diets when alcohol departs, and my dad had made a big investment in cookies. His third wife, my stepmother Liz—we called her "Third-and-Final"—encouraged this effort, but since she was at the time appearing in eight shows a week on Broadway in Neil Simon's hit *Brighton Beach Memoirs* with Matthew Broderick, Dad went to Miami solo. While he was checking into the Institute, the admitting doctor informed him that he was in the midst of a heart attack.

My father was instantly transferred to Miami Heart, one of the best places in the world to find oneself in the midst of a heart attack. There, he underwent quadruple bypass surgery, alone. His other two daughters were busily raising young families in Orlando and Warren, Connecticut, respectively. I was in London. After the surgery, Dad recuperated at the Pritikin, but he was still extremely frail and it was clear that he'd need someone to shepherd him safely back to New York. As the sole child-free and job-free offspring, I volunteered.

Arriving in the strange community of Miami Beach for the first time, I saw none of the fabled nightlife, tasted no Cuban delicacies, barely spied the ocean on the one night spent in a 15th floor hotel room, because I had eyes only for my dad. What a ridiculous thought, that he'd needed to lose weight! In the process of the surgery and subsequent stay at Pritikin, where even the salad dressing was oil-free, he had dropped a third of his body weight. His skin and hair had lost the luster that comes from a modicum of fat in one's diet. He appeared haggard, uncertain, wobbly on his feet. *Who is this old man? Surely this is not my dad!* I was inwardly shell-shocked but maintained my usual perky façade.

* * *

ED BINNS HADN'T EXACTLY FOLLOWED the proscribed path for a poor Quaker kid from Philadelphia. The youngest son of six boys born to a cigar-chomping, alcoholic father and a soft-spoken, perpetually exhausted mother, my dad had a bowl haircut—the kind that is literally created by placing a bowl on a child's head and cutting around the rim. During the family's ill-fated attempt at homesteading in Oklahoma, one of the brothers, Lemuel, died of a mastoid infection when he was ten months old. Had there been a hospital nearby, he would have survived. Another brother, Clarence, a beloved spirit and promising medical student, drowned on his honeymoon at the age of 26, when my father was nine. When their canoe capsized on a lake in the Adirondacks, Clarence saved his bride but succumbed to the cold water and cramps.

Joe, brother number two, became the manager of the Plaza Hotel in New York City and, later, the Waldorf; his daughter, my cousin Ruth-Anne, when asked where milk comes from, famously replied "room service." Arthur, brother number one, was 20 years older than my father and already an influential captain of industry in Philadelphia when my father was still a pre-teen. Their father's health was already compromised from years of heavy drinking, plus working as an engineer on cold factory floors and in pump-houses. Clarence's death may have sapped their father's will to live; he died at 56.

Thus, for some years Mother Binns was left alone with little Eddie, the fourth living son, a.k.a my future dad. Their mother-son bond was strong; she was a devout Quaker who believed above all in "Plain Living and High Thinking." When Eddie gravitated toward the drama department at University of Penn, the two eldest brothers ridiculed him—they looked down on their youngest sibling and his wasteful, frivolous acting career. Later, they publicly excoriated his struggles with alcohol. They saw in his drinking a reminder of their own father's behavior, which they blamed for their chaotic, dirt-poor, and peripatetic childhoods. To these brothers, making money and a name for themselves was paramount. Both succeeded handsomely.

Just after college, my father joined a group of good-looking young men cooling their heels south of the border in Mexico waiting for America to enter World War II. They believed that the isolationists would eventually have to give in, and when America joined the allies in war these raucous, muscular, masters of their own universe would cross the northern border and join the army. my dad was unlike them in one important way: he was a Quaker, from Philadelphia, a supposedly committed pacifist. Yet he was ready and eager to go to war.

In Mexico City, the boys started a theatre and produced plays, drank heavily, laughed uproariously, and fancied themselves communists. His buddies called him "*Señor Frijoles*," because, when pronounced with a Mexican accent, his name sounded like "Mister Beans." In later years, the flirtation with communism would come back to haunt many of them. My father was one—the big Hollywood studios blacklisted him in the Fifties. Binns family legend says that he lived with a prostitute on the beach during those two crazy years in Mexico. I don't know if that was true—he never mentioned it to me. It may have been a construct by the judgmental brothers of his supposedly wanton ways. But I do know that the memory of that time in Mexico City caused him to despise the zeitgeist of any hot-country expat community.

When he was blacklisted, my dad came close to losing his mind, his family, and his self-respect. He went from being a working actor with his own series—*Brenner*, a father-son police-team noir in which he co-starred with James Broderick, father of Matthew—to scrabbling for line-free roles or as an extra. He lost any trace of sobriety that might have been left after fifteen years of hard living, a shot-gun marriage, the war, the descent of his first wife into mental illness, the birth of two children he was unequipped to care for, and lightning-fast, if brief, success in film and television not long after the war. He descended into what he would call classic alcoholism while waiting for the blacklisting to end. It was a long wait; although he slowly and painfully rebuilt his career as an actor, his sobriety was mostly elusive for a total of thirty years. my dad periodically went AWOL for long periods of time, then showed up and asked for money; his two older brothers gave it to him with obvious rancor. In turn, he harbored a profound animosity toward them for the rest of his life. Mother Binns walked a fine line between her warring sons but in the end was unable to protect her youngest from their contempt.

The next-eldest son Johnnie was always non-judgmental, apparently the glue that held the family together as their mother's health also began to deteriorate. Johnnie was a good friend and moderator to Eddie when the elder two brothers withheld their approval. When my father's first wife Kaddy's mental health declined and she was institutionalized, Johnnie and his wife Faye were drafted to look after Eddie's two very young daughters—later, my half-sisters. It had become clear that, as a struggling actor in New York City in the decade after WWII, my father didn't have the time, inclination, nor ability to do it himself. Number two son Joe's daughter Ruth-Anne, a beautiful young woman perhaps over-enjoying all the fruits Manhattan had to offer, was also often tasked with baby-sitting the two confused little girls, though she was barely out of her teens and had her own difficult relationship with alcohol.

It took me a very long time to admit that this man, my titular father, had zero talent or desire to be an attentive parent.

* * *

AT THE MIAMI AIRPORT I insisted on a wheelchair for Dad; he mounted a brief and lackluster protest. I was completely unfamiliar with being in charge of a parent; this role-change had happened way too soon. In the mad scramble to get him on the plane with his dignity intact, I left my only winter coat behind in the terminal. It was December.

Once I had installed him back in the tiny, brick-walled apartment on 31st Street between 1st and 2nd Avenues, I spent two nights on the fold-out sofa just a few feet away from the quintessentially New York street sounds. Dad was comfortably ensconced in his burgundy plaid Brooks Brothers robe in the back bedroom, which overlooked a snowy courtyard. Liz juggled her eight performances a week with attentive Dad-care. I felt sure that her ministrations would soon have him back to his usual fighting fitness, so I flew home to London.

Dad would be the first to say it: The show must go on.

LOADING THE BIG TRUCK WITH CILLA, FULHAM

every now and then it falls apart

LONDON, 1989

"DIDJA GET YOUR LEG OVER, MATE?"

In Britain, *getting one's leg over* refers to the act of having sex. In my multi-national household, no one was getting their leg over. The marital bed sported a huge lump in the center because no one ever spent any time there. Sad little hollows on either side cocooned two members of a marriage in which physical intimacy was largely a thing of the past. I was 35. On Valentine's Day, five short months after settling into Daisy Lane, Joffrey suggested dinner at The Blake Hotel in Knightsbridge, just behind Harrod's. The dining room was cozy, sparkling, civilized—about as far from the muddy wilds of Hampshire as you could get. My menu that night was priceless; literally—because I was *the girl*, my menu had no prices on it. I ordered the goat cheese soufflé and noisettes of lamb. Joffrey ordered the seared grapefruit salad and tournedos with an unctuous red wine reduction. The surroundings and quietly confident service should have invoked calm reflection, but Joffrey seemed oddly manic. Little did I know that, rather than the celebration of a rewarding new life, this night was the very beginning of the Crash of '89.

"How'd you like to go to Tokyo for a couple of years?" he asked.

"Huh?"

Over the Montrachet, Joffrey proceeded to float a very strange plan. He would request a transfer to the Tokyo office, he said. There was a substantial premium in compensation. I could teach Japanese ladies to cook Western food, he said. We'd save money and return in two years to a far more comfortable lifestyle, he said.

Again: Huh? I am totally baffled: to me, the lifestyle is already plenty comfy and I am in love with London after my years-long purgatory in the pages of Country Life *magazine. This plan had come straight out of the blue; it had never even been broached in passing conversation. I'm a team player, sure.* But I soon realized that something was very wrong. The odd and unwelcome dinner conversation hung in the air like a spare prick at a wedding as we made our way back to Daisy Lane and into the safety of sleep.

At about 3:30 the next afternoon, the phone rang.

"My left arm is numb, my chest feels tight, I'm dizzy, I need to come home."

I thought quickly. *If I try to drive to the City at this hour, I'll be mired in traffic.* "Take the tube to Chelsea. I'll come get you there."

With a month still left on my driving ban, I nevertheless jumped into the Range Rover and sped down to Chelsea Tube Station to fetch him. He still looked almost exactly like Hugh Grant but there was a new tremble in that dimpled chin. Swerving around corners, I screeched into a rare parking spot in Harley Street, where our doctor ruled out a heart attack in favor of what he called "acute anxiety," a.k.a. a panic attack. He prescribed beta blockers. I still didn't have a clue what was going on. I did the wifely English thing and put Joffrey to bed with some warm milk.

The next morning, I phoned his office to say he'd be taking a sick day.

"I don't feel up to making the call," he'd whimpered.

In five minutes, the phone rang. It was the Managing Director, Ward Stephens. "Joffrey must come in today because we are going to fire him."

When I raced up to the top floor to breathlessly report this conversation, Joffrey looked like a ghost; silent as the grave. Quite suddenly I became the only adult in the room. Again, I had some illegal driving to do. Sitting outside the glassed-in conference room on the 35th floor, I could see a bevy of suits gesticulating at Joffrey, as he sank farther and farther down in his leather chair. It seems he'd bought a stock, betting it would go up, as traders do, and he had done every day for fifteen years. But it had gone down. He'd been afraid to tell anyone or mark the lower price on his nightly position sheet. Then it went down some more. He'd lost some money for the firm, but gained nothing at all for himself except black, abject fear, like a baby abandoned by its mother on a dark street-corner.

What Joffrey had done was not against the law, but it was against the rules. Ward Stephens, as his direct superior, *should* have seen the deteriorating value on the nightly mark-to-market sheet. That was his job. Before the Crash of '87—known in the industry as Black Tuesday—it wouldn't have made much of a difference, but now the rules had changed.

When Joffrey emerged from the conference room, he no longer resembled Hugh Grant. As of that very day, "Mother Morgan," as the white-shoe firm was frequently called by its employees, ceased his salary, took back both of our cars and all the annual bonuses that had been placed in an offshore tax haven in the Cayman Islands over the past several years. In less than a week Joffrey went from a man making too much money for his age to a broke and broken man who, when he sleep-walked out of the office that day, mumbled in my general direction, "I can never work in this business again."

Who am I to argue with that plaintive cry?

After seven years, it suddenly looked as if my life in England was coming to an end. Instead of bemoaning my fate or mourning my just-begun London renaissance, I stepped into my adult shoes and began to plan our departure. Sure, I could have admonished him to buck up and carry on, but that option felt like a selfish and cold-hearted move in the face of his acute distress and apparent meltdown. Had I done so, my life would have played out in a profoundly different way. His, too.

I most definitely did not want to leave London, but there was no room for my own self-pity: his sucked up every shred of the available oxygen. As a life-long champion of the underdog, I saw his deep and abject fear; his sudden crippling loss of self-confidence, and my instinct was to take him at his word. I would use my powers of crisis management to make it all better. *I am awesome in a crisis.*

My first move was to initiate a court case against Morgan Stanley for wrongful termination and illegal withholding of the offshore bonuses. A kind lawyer friend was willing to handle the case on spec. I had to drag Joffrey down to The City for the meeting—he was ready to walk away like a beaten dog, but I insisted he stand up for his rights. In the meeting he was like a stumbling, mumbling wraith, the old friend shocked at his demeanor and appearance. But the case was now a reality. I firmly believed it was something that had to be done for his future sanity, not to mention our financial survival without his cushy job. But I wasn't holding my breath. *This is like David and Goliath except for this time Goliath (a.k.a Morgan Stanley) has the rock.*

The lovely little house sold in three days. *Wait—so many memories here waiting to be made!* I had a big garage sale and gave the plants away. I wrote an inventory, translated it into French and Spanish in order to secure a French transit permit and a Spanish import permit for personal effects.

I rented a three-ton truck and we said goodbye to our home, our friends, Joffrey's salary, and our joint financial security. Now, it was hello to life on a small, fixed income, earned by the proceeds of my Daisy Lane didn't-ever-get-to-be-a home. Awaiting us was a tiny, unfinished vacation house we'd been building on Spain's Costa del Sol, but hadn't yet seen. It was supposed to be an investment and occasional vacation spot, a precursor to the home we would someday inhabit in the South of France. Spain was certainly never intended to be the final destination. Known then by some Brits as the "Costa del Crime," coastal Spain was a place of blustering, pale, and sweaty northern European tourists and snowbirds, cheap booze, and expats who happily used the local health care system but declined to learn the language nor pay Spanish taxes.

This new life was rife with financial uncertainty and, for Joffrey, a crippling loss of confidence after he'd been fired by one of the top investment banks in the world. The Mother Morgan-provided nest-egg that had been sitting safely offshore in the Cayman Islands—far from the British tax collector's eyes—was gone without a trace. It was a victim of the legal contortions that elite lawyers can affect when they are intent upon screwing an ex-employee. A small bank account in Jersey, Channel Islands contained the equity leftover after the house sale, but it wasn't enough to live on; we would have to find another source of income sometime soon.

Waiting to be loaded onto the cross-Channel ferry, I wrote on the dusty side of the big truck with my finger: *Rumbo al Sur*. Heading South.

In the port of Malaga

CHAPTER 18

inflection point

FRANCE AND SPAIN, 1989

I AM THIRTY-TWO.

I am driving a three-ton truck over the Pyrenees. In the back of the truck are all of my earthly possessions—except for the full set of Wedgewood wedding dishes, Royal Gold pattern, including the precious "cream soup bowls," which I had left behind in my mother-in-law's coat closet in Twickenham. Oh, man, I remember how much I wanted those cream soup bowls. What a coup it was when I finally had six. But that was then.

The truck is so large that it has airbrakes. What are airbrakes? I have no idea, but right now I'm petrified to tap them, even though I'm hurtling down the mountainside in the passing lane with a tour bus on my right. I have just now realized that the truck is going way too fast. If I don't tap the brakes, I may lose control and sideswipe the median which helpfully separates me from the traffic heading uphill, on its way north to the French border. If I do tap the brakes, might it set in motion a shimmy I'll be unable to control? Either choice feels like death.

It doesn't help that the steering wheel is on the wrong side of the truck's cab because of course we'd rented the truck in England. This makes passing another vehicle akin to firing a gun with both eyes closed. On the other side of the cab, slumped dejectedly against the door and awash in his own inner torments, is my husband. He is wan and white and possibly whimpering. In between us on the seat is a huge stone lion with ram's head in its mouth. It is about the size of the largest St Bernard dog that ever trod the earth and weighs nearly 200 pounds.

Six weeks earlier, I'd been the wife of a dashing Euro-bond trader at one of the world's swishiest investment banks and lived in a four-floor townhouse just off the Fulham Road in London. Suddenly I, we, were unemployed Euro-trash bolting south to hole up in a small unfinished vacation villa on the Costa del Sol. Joffrey's sole ambition is to lick his emotional wounds. Indefinitely.

How am I doing? I have just started to sense a life of adventure opening up, far from the stultifying class system and appalling weather of rural England, where I have been serving with few vocalized complaints for seven years. As I move past the tour bus with agonizing slowness—notwithstanding the fact that both vehicles are bombing downhill—my knuckles are clamped onto the steering wheel in a death grip. Out of the corner of my eye I glimpse a row of faces watching my slow progress, English tourists on a package tour by the looks of their coach signage. My adrenaline pumps for hours after I make it safely back into the right, outer lane, where the steep mountain walls are speeding by just inches away from my driver's-side window.

I am no longer a tourist.

WATER-SKIING OFF THE COSTA DEL SOL

CHAPTER 19

that was then, this is now

SPAIN, 1989

EVER SINCE I'D MET JOFFREY, I'd sat back and let myself be taken care of. It had been a comfortable, non-threatening, and seductively easy existence. But in that disturbing two-step dance that sneaks up on kids and parents, old friends, young kids, and sometimes, married couples, I had to change positions and become the caregiver in the little family. Looking back a few weeks, I might have known this was my new role as I sat outside the Morgan Stanley conference room and watched my husband shrink into himself.

When faced with a crisis that demands A Big Project, I approach the pinnacle of my female powers. Strict control is my condition of safety, my lifelong defense against the constantly encroaching chaos that had always surrounded my mother. The day before the downhill dash in the Pyrenees, we'd pulled up to the border crossing between France and Spain. The stress of the past few weeks was finally catching up, and we were both exhausted. We were driving into the unknown, and it was no longer such a cinema-worthy adventure. The grim, sun-glassed and mustachioed Spanish border guard perused my 24-page fully translated inventory. On the cover page of the list, I'd typed "Used Household Goods" in three languages. He waved us over to a side lane and gruffly directed Joffrey to open up the back of the truck.

"Let me see the television," he barked in Spanish, riffling through my pages.

"*Si, immediamente, Señor.*"

Joffrey attempted to ratchet down the lift-gate, but this was easier said than done since the inexpertly packed contents had apparently shifted *en route* and something was wedged up against the inside of the door. When the door was finally rolled up a single lawn chair instantly fell out, narrowly missing the guard's head. Behind it was an impenetrable wall of boxes and furniture. *Is that actual disgust on his face?*

Giving up on spotting the TV, he compromised: "Okay, *esto!*" pointing at a smaller box that looked accessible. Joffrey pulled it down and opened it up. Inside was a jar of Dijon mustard, a hairbrush, and an answering machine, the last items I'd grabbed as we departed forever from the pretty little house at 18 Daisy Lane. The guard was nonplussed. He waved us on with a palpable air of relief, and our truck lumbered back onto the *Autopista*, heading south. Always south.

When we hit the high plains of Spain—where the rain reputedly stays—thousands of olive trees stood sentinel in mute and immovable witness to our passage. Many, many olive trees. After my trauma crossing the Pyrenees, Joffrey took over driving and I fell asleep. Hours later when I woke up there were still olive trees as far as the eye could see. I draped a towel over the lion in the middle so I could use it as a book rest to peruse the Spanish Michelin Guide—purely out of boredom, of course. Security concerns and the size of the hulking truck with all manner of valuables packed inside had led us to vow not to detour for food on this trip. *I always detour for food!*

"Look!" I cried, "there's a one-red-knife-and-fork in this little village that's only a 10-minute drive from the *Autopista!*"

Of course, we both wanted to go off-plan to find the place. *This feels like a slice of normal in the midst of a slow-motion nightmare, and we need a little normal.* The steep and narrow road up to the village should have been an instant deterrent. But in the thrill of the hunt, Joffrey became animated—something I hadn't seen since the odd conversation about going to Japan at the Blake Hotel two months before—so we persevered, and found the tiny, old-fashioned eatery right on the main square. The square was charmingly outfitted with wrought-iron balconies on the second floor of almost every building. A bit New Orleans-esque.

Sitting at the little table scarfing *jamon* and *alubias* (Spanish-style pork and beans), it felt almost like a vacation. There had been many of these over the past seven years. Mother Morgan—for so long a selfless provider—had been generous with both vacation time and money; driving trips to the continent with Michelin Guides for France, Spain, and Italy were frequent and easy. I became more of a European with every passing year. But that was no longer our beautiful life. The illusion of normalcy that briefly overtook us in the little square in the Spanish village was short-lived. Returning to reality, we climbed back up into the cab and set about to rejoin the *Autopista*.

Not so fast.

Miraculously, the top of the truck was suddenly too tall to squeak past the wrought iron balconies that jutted out over the lanes leading out of the square. How we'd gotten it in there in the first place was a mystery. A gaggle of black-clad Spanish matrons gathered to watch us make fools of ourselves. Shouting and gesturing, Joffrey tried to direct me, but we were getting nowhere fast.

"Just back it up a bit, left, no right! Okay, now forward. Crank the wheel, Brig!"

Gritting my teeth: "I can't, damnit! Why don't YOU do it, if it's so bloody simple!"

"I don't know why we even tried to come up this bleeding road in the first place!"

Because of course *it's my fault.*

Eventually, we scraped the top of the cab underneath a balcony, leaving behind paint, self-respect, and a wad of pesetas for the home's owner. The bubble-top of the truck's cab looked like someone had tried to plump a pillow with the edge of their hand. The townsfolk were unimpressed.

At last we reached the coast. We spent many hours passing through maritime customs screening in Malaga, where my carefully typed inventories were perused, approved, and discarded. Finally, we were headed west instead of south, to the small town of Estepona. Two years earlier we'd bought a postage stamp of vacant land with a stunning view of the Mediterranean and North Africa just outside of this little community. A 1300-square foot vacation villa we'd never laid eyes on was supposedly very close to completion. No one had ever imagined we'd actually *live* in it full-time; thus, the house had no laundry/utility room, no storage space or even garage, and three bedrooms not much larger than our closets in Hampshire, one of which was subterranean and would prove to be an excellent place for cultivating mold. As the dirty truck trundled over the last rise and pulled up in front of the whitewashed house, we were like a modern-day Joad family, finally finding permanent refuge. There seemed to be no front door, and the small, steeply pitched garden was still a messy construction site. *This will be our port in the storm.*

ON THAT MOMENTOUS APRIL DAY when the *Rumbo al Sur* trundled over the crest of the hill in the "urb" (*urbanization*, a.k.a. small development) of Bahia de Casares and we first saw the almost finished version of the little house—which I named Las Gaviotas after the town next to the Hollister Ranch above Santa Barbara—we had no comprehension of the bucolic life that we might create there. What we did have was worry, most of it financial. For a couple that had been richly taken care of by Mother Morgan for years, it was an unfamiliar and visceral shock, quickly morphing now into a steady-state vibe of deep unease.

The house was all about the view. It was tall rather than wide and anchored on a steep hillside with houses on either side and below, but nothing except scrub up above. The face it presented to the upper road was almost blank. It looked tiny and squat, just a few steps leading up to an unassuming front door. Seen from the parallel road below, however, the split levels were apparent; it felt tall and interesting, with a picture window almost as big as the tiny living room itself offering 180-degree views.

There was no one-way truck rental available between England and Spain, so the truck had to be driven back to London empty, and as soon as possible to avoid extra fees. One of our bright ideas had involved loading it up with huge terracotta pots to sell at a tidy profit back in London, but there wasn't time, nor any packing service to ensure they didn't arrive as mere shards. We had to unload the truck immediately. Luckily, the builder, alerted to our way-too-early arrival, provided two extra sets of hands and muscles as his team rushed to finish the house we were already moving into.

As I supervised the installation of my sky-blue sofa, a couple of women were applying the final coat of *cera roja* (red wax) to the five-pointed terracotta tiles that spread luminously throughout the compact floor plan. That wax is the secret to the rich and deep red color of such tiles. I spent the first night trying to remove splatters of red wax from the base of my sofa. But I did know right where the sheets were: in the box marked "First-night bedding." The mustard went into the brand new, empty fridge. The answering machine headed into semi-permanent storage since there was no phone line. Sure, you always need a hairbrush.

We need a cheap car, like yesterday.

The view of the Mediterranean was sublime.

THE NEXT MORNING, JOFFREY DROVE OFF in the big empty truck and left me alone. And I mean *really* alone. Imagine, if you will, the state of technology to which I'd suddenly descended. No vehicle. No friends. No cell phones. The waiting list for a landline was four years long, according to the builder. No computer, no internet, and no

English-language television. But Spanish news was good company as I began to unpack many tidily labeled boxes. I was fast becoming a pro at international moving, but at that point there was nothing on my horizon but the crouching profile of Morocco.

It took Joffrey several days to drive the truck back to England and then fly back down to Gibraltar, the closest airport. Spanish network news was breathlessly reporting historic unrest in China; there was a tense standoff in Tienanmen Square as brave students confronted the iron might and uncaring soul of the Chinese government. It was several worlds away from that hillside on the Costa del Sol, but my heart was breaking for China.

If I'd made a different decision back in New York almost ten years ago, I'd likely be in China right now.

LETTER FROM ME TO MY MOTHER, MAILED FROM SPAIN, AUGUST 1989

Dear Mom,

For a long time, I've had so many things that I wanted to talk to you about—I wanted your advice and I wanted to run home to Mommy and say, "Things are bad out here, I'm eaten up with misery, self-doubt and indecision, you never said this would happen to me—what should I do?" You've never been that kind of mother, but ... I kept fooling myself that maybe just once you'd listen to what I had to say ... maybe help me figure out what to do with the rest of my life, like other mothers seem to do.

Every time I speak to you and every letter you write is all about you, and anything concerning me is something I've done wrong. Time after time on the telephone, we talk for 40 minutes about you, and my lack of perfection in one area or another, and as soon as I try to talk about my life —I need to share because I'm a foreigner everywhere and no-one really understands me—then you're suddenly late to go out and if it's your call it's because it'll cost a fortune.

I've been here four months and I haven't even had a card from you.

Perhaps I'm being old-fashioned, but I need some help here, and although I have some terrific female friends, I don't see why I can't talk to my mother about what's happened to me. Why should I be telling a very nice 42-year-old lady whom I've only known for a year that my husband doesn't ever touch me, that we haven't had a regular sex life since late-summer of '84, that he won't discuss it and claims there isn't a problem, that we had four sessions with a marriage guidance counselor and got nowhere, that I cry myself to sleep two or three times a week trying to figure out what I'm doing wrong ... I feel petrified about financial security, my future—whatever it will be—and where the hell I'm going to be 10 years from now and what that woman would say to this woman now if she could ... I came to California in March because I thought it was the first time both of my parents had been in the same town for ages —I needed my parents, I needed help and I need it more now, but that trip was a fuck-up only you and I could have managed.

How I've found myself, or gotten myself, into this position at age 31 3/4 is absolutely beyond me.

Love, Brigit

FROM MY SPANISH OVEN

rising to the occasion

SPAIN, 1990

JOFFREY WAS AGAIN VERY CRANKY. It had been four months since the *Rumbo al Sur* crested the hill, and the house was starting to feel finished, but the lawn was still just a hill of dead-looking, little brown sprigs of someone else's lawn. That's how you make a new lawn in Spain: snip about 300 little pieces of the viny, weed-like plant that serves as grass in this sauna-like climate, then stick them in the dirt, and add water. Every day. At first, they all appear to die, then after a few weeks, magically, each one sends out a hopeful green runner; eventually the runners overlap and look like a netting of pretty green lace over the dirt.

At some point, months down the road, there are enough runners to completely cover the ground. But now, of course, they're off and *running* in mad abandon, and you have to start trimming them. Not with a lawnmower, at least not at first. With scissors. Being English, Joffrey is obsessed with this nascent lawn, but the process of watering the muddy slope every night releases in him some deep-seated anger, perhaps even rage. He does not want to be standing in the mud outside a tiny house inhabited only by his "trouble and strife"—Cockney rhyming slang for *wife*.

Joffrey would prefer to be lunching with his mates in the City, perhaps at the City Circle—a.k.a. "Titty Circle"—where all the waitresses went topless.

"Fucking hell, this is *not* what I signed up for!"

He put up a hand-lettered sign in the center of the slope, facing down the hill toward the next road in the little neighborhood of about twenty houses. "*No Pisar al Cesped*!" The neighbors just across the road appeared a bit standoffish, waving briefly as we floundered, then scurrying indoors. We found out later that our sign meant, basically, get the fuck off my lawn. *It is a great way to meet people.*

SPAIN'S COASTLINE IS ANOTHER COUNTRY. There is a strip of land all along the Mediterranean that is not really Spain. In some places it's only a quarter of a mile deep; in others it reaches inland by several miles. The denizens of this strip are largely non-Spaniards and non-Spanish speaking, although long-time residents do pick up enough to get by surprisingly well, especially if they work or live with, or love actual Spaniards. It's a state-less Disneyland of fast cars, lumbering super-yachts, hundreds of golf courses, and faux-gold jewelry.

Inland, stunning white villages are strung precipitously along the coastal hills like luminous pearls, quiet in the piercing sunlight and, with a few exceptions, mostly untrammeled by tourists. Ronda is one of the most famous, for its gorge and its bullfights. Ten miles up a windy road just above my house perches another white village, Casares, and the builder told me we should go there to pay our property tax. At this point, Spain was just beginning to deal, or rather not deal efficiently, with an influx of homeowners from Northern Europe. We were encouraged to register, pay our taxes, and generally contribute to our adoptive country. This did not go over well with some Brits, who felt they were special enough that legal responsibilities should not apply. But in my identity as a proud bleeding-heart liberal, up I promptly trundled to Casares, Spanish checkbook and paperwork in hand.

"*No hay casa en 105 Bahia de Casares*," said the court clerk. There is no house at that address.

I demurred: Yes, there is, I live in it and here's the sale contract, including the address. Bureaucracy is a bitch. He refused to take my money.

Across the road at the bottom of our postage-stamp property, our neighbors Olga and Graham had forgiven us for the tone-deaf "*No Pisar al Cesped!*" sign and become our friends. He was English, a maritime engineer, and top dog at the Sunseeker speedboat dealership in the nearby port. Olga was a boisterous Peruvian princess accidentally relocated to Spain and ready to make it work for her, no matter what. One day, Graham announced that there was "a steal" to be had in the form of a dilapidated 16-foot Shakespeare speedboat. It was sleek and small and sported a festive yellow and white exterior, but the interior was lacking in many accoutrements necessary for such a boat. Like an engine.

The two new friends split the minimal cost of the purchase, and Joffrey set out to do the substantial physical work of rebuilding it, under Graham's supervision. First, he ripped out the mouse-chewed seats and re-upholstered newly made forms with brand-new foam and plastic, then re-carpeted the interior surfaces for slip-free cruising and executed a myriad of mysterious but detailed instructions from Graham. For several months he hunched over the boat in the driveway of *Las Gaviotas*, his back going mahogany brown in the Spanish sun. When the boat was ready to launch, we smashed a split of cheap Cava across her bow.

In the early mornings the Mediterranean is smooth and glassy. You are supposed to have a driver *and* a spotter when waterskiing, in case the skier falls, and the driver keeps on motoring along oblivious to the empty rope bouncing along in the wake. But Joffrey and I are above this. On the days when it's our turn to use the boat, I drive and he skis, then vice versa. This isn't a party boat. It's like a maritime version of an MGB: good for one thing only—skiing, and at that it excels.

I first learned to ski on Shaver Lake during summer camp and honed my form on the Columbia River while at Lewis & Clark College. Even though I still weighed barely more than 100 pounds, I could lean over so far that my body was almost parallel with the water, and throw up a graceful curl of water like a pro. This is the only physical sport in which I have ever had even the slightest bit of proficiency. In fifth grade I was kicked off the volleyball team after the ball hit me in the head so many times they thought I had a magnet in there. Snow skiing was a mystery to me: Why would one want to be cold? Cross country skiing? A cold *and* ludicrous effort for minimal forward motion. Tennis?

Joffrey tried once to teach me but quit in disgust, telling me "You've got *no* ball-sense!"

Water skiing is my sport. Our morning skis punctuated the days of our new and still-unfamiliar existence. Skiing kept us from seeing our lives as direction-free.

While Joffrey dropped further into self-pity, I was more sanguine: The terra cotta-tiled terrace had a 320° view of the Mediterranean; across all that glassy-smooth water, Africa enticed. In Algeciras, you could grab a hydrofoil to Tangier for the day, and I did so with a group of new girlfriends, plus one very exhausted male friend tasked with shielding us from any overly aggressive hawkers.

The little living room was frigid with its inefficient fireplace, the one I'd been fighting with since my arrival in freezing-cold March when I realized someone (me) had neglected to install a heating system in the house. In mid-May, the room was temperate for about five minutes before shooting rapidly up over 99 degrees. Of course, there was no air-conditioning. But I had decided to embrace this new life, to bloom in the sun like the nasturtiums in my hopeful little vegetable garden.

My short time in Spain had already begun to change my cooking habits. Butter, cream, and red meat were showing up less often; salads, poultry, and vegetables had begun to assume a greater role. The markets on the coast were strong on cabbage, potatoes, onions, peppers, and hard, pink tomatoes, weak on exotics such as arugula and fennel; huge heads of romaine were in good supply. There was absolutely no basil, nor pre-made pesto, in the entire country. So I planted what I needed, using seeds collected on the drive down through France: green and yellow zucchini, arugula, mesclun, flat-leaf parsley, chives, of course basil. A nursery on the road to the white village of Ronda supplied me with woody herbs like rosemary, sage, and oregano, and they quickly made themselves at home. The hill behind the house was already covered with wild thyme. Yet I was still cooking in a largely Anglo-Saxon style. This would prove to be a financial savior when I began catering to support the family, since virtually all my clients were Brits.

On the plus side, there was great olive oil, myriad styles of chorizo, cheeses from *Cabrales* to *Tetilla* to 85 versions of *Manchego*, earthy *jamon Serrano*, and imported Italian polenta. But the bread became stone-hard within hours, the butter tasted nothing like butter—at least to me—and the bacon was, well, weird. A hybrid between British and American bacon, it lacked that cured porky flavor to which vegetarians are so often fatally attracted. After a few months I realized that when the tomatoes were picked—unripe of course—for shipping, quite a few escaped the boxes. These escapees littered the sides of the fields where, left unattended, they ripened to glossy, deep-red and flavorful transcendence. No one seemed to care, so I gleaned them late in the evening when the farmers had retired to have a *tinto de verano* in the *finca* (garden), then let them ripen on the counter into true, deep tomato-ness. In our own garden I grew the perky yellow pear tomatoes needed for my simpatico dinners. There was a fantastic fish market, but Joffrey didn't eat fish. Not any fish. At all. *Hello? We're in Spain here. On the Mediterranean Coast.* This cry fell upon deaf ears.

For all-important items such as butter, bacon, puff pastry, and dependable hard-wheat flour for the bread I planned to make, I drove to Gibraltar, i.e., another country. Gib has been a British Protectorate since 1704, but Spain has never acknowledged British sovereignty over the isthmus. Chaos has repeatedly ensued. To show my passport every time I needed groceries might seem excessive, but hey, Gib was just 35 minutes from my house. In a perfect world I could just drive across the border, pull straight into the Safeway parking lot, shop, lug out the bags and place them conveniently in my car, then drive back across the border and rapidly home. Problem was, the world hasn't been perfect for Gibraltarians for some time, and they have been, for generations now, pretty pissed off about it. So, in the only civil-servant approach available to fight back against the despised Spanish, shortly after I moved to Spain the Gibraltarian civil servants instituted a crushing "go-slow" campaign at the border. It was not uncommon to spend an hour in the "queue" waiting to drive across. Snack-sellers hawked their wares to those waiting in their cars, and people hob-knobbed with their similarly inconvenienced neighbors. The delay was bloody irritating.

But I was not about to stop shopping at Safeway, so I just parked in Spain and walked 75 feet across the border and then across the airport runway—unless a plane was landing—and into the store. Later, when I was catering a party and needed hordes of supplies, this became a less joyous process.

With deepest apologies to the Gibraltarians, I think Gibraltar is a disturbingly strange place. The architecture is far more Northern European than Mediterranean, the bank-lined little streets and shops cramped and cluttered, reminiscent of what I imagined northern England had been in the 1960s. In fact, much of Gib was impossibly old-fashioned. When the land border with Spain was closed by Franco in the late 1960s, Gibraltarians were left to inter-marry and develop a strange chip-on-the-shoulder society whose main claim to fame, other than as a minor center of offshore banking, was hosting John Lennon and Yoko Ono's wedding in 1969. They'd been rebuffed from tying the knot either on a cross-channel ferry or in France (their first and second choices). Gibraltarians have been dining out on this fortuitous, last-minute event for two generations.

By the late eighties the border was open again, but the legacy of extended seclusion was clearly visible in the phone book: Arguably, about ninety percent of residents of the protectorate shared the same five surnames.

Once again, I was an American amongst Brits, only now they'd been joined by Scandinavians, Germans, even a few Russians. Yes, of course, there were Spaniards, too, but the integration between expats and locals was uneven. The Brits complained when their plumber didn't speak English. I started twice-a-week Spanish lessons, but money presented a more pressing need than learning the language. In reality, we were far from poor: the fire sale of our London home had yielded a tidy sum. It was yielding late-eighties-style interest, i.e., 14 percent in an offshore bank in the Channel Islands. But neither of us could conceive of any real income-generating activity we might pursue in southern Spain, so we'd decided to live solely on the interest, never touching a penny of the capital. Not even halfway through our thirties, we had retired. Far from finding our reduced financial circumstances problematic, I had embraced the challenge. I would make my own clothes, grow vegetables and bake bread, switch from Clinique to The Body Shop. Nevertheless, at least *some* additional income was a pressing necessity.

After the takedown in the Morgan Stanley conference room, Joffrey had frequently repeated that he could "never work again," so if I wanted to do more than simply subsist, it was up to me. My sympathy for the underdogs in life prevented me from feeling put-upon by his wimpiness, and in fact I began to stride forward into this new world where I would be the responsible, bread-winning partner in the marriage. When I'd met Joffrey, I'd wanted nothing more than to stop worrying over how to pay the next month's rent. But somewhere along the way I had figured out that with responsibility comes self-determination. Without it, one could become a kept woman, a recipient of the dreaded, "Don't worry your pretty little head" admonishment. Although it might be a comfy way to live, such a position was untenable to an American of my vintage and heritage. British women seemed quite comfortable with this disempowering status-quo—at least the ones I came across in the investment banking and culinary world—but my liberal, women's empowerment tendencies were just beginning to come awake after a seven-year slumber.

It was time to put my spendy culinary education to use earning an actual crust. My little green flyers trumpeted "Glorious Food by Brigit," a "California and London-trained chef" offering "private catering for cocktail parties, sit-down dinners, and picnics or 'boat-nics.'" I puttered around the moneyed marina enclave of Puerto Banus in our battered 10-year-old Peugeot 205, slipping them under windshield wipers.

My first job was a birthday party for Olga and Graham's two-year-old son Alex. The menu:

> *Shrimp and Sun-Dried Tomato Mini-Pizzas*
> *Spinach and Goat Cheese Quiche*
> *Pork Satay Sticks w/ Ginger-Soy Sauce*
> *Caesar Salad*
> *Tomatoes, Basil, and Ybarra Olive Oil*
> *Garlic and Rosemary Focaccia*

The kids ate a locally-made ice cream cake—being that I've never been much for desserts—or rather, smeared it all over themselves. The adults warmed to this sunny, culturally diverse menu like a current of fresh seawater flowing across the virtually land-locked Med. At the time, expats often picked up Spanish specialties from a restaurant, or asked their Spanish cleaning lady to cook, but a more modern, multi-cultural approach to catering was not available.

In the wintertime on the Costa del Sol, hardly any actual money changes hands amongst the relatively small year-round expat population. The wealthy summer people leave, and the younger working folks create a sort of barter economy. I traded catering for Alex's birthday party for his father's help installing a wood-burning stove in the minuscule dining room. This was a vain attempt to warm up the ice-cube of a house. And yet summer was coming, and with it, the hordes of pasty-white vacationers and second-home owners who annually flocked to the coast to shed their inhibitions—and clothes—with the helping hand of alcohol. The summer people enjoyed any excuse to dine and sip on their patios and boat-decks, and my catering business began to gain some traction. But a problem soon arose: there were no equipment rental companies in that part of Spain. So I became a rental company, too. I stored glasses, plates, tables, chairs, flatware in a small lock-up in the village of Estepona. I ferried them back and forth in the boot of the trusty Peugeot.

At this point a telephone was still far away, which made doing business difficult. Each day, I journeyed down to the village to pick up faxes and messages at the "Service Center." Soon others wanted to rent glassware for their own events. Joffrey functioned as my server, once dropping a couple of green beans in the lap of the evening's hostess. He also helped stack and clean the equipment before and after rentals. The feeling of being in charge of the family unit of two picked up speed, and I liked it. I even earned enough to buy a locally made china hutch for the kitchen. Many of my menus were straight from the pages of Martha Stewart's first glossy tome, *Entertaining*. I typed the menus and the invoices (always on green paper) with the manual Olivetti I'd used to type my thesis at the bordello outside Taipei.

"Why can't we have sausage rolls?" my British clients often wheedled.

Not bloody likely. You'll have artichoke heart and lamb skewers with aioli, and you'll like it.

I was partial to serving crudités with Roquefort dip nestled inside a scooped-out red cabbage. I made salmon mousse in a salmon-shaped mold. I layered three different colors of omelet mixture, then cut the resulting frittata-like stack into sassy squares. I stuffed chicken breasts with wild mushrooms and hazelnuts and sliced them on the bias. I folded filo triangles with abandon. I went through bamboo skewers like a French fisherman through *Gauloises*. This was groundbreaking food for that place and time, and the Brits and other Northern European expats ate it up.

In Los Angeles there was a clubby little bookstore near the Beverly Center called The Cook's Library, run by a woman named Ellen Rose. Not long after I arrived in Spain, she and I started to exchange letters. I yearned to feel some kind of a connection to California, especially its food, so about once every six months Ellen sent me a few recent cookbooks. Slowly my cooking style began to shift, away from the oh-so-perfect Hamptons-esque style of Martha toward a more rustic, outdoorsy style. I was able to find avocados and goat's cheese and added them to my menus. I proposed Monkfish Medallions in Saffron Mousseline Sauce. The clients were game. *Sort of.*

Early on, I had discovered a fly in the ointment: the baguettes in Spain were unacceptable. *This is not bread I can serve at an elegant party catered by "Glorious Food by Brigit."* The pages of Alice Water's pink cookbook offered up a sourdough starter that involved fermenting potatoes. *I'll try anything.*

I fed my sourdough starter and watered it and coddled it, and in return the starter gave me exactly what I wanted. My loaves were so impressive, so different from the Spanish bread, so rustic, that I had to cry. Catering clients ate it up and wanted more. Though working with a single home-oven limited my output, I was still able to create finger-food for eighty guests at an event down at Puerta de La Duquesa for Sunseeker Speedboats.

I am big-time.

ABOUT THE TIME THE TELEPHONE was finally installed—two years early! Yay!—We suddenly started to see advertisements for live Maine lobsters on the coast. This was cause for great excitement. Not a lot happened in Spain, and I suppose by that time I had grown weary of the superb and succulent spiny lobsters—known as *carabinieri*—that were readily available in Marbella's cavernous, pungent fish market—the one into which Joffrey stubbornly refused to step.

My closest friends in Spain, a summertime-only English couple fast morphing into life-long friends, decided they'd like to throw a lob-ster blow-out. It would be festive, impressive, and fun, not to mention quite a splurge. As the resident food-obsessed person, I was enlisted to orchestrate the event and prepare the lobsters, carte blanche. Honored and excited, I contemplated my approach. I visualized a green and yellow theme to accompany the pink guys. First up: a fresh tarragon mayonnaise using the best local olive oil. Then came a lemony roast-ed yellow-pepper sabayon. I poached the lobsters gently in a true court-bouillon. After they cooled, I surgically removed the meat from the shells. With a bit of work each claw piece emerged perfectly intact and prettily pink; the tails were gloriously plump, glossy, and rosy. At serving time, I flooded one side of each large plate with the pale green mayo, the other side with the sunny sabayon, then drew a skewer back and forth along the dividing line, still under the impression that the oh-so-eighties "Rorschach" effect was in some way cool. I perched a tail on one side, two claws on the other, and garnished the plates with tarragon sprigs and a few of the spiny legs. These lobsters were ready for their close-up!

Resplendent in mostly white and gold nautical themed outfits, the multilingual guests were assembled at a long table on the lawn, sipping sparkling *cava*. As I proudly and carefully carried the precarious con-structions to the twelve recipients, I snuck a peek at our hosts. They looked like two little kids who'd had their favorite teddy bears taken away. Where was the melted butter, the hammers, the crackers, the bibs, and, for that matter, the rest of the (damned expensive) lobsters? The table was mostly silent as people delicately cut into their naked little lobster tails.

At first, life in Spain had been terribly new and exotic. Joffrey had initially struggled with the humiliation of sharing one tiny Peugeot 205 between us after having owned both a Ferrari and a Range Rover, but I was so happy to be living in the sunshine after all the gray years that the car we drove made no difference to me. About two years after we'd arrived several things happened that changed our lifestyle. We fi-nally made our way to the top of the list and got a home telephone. My catering business was thriving. And from just writing a monthly recipe for the English-language magazine on the coast, *La Vista*, I graduated to being its editor.

My editorial integrity was out of place at *La Vista*. Nicky Faulconer, something of a hustler with a strong South London accent—*Omigod now I'm starting to classify people by their accents!*—had started the magazine, envisioning a vehicle for free ads to promote his restaurant *Payasos* (clowns). But the little rag grew into a venue for classified ads and helpful info for non-Spanish-speaking denizens of the Costa del Sol.

I was brought in to provide a monthly recipe in return for a quarter-page ad for my catering business, but Nicky tired of the editorial responsibilities after only a few months. I was elevated to Editor-in-Chief, with an actual, if tiny, salary. As the owner, a.k.a. the publisher, Nicky did keep one responsibility: restaurant reviews. Every time he described a salad as "crisp"—this was every time he mentioned a salad—it drove me absolutely insane. *La Vista* was the kind of magazine in which an article about foot health would appear directly opposite an ad for a podiatrist: it was 100 percent pay-to-play. I certainly didn't have *carte blanche* to change the magazine into an expat's version of *The New Yorker*—the business model suited Nicky well, and he wasn't inclined to change it—but I *was* able to stealthily inject some credibility into the 32-page black-and-white glossy.

I had a fantastic graphic designer named Peter and a stellar ad salesperson, Diane. In a tiny office above Payasos, we three labored every month to produce a respectable, interesting, and financially solvent product. I hand-delivered the precious, laid-out pages to the printer in Estepona every third week of the month. A few days later I picked up 4,000 finished copies, which caused the Peugeot's chassis to ride about one inch above the tires as I drove up and down the coast delivering free copies to hair salons, restaurants, gyms, country clubs, and golf courses.

And there was another big change at about the two-year mark: Joffrey—who had played at Junior Wimbledon as a teenager before giving up tennis to become a City Gent—started teaching kids of various nationalities how to play tennis a few days a week, at the local country club. At about the same time, he began selling insurance and annuities on commission for an English guy with a small agency down the coast in Marbella.

Outwardly, things were moving into a new, more settled phase. The self-respect that had been obliterated when Joffrey was fired was finally beginning to return; he'd finished crying in his beer. He was also tired of being poor. After years of being embarrassed that I was an American, with no job to call my own and no children to keep me fulfilled, I had blossomed. I was working, and I was good at what I did. Though it was still heavily weighted with Brits, the offshore international community on the Costa del Sol afforded a refreshingly liberal class system. In the sun, with copious amounts of wine flowing, the Brits forgot to be judgmental.

Socially, Joffrey gravitated toward the gold-chain brigade, as I called the folks who gathered down the coast in the swanky, jet-set domains of Marbella and Puerto Banus. I felt more comfortable up the coast in Sotogrande, an elegant and restrained community that tended to attract a more worldly demographic. In the summer, we still frolicked with our favorite visiting Brits, but as winter loomed and the population shrank, our circle of chums began to diverge. We were starting to inhabit two very different worlds, and with this branching-out came less dependence on the marriage as a safe haven.

I WAS LISTENING FOR THE TELLTALE GURGLE that indicated the water was on its way back to our pipes. The little urbanization of Bahia de Casares was built on a hill just a stone's throw from the Mediterranean, and the water supply for the twenty or so houses came from a tank at the top of the hill. Sometimes. Before the telephone was finally installed, we had what I call "no-tech days." No water, no electricity, and, of course, no phone. After the phone *was* finally installed, amid much celebration, we often had "low-tech days," in which water *or* electricity might be present. Or neither.

The water and electricity were phantom-like; they existed when possible and the memory of them when they were not present was wraith-like. You knew you were supposed to have these conveniences, but it was equally familiar to exist without one or both. There was no electric or gas heating in the little house anyway, so an open fire had always been the only source of heat during chilly winter evenings. But once the satellite television option kicked in, the blue light of the TV was a welcome hearth at which to warm our hearts and minds. Without it, the winter nights were dark and chilly and lonely. On our second Christmas in Spain, Joffrey gave me a generator. This is arguably still one of the most wonderful gifts I've ever received. The generator didn't help with the water issue, but we were blessed with a swimming pool whose water was perfect for the bucket method of flushing toilets and, when warmed on the propane stove, washing dishes and bodies. On those nights when the rest of Bahia de Casares was dark and certainly rather smelly inside, our tiny home was still a comforting beacon of light and cleanliness on the hill, like the bridge of a tanker alone up high on a wine-dark sea. I had become its Captain, with Joffrey as my First Officer. A mutiny in the face of this bounty seemed unthinkable, but below decks the rot was spreading.

Merry Christmas! Happy New Year!

the LAKOSes

MOM IN THE BAHAMAS @1954; ME IN SPAIN @1990

WITH DAD AT THE RANCH

under a microscope

SPAIN AND ITALY, 1990

WE HAD BEEN IN SPAIN FOR ALMOST THREE YEARS when finally some members of my family came to visit. With the arrival of the long-awaited telephone line, making plans was a piece of cake compared to the years when we were cut off from civilization. Although we'd developed somewhat different circles of friends, we now had a social life that even extended past the summer months.

Enter my dad, stepmother Liz, and wildly intelligent 8-year-old niece Lily *sans* her mom, my sister Nancy. They would come to visit us; they would see the way we lived in my fourth and latest European home. I was beyond excited. At 75, Dad was three years past his quadruple bypass, which had exacted a huge toll on his health.

When Joffrey and I went to pick up the trio at Malaga airport, poor little Lily's suitcase had failed to arrive. I felt terrible for this unfinished small person, whom I hadn't seen since she was just 5, and had missed desperately. The first order of the day was a swim in the pool from which, I proudly trumpeted, you could see Morocco. Lily looked silly—and felt embarrassed—in one of my black bikinis; Dad and Liz were thrilled with the tiny house, vocally appreciative of all the work we'd done with the steep garden. After so many years in Spain with no family, no faces from my former, pre-Europe life, I was brimming with pride and enthusiasm.

We showed them the points of our interest: our favorite beach bars (a.k.a *chiringuitos*), the moneyed marina of Puerto Banus—summer-populated with Europe's leathery glitterati—and the stunning views of Africa out my kitchen window across the sun-striped sea. I cooked creative dinners, and we swam laps in the pool-with-a-view, just outside our back door.

Chiringuitos are the life's blood of Spain's coast, one of the main reasons Northern Europeans flock to the shores of the Med despite slightly brackish water and floating medical debris from Gibraltar—part of the Gibraltarian campaign to piss off the Spanish. A dirty little secret: The closer you get to the pinched-together mouth of the Med at the Rock of Gibraltar, the less forceful the circulation of the sea; this frequently results in cloudy, even dirty, water.

Chiringuitos are strung all along the beaches of Spain and, although many of them are seasonal-only, they provide a generous income for all involved. They are only related to restaurants inasmuch as a floating raft is related to a cruise ship. A good *chiringuito* has not just great food and plentiful adult beverages, but also familiar faces of all colors and nationalities. Your bartender will know that you only drink white wine at lunch and that your favorite sunset beverage is a Lumumba. You will know that his son is studying math and plans to become an engineer. The chef will go to the big fish market in Marbella daily, and upon advance request will present a whole sea bass encrusted in salt, or mount impeccably fresh sardines on wooden stakes perched over a campfire in the sand until they are salty and crispy. You can go barefoot while dining in a *chiringuito*, and most people did. But you had to wear a bikini top, even if you whipped it off the moment you descended from steps to sand. Sadly, highly regulated America has almost no similar establishments, but you'll find its relatives studded along the coastlines of France, Italy, Greece, and Turkey. That right there is a reason to live close to the Med.

At our favorite *chiringuito*, Hawaii Kai, the thatched-roof, open-sided wooden platform holding the bar, kitchen, and about fifteen tables was situated directly across from the outdoor shower provided for sandy beach bums to rinse off before coming over to the food and bar-service areas. This was not mandatory, but after lounging around on a beach chair all morning, it was nice to rinse off before installing oneself either at the bar or a table for an extended lunch. Back then, all around the Med, ninety percent of women over the age of 21 went topless at the beach; the chaps at the bar had an excellent view of the bevy of almost-naked beauties who availed themselves of the shower. My father seemed to find this less amusing than we did. I could feel the drip, drip of his disapproval emanating like poison dripping from a rattlesnake's tooth. *Wait—wasn't this harmless fun? Humorous? Glamorous, even? Perhaps not.* Looked at through his eyes, my pride in our lifestyle ratcheted down a few notches.

After a week, we four—*sans* Joffrey—flew from Malaga to Rome, where Dad hoped to revisit haunts he hadn't seen since just after WWII when he appeared in a film called *Teresa* with Pier Angeli and Rod Steiger. Robert Wagner had an uncredited bit part as "G.I."—did they compare notes years later on the Italian set of *It Takes a Thief?* Dad had stayed on for the summer with his first wife Kaddy and my two, then-small half-sisters. His rose-colored memories beckoned.

Joffrey hadn't been invited on the Italian journey, and he sulked unsubtly at this perceived slight. My dad was footing the full bill for the four of us, and I was too grateful for his largesse to speak up as an advocate for Joffrey. At the time I didn't feel guilty. I knew he felt slighted but chose to overlook the petulance he rained upon me when we were alone. It seems clear in retrospect I had dealt a body blow to the fragile self-confidence of my once blue-eyed boy. *Perhaps his new-found confidence is only skin-deep?*

As a ten-year resident of Europe, I was designated official driver for the week's Italian explorations. This role I botched hideously on one occasion, mistakenly taking the off-ramp to Florence (*Firenze*) instead of continuing to Venice (*Venezia*). This required two hours' worth of embarrassing backtracking. The atmosphere in the car when this came to light was not a happy one. I had disappointed my father, who did not need to spend two extra hours in the car at that point in his frail existence. Disappointment from a parent was a reaction I'd been used to for most of my life, just not this particular parent. *I feel absolutely horrible.*

Although I had worn my best blinders and tried to pretend it away, my father's weakness had been worryingly noticeable during those two weeks. The three years since the quadruple bypass had been happyish ones for him, but not healing. As we walked over the bridges and down the alleyways of Venice, he lagged behind. His strict diet prevented him from eating a whole range of things, many of which he could not remember.

"Am I *allowed* to eat this?" he wheedled Liz, only partially in irony, as we sat at a convivial little fish restaurant beside a limpid, slightly smelly canal. It embarrassed me to see him reduced to begging; to hear her speak to him as though he were a child.

"Ed, you know you can't have that much olive oil on your salad. *Brigit* knows how to make a balanced dressing—Brigit, can you show your father how to do it?"

Part of me wanted to show off to my dad, to prove that I was a sophisticated and capable denizen of Europe, but I didn't imagine there was anything I could possibly do *better* than he could.

"It's about two-thirds olive oil and one-third vinegar," I mumbled into my napkin, gazing away across the piazza so I wouldn't have to see his rheumy eyes and quizzical look. My *dad is the life of the party, the funniest guy ever, with the quickest wit, master of the non sequitur, and a vicious punner. Not this frail and stooped man.*

One night in our Venetian hotel, Liz came to me. "Your father wants to speak to you alone."

She waited in the hotel's tiny, tiled lobby while I climbed the narrow stairs and found their room. We were just two days away from saying goodbye. I sat on the edge of the bed in the darkened hotel room where Dad was resting with a cold cloth over his forehead. I was a little nervous about what would come next. There had been close moments between us in the past, but I'd been living in Europe for almost ten years, and our recent relationship had consisted mostly of newsy letters. In spite of his reduced physical state, he was still my Rock, and I wanted so very desperately to please him. In the dusky light coming in the window from the narrow alleyway, I could barely see him as he began to tell me things no father wants to say to his daughter.

"Your situation in Spain is very unhealthy. Joffrey is a weak man. I know this because he reminds me of myself as a young man," he whispered to me. "Get away from him and get away from there."

Our lifestyle—existing on a small, fixed income in a seasonal resort town filled with loud and ostentatious tourists, fast cars, and humongous yachts—was not the life he wanted for me. It reminded him of the contempt he felt for the expats he'd known in Mexico City before WWII. My job, freelance catering plus a little local journalism, was not challenging my intellect or my soul. It wasn't about the lack of money—my dad would be the first one to celebrate the pure creativity that can result from being broke—it was the lack of a stimulating intellectual environment. Dad had a rather vicious contempt for the vacuous small-mindedness that pervades expatriate communities in a warm climate. He feared for my health and sanity. He wanted to be proud of the adult I had become.

I was shocked—or *was* I shocked? Was Dad telling me something that deep down inside I had sensed? Or that I already knew? I peeled back the layers of the onion and saw decay, mold, a blackness and loneliness that I would have had trouble putting into words. I, who was normally so good with words.

Does my dad know me better than I know myself? Or is he looking back at his own personal regrets through the prism of time and his youngest daughter's life?

I felt like I'd eaten a huge ball of raw cookie dough and my chances of digesting it without abdominal disaster were slim. Back in the room I shared with Lily, I kept up my amusing big-girl banter—we forged a language during that time that would salve us both as she grew into a vital young woman, my not-daughter. But in the dark of those last two nights in *Venezia*, my brain and heart were stumbling toward a finish line that had suddenly appeared out of nowhere. There existed the possibility that a door was opening to allow in a smidgeon of pure, clean light.

But wait—what if my dad's opinion of me is based on his own life, rather than mine?

AT THE HOLLISTER RANCH when I was little, I followed Dad along the beach as he collected mussels from the rocks. Back at the Ritz, I perched on a stool as he dumped them into a tall, dented aluminum pot, added a touch of wine, and clapped the lid on top. A few minutes on the heat, gently jiggling the pot, he showed me, was all it took.

"*Voila!*" he cried and lifted the lid.

Miraculously to my wide-open eyes, the crusty and threatening bivalves had opened to reveal smooth, neon orange creatures who took to a bath of melted butter like it was their natural habitat. The possibilities for shellfish and butter skipped ahead of me, crooking a finger back as if to say, this way lies your future. Years afterward, in New York City, Dad and I sat together at a lunch counter in a brightly lit hall. Vast, cavernous, bustling with diners from all points of the compass, Grand Central Station is a beloved landmark of Beaux-Arts architecture, and the subterranean oyster bar was and still is its most venerable eatery. When I was 25 and safely away from our shared enemy, Dad introduced me to oysters his way. His preference was for Blue Points, live on the half-shell.

"Do you *do* anything to your oysters?" he'd ask, his scornful tone and glare signaling disdain for anyone who added more than a spray of lemon. But in those halcyon days of my young adulthood just after college, with the half-sisters elsewhere, it was for once just Dad and me. At that bar, we rekindled a relationship that had curdled under my mother's merciless gaze in the decade since their separation. He had escaped, cleaving to his East Coast while I clung to my beloved West, where she was always inescapably present.

But suddenly I was a fully employed denizen of New York City, ripe with self-determination and eager to grow. Under the cool, disinterested eyes of the uniformed oyster wranglers at the Grand Central Oyster Bar, Dad showed me his spiritual home. Not his true home on the wrong side of Philly, where the large, poor Quaker family famously subsisted on thin pepper-pot soup with rubbery strips of tripe (the quintessentially Philly version, not the Jamaican). Instead, this home was the gleaming canyons of New York. Here, my father had long ago cultivated and finally assumed the civilized life of a working actor. I suddenly saw him as a man made up of equal parts gravitas and corny humor, a man worthy of my respect as well as my love. It was a view that had long been obscured by the shadow of a self-involved woman. I soaked up his wisdom, humor, and street-smarts like the bread we later used to mop up our creamy, buttery oyster stew.

At the juncture of youth and adulthood I had found a rich bounty not unlike that which exists at the end of the land and the edge of the shining sea.

MANY YEARS AFTER DAD'S DEATH, I listened to some tapes he had recorded about his life not long before it ended. He had married my mother, he said, because he thought she would save him from himself and his alcoholism. *Had he ever loved her? It is too late to ask.* When she couldn't save him, he'd had no choice but to do it himself or most certainly lose his life. And then, without love, there were no ties left to hold them together. The hugely damaging process of their separation and eventual divorce involved myriad lawyers, damaged friends, and routinely set me right in the center of a hurricane that didn't abate until fifteen years later. The volume of correspondence is biblical. One thing my mother did well—too well—was write scathing letters. *Sadly, the gift of stab is one talent I've inherited.*

THERE WAS ONE MORE PEARL of wisdom/mini bombshell that my dad dropped on that portentous late afternoon in Venice, but at the time and in the face of the other revelations, it didn't make too much of an impression on me.

"By the way, you don't know this, but you are Jewish," he said. "Your *grand-mère* Barbara-Legere was 100 percent Jewish, your mother is half, but they never wanted anyone to know. I always thought it was very odd."

"Wow," I replied, almost immediately banishing this unexpected revelation back behind my marital concerns.

Religion had been a non-issue in our family my entire life. I attended a Presbyterian Sunday school in Brentwood at the age of six, but when my mother discovered they were giving us kids candy she pulled me out, never to return. I had enjoyed the garishly illuminated scenes in the Bible, and thought Jesus' long wavy brown hair and hippie-ish robes looked kind of hot. My dad's Quaker heritage was the source of some good family stories, but I never once set foot in a Quaker Meeting House. Joffrey was C of E (Church of England), like most English people. We had never discussed religion; neither of his parents ever brought up religion nor attended a church service. The closest they came to any kind of ceremony was the insistence that Joffrey and his father both wear top hat and tails to our wedding in Connecticut, to the fascination of the American guests.

Finding out I was a little bit Jewish, although a surprise, didn't seem particularly life altering.

Is there such a thing as "a little bit Jewish"?

BACK IN ITALY: Dad, Liz, and Lily's flight home to New York was scheduled to leave Venice before mine to Malaga, so I dropped them at the front of the tumultuous terminal and went to return the car. There was some sort of paperwork snafu at the rental agency, and as the minutes dragged on and the time for their departure approached, I went from mildly anxious to irritated to bone-chillingly petrified. It came to me so suddenly that I felt I'd been sucker-punched: if their plane left before I got into the terminal, I might never see my father alive again.

Finally released from the agonizing tyranny of bureaucracy, I covered the distance between rental desk and international terminal in a heartbeat, a madly dashing Flash Gordon in espadrilles. I rushed through check-in and into the waiting room, heart in mouth, gasping for breath. There they still were, ensconced comfortably on a padded bench, writing postcards; their flight had been delayed for several hours. I swallowed my terror and managed to engage in some idle reflection on the success of our journey.

Dad said nothing further about Joffrey or our lives in Spain. At eight, Lily had made her first trip to Italy even younger than I, at eleven, and I was thrilled to watch her process the experience. In the end, my flight left before theirs, and I hugged them all quickly and democratically, awarding equal time for each hug. Flying back to Malaga, my thoughts were like a hummingbird, never stopping, never resting. The heart-to-heart conversation with my dad held so much to reflect upon that I didn't even know where to start. *But I must start. I know, let's make a list of the pros and cons! I'm never happier than when I have a juicy list.*

After two and a half years of adjusting, life in Spain was comfortable and non-challenging, but empty. Sure, it had elements of fun, but it was also like being retired at the age of 35. It was hard to dodge the reality that I no longer respected Joffrey as a man. Gradually, as we had drifted apart, I had come to see him in a wholly different light. I confess that I secretly judged that he was narrow-minded, shallow, self-interested, and uncultured—sounding in my head rather like my mother for a sickening, revealing moment. Sex was still a rarity. *I guess it's tricky making love to your critic.*

As well, I had accomplished his rescue from the Morgan Stanley crisis, so he was no longer the underdog in need of my support. Wasn't I capable of doing better, in almost every way? Hadn't my success at catering and editing *La Vista* showed that I could accomplish more in life than just surviving? I had become a big fish in a small pond, but I wanted to take a stab at a bigger pond. We didn't fight; it wasn't about that. We just had different worldviews, and mine was broader. That inflection point in our lives, hurtling down the Pyrenees toward a shiny new life in Spain, had begun a slide of a different kind. After almost ten years, the marriage had simply petered out so quietly that I'd needed a big nudge from my dad to open my eyes.

By the time the plane touched down in Malaga, I was filled with a quietly building resolve to walk away from my nine-year marriage. I didn't have a financial—or any kind of—plan, but suddenly the prospect of canceling various long-made arrangements with friends and family in Europe seemed less impossible than it had when Dad had first planted this seed just days before. Life was about to change; who cares if Christmas in London falls by the wayside. Eventually, everyone would know, and I would survive their knowing.

Joffrey was waiting at the gate, wearing his lop-sided grin. My glance veered away guiltily. On the hour-long drive from Malaga airport back to Estepona and home, I was quiet in the car, nibbling experimentally at my secret resolve. Suddenly a large, lanky, gray dog darted into the middle of the busy *Autoroute del Sol*, and in an instant he was hit by a huge truck, spun around, and blasted to smithereens. It happened in a split second; in the next one, our hands instinctively reached out for one another and glued themselves together in the kind of silent, strong understanding that would seem to signify a good marriage, but in fact was more about what had happened to our Boss back in London. It was a kind of brotherly-sisterly connection that had nothing to do with romantic love.

Back at *Las Gaviotas*, I hatched a complicated plan. As I was the one planning to leave the marriage, it felt totally uncouth for me to ask for even a penny from the offshore joint marital account. Thus, I would be walking away literally penniless. I wrote to Dad and Liz sketching out the following scenario: If they would offer me a loan of ten thousand dollars, I would buy a car in Germany, ship it to New York, and then drive it across country to Los Angeles, where I would be able to sell it at a decent profit due to the difference in car values between the two countries. I would pay back at least half of the loan immediately, then I'd get a job and pay the rest back as soon as possible. *You suggested I leave, Dad. Are you willing to help me do it?*

The answer was no. Both dad and Liz judged my plan to be at best rickety and at worst highly improbable. Sure, they were "terribly, terribly supportive." They just didn't want to make that support financial. Once again, my dad was leaving me to flutter in the wind. I was completely left alone with my thoughts.

And I had no Plan B.

SAN FRANCISCO BAY

CHAPTER 22

men, interrupted

JOFFREY WAS IN LONDON, staying with his mother. He had gone to help the little white-haired, blue-hatted Queen Elizabeth look-alike with some paperwork. They were selling the family home, a two-up, two-down on a cookie-cutter street in the rugby-centric, Heathrow-adjacent suburb of Twickenham. Marjorie had lived there alone since Joffrey's father Ron had passed away.

I was still in Spain, and one night I had dinner with some simpatico neighbors. I returned home at about 11 p.m. At 4 a.m. I was jolted awake by our new telephone, ringing madly. On the other end of the scratchy line were my stepmother Liz and half-sister Nancy in Connecticut.

"Your father died this afternoon," they told me, as I hunched awkwardly over the landline in pitch darkness. The floor of my tiny bedroom seemed to drop away so suddenly that I was suspended in mid-air with my stomach somewhere miles below. *Am I awake? Is this a nightmare that I will safely awaken from with my family intact?*

No.

They apologized for waking me with this shocking news, but the reasoning was this: It's late on the East Coast; if they go to sleep, it will be halfway through the following day before they can call me. And they know that I need to know. To make plans. We were on the phone just long enough for them to relate what had happened: Dad and Liz were driving from New York City up to Connecticut, Liz in the driver's seat, my dad on the passenger side.

"What a beautiful sunset," he had said to Liz, and then slumped over against the window. It was a dark, gray, and overcast day; the sun was nowhere in sight.

At the hospital, there was nothing to be done. Nancy was there in an instant, but our dad was gone, forever. *All the things we didn't say will never be said. The memories, the apologies, the congratulations, the answers to questions we forgot to ask; there is no chance now.*

Liz and Nancy were both exhausted and confused; calling me seemed to have been the last and very difficult thing either of them could do on that unimaginable day.

When I hung up the phone, I had no clue what I should be doing, home alone at 4:30 in the morning. I had become an orphan—the continued existence of my mother didn't seem to count. I sleepwalked into the bathroom and got into the shower. Auto-pilot instructed me in how to use the soap and shampoo while my mind refused to process this new state of the world. But halfway through the shower I realized that I was on my way to New York. *I seem surprised. Where else would I go?*

My next task was to find Joffrey.

"Oh dear, Brigit, I'm terribly afraid he never came home last night," crooned Marjorie in Twickenham in, I supposed, some drastically inadequate attempt at consolation.

When we had uprooted from London two years before, I'd left my winter coat in Marjorie's downstairs closet, along with a few other items that were deemed inappropriate to the Mediterranean lifestyle— like my wedding china. Now I was suddenly going to New York and Connecticut in December. I had no winter clothing with me in Spain.

I could hardly deplane at Kennedy in the first week of December wearing my homemade yellow linen outfit with the shell sleeves and ankle-length skirt.

The only way to get to New York from where I lived was to fly from Gibraltar to Heathrow and then on to Kennedy. I needed Joffrey to bring my coat to Heathrow and meet me between the flights.

I knew Joffrey had been having dinner with one of his old City friends, and I called the friend's home at six o'clock in the morning. The man's wife told me he'd already left for work. After booking last-minute flights with British Airways and arranging a ride to Gibraltar, I was able to reach his old friend on the trading floor.

"I left Joffrey in the Strand after dinner and drinks, at about midnight," he offered in a distinctly hungover tone.

"Where was he going?"

"Haven't the faintest, love, sorry."

Very soon it was time to leave for the airport, and just before I left, Marjorie confirmed that there was still no sign of Joffrey. I gave her my flight details and hoped for the best.

As the plane lurched sickeningly toward the English coast, I felt the loss of not just my father, but the potential loss of my husband as well. Four months ago, I'd wanted nothing more than a parting from him. Suddenly, I felt an immense loneliness, as though I'd fallen unnoticed from a party-boat that was now sailing blithely on without me. *I am not equipped for this. This isn't my life.*

But when I arrived at Heathrow, I saw him across the terminal, rumpled and unshaven, holding my winter coat. We ran toward each other as in some demented slow-motion Irish Spring commercial, bounding, seemingly in slow motion, and then colliding like bumper cars and embracing fiercely in mutual grief and disbelief. He was radiating the smell of fermented fruit from his very pores—the reek of a vicious night of drinking capped off with fear-sweat and unbrushed teeth. But he was there.

"But where *were* you?" I pleaded through my tears.

"I fell asleep on the Tube after dinner and woke up at the end of the line."

I know he is lying, but I don't care. He could have had a perfect lipstick print on his cheek and I will still believe what I want to believe, which is that I still have one of the two most important men in my life. He is alive, and even if somewhat imperfect, mine. Joffrey said things about my father that made me cry for the first time that day. He said I must believe his story—never knowing that I already did—and that I was the most important thing in his life.

I continued my journey in a zombie-like dream-state: On the flight from Heathrow to Kennedy. On the bus to Port Authority. On another bus up to Danbury, where Nancy collected me. Three days later, Joffrey turned up in Connecticut, looking and smelling completely normal. The family embraced him, and so did I. The lost night had been banished, at least for a time. We had crossed an ocean, literally and figuratively. But we had each crossed it alone.

I was touched that Joffrey had made the effort and borne the expense to join us. This time was about dad, his three bereaved and bereft daughters, and his beloved and loving wife Liz, not about a dishonest husband and a suspicious wife.

My high school friend Junie Lockhart—daughter of TV dog *Lassie*'s mom—managed to track me down via her mother's agent and my dad's agent, even though we'd been out of touch for years. She called the house in Connecticut to express condolences, but also to ask an important question: "Do you think you will watch your dad's movies now that he's gone?" Junie was heartbroken in advance and curious how she would feel when her mom eventually passed. I'd already watched my dad in *Oliver's Story*, though none of the others in the house could stand to see him on screen.

Joffrey stayed for a week and then returned to Spain. I stayed another ten days and then planned to join him for the Christmas holiday. This caused a Cat 5 hurricane from the woman scorned, my mother, who had just thrown her back out.

"It's almost Christmas, why can't you come to Los Angeles? You've just spent almost three weeks with your *father's* family! Why wouldn't you want to come to Los Angeles and spend Christmas with Your Mother? You're already halfway here!"

"Because, Mom, my home is in Spain with my husband, and I want to spend Christmas with him."

She was mortally wounded, as if by a spear of silver launched into a vampire's heart. After all, she *needed* me, and Joffrey would understand. Or so her logic went. I examined my knowledge of her marital and maternal histories and called British Airways.

I returned to Spain, suddenly resolved to cling to my husband like an encircling vine. My plans to leave him were abandoned, forgotten; I had been remiss—I had accepted and adopted my dad's opinion because I loved and respected him. But I had been wrong. *Right? Right?*

There was nothing wrong with a settled and relatively comfortable life. Many people would kill for my life in Spain. I had jumped to judgment based on someone else's opinion, not my own. Joffrey was the only man left standing in my life. I clung to him with an almost religious fervor. *I will make this thing work because it is all I have left.*

Arriving home, I became a fierce baker. My carefully cultivated sourdough starter had turned sluggish and gray while I was in Connecticut; I fed and nurtured it, and eventually it perked up, sending hopeful bubbles to the top of its previously bland and flat surface. I worked the dough with strength and rhythm; the repetition of punching and folding like a religious ritual even for a non-believer, a meditation upon the miracle of life, or at least what was left of it. With a straight razor, I slashed the tops of the poofy, risen loaves, pregnant with promise; the dough parted like a quick-blooming flower. My loaves were golden, firm, life-giving, tangy with sour notes, the perfect partner for good English butter from Gibraltar, and sea salt. I smeared thick slices with mushy-juicy tomatoes, drowned them in local green olive oil, showered them with my own basil and arugula. Stale loaves were reduced to chunky breadcrumbs, combined with garlic and Italian parsley, then rained down over salads, pasta, sliced tomatoes, grilled zucchini. More than just sustenance. *Survival.*

"Why don't you sell your bread?" more than one friend asked, "It's incredible!"

"Why don't you sell your children? They're really nice too." Thought, but never uttered.

Eighteen years later I will find condolence letters written to me after my father's death tucked into the pages of *The Italian Baker*.

There was work to be done. I quickly commenced an ambitious project. The broken marriage could and *would* be fixed. Forgetting—with the nearsightedness that occurs when marriages go into meltdown mode—that I had so recently been the one wanting out, I spent a very full, but in the end fruitless, year trying to force my vision into reality. Along the way I gained confidence in my independent earning power and cooking skills.

And I also gained the small, vulnerable creature that would be of immense comfort when the going got so hideous that I ultimately had to get going—her name was Wiggy.

THE TRAUMATIC LOSS OF BOSS the Ridgeback not long before our departure from London had left me without a dog. Such a situation could not stand. We Legeres were dog people; it was one of the few things—besides certain types of food—that my mother and I could agree on. When she lost her precious dog Cassie, I felt a deep and profound sadness for her. This was rare.

The owner of a wine shop in Sotogrande contacted me about renting some wine glasses for an event. We scheduled the pickup and Beamish, owner of the eponymous shop, duly arrived one afternoon and knocked on my door. When I opened it, I was immediately brushed past by a curiously confident, muscular but diminutive, short-haired dog with deeply brown eyes and a perpetual cockeyed grin. It wasn't hard to imagine a cigar hanging out of one side of his mouth. He trotted off to investigate my kitchen without a backward glance.

Squatting down at dog level, I investigated him back. Immediately, unable to resist the closest thing to a burrow, he demonstrated his terrier background by scuttling back and forth underneath my crouching legs, never for a moment evincing any slavish dog-like pursuit of affection; rather, he coolly permitted my admiration.

"Sorry," said Beamish in that sing-song way that Brits have of using the word "Sorry" in hundreds of situations which non-Brits might never contemplate, "Staffies are rather forward, I'm afraid."

"What's a Staffy?" I was falling precipitously and permanently in love.

"Winston's an English Staffy—Staffordshire Bull Terrier," said Beamish in his plummy accent. Evidently this was the most popular breed in England. I had somehow missed them during my tumultuous, decade-long love affair with Rhodesian Ridgebacks. Winston was an intensely doggy kind of dog: far smaller than a Ridgeback, but not a precious little yapper. He tolerated my attention and then actually smiled at me. This bully breed has a wicked sense of humor, and at 35 pounds is not too big to pick up if trouble should arise. Plus, he had blissfully short hair. I was sold.

Winston came from a breeder up in the white village of Ronda. I reached out through various channels and heard about a recent litter. On the appointed date, Joffrey and I piloted the Peugeot up the winding road to that hilltop village of deep chasms and throwback bullfights and met the puppies. They'd been born two weeks to the day after my dad died. And of course, we met the parents. They were every bit as charming as Winston—his fabulous traits appeared to be breed standards. We picked out a lurching, top-heavy, round little pup—the smallest of the litter—*I refuse to say runt—I just want to protect her*—brown-black brindle all over except for a white blaze on her chest, two front paws that appeared to have been dipped into a tall, cool glass of pure white cream, and soulful brown eyes. She piloted herself along the gravel courtyard of the breeder's *cortijo*-style home like she was on a guided mission, right toward my waiting arms. Two weeks later, we brought our own little "Scud" home—the first Gulf War had just broken out—and she finalized the highjacking of my heart.

Liz called from New York.

"My goodness, there's a war there!" she worried across the ocean, "Do you want to come home?"

My "other-mother" in California, as she was beginning to be known in my mind, did not reach out.

"I *am* home." And I meant it. This man and this dog were my family now. Scud had been renamed Wiggy after only a week, when her sweet disposition made it clear the missile moniker was totally inapt.

"And besides, the war is over a thousand miles away from here."

When she rooted around on the thyme-studded hillside above the house Wiggy acquired the nickname "Wild-Thyme Wig."

And now we are three.

A LOCAL MAGAZINE INFORMED ME that Segovia was the self-described suckling pig capital of Spain. *This is like a perfumed invitation.* As soon as possible, I scheduled a trip up north with Joffrey. Approaching the hill town from Spain's great central plain, we briefly admired the high Roman aqueducts radiating outward, then located the small, very basic hotel and checked in—food, as always, taking precedence over sightseeing and comfort. It was just 5 p.m., and since dinner in Spain starts at 10, we had several hours to stroll around the town and decide which restaurant would receive our business for the evening.

As promised, there were many, many suckling pig restaurants in Segovia; they clustered cheek-by-jowl along the main and side streets. Proud of their star attractions, all the restaurants featured a refrigerated glass compartment at the front of the establishment for displaying them. The "them" was where my problem arose. With little pink trotters placed snugly on either side of little pink snouts, and little hind trotters stretched out to the rear, they lay piled on the counter as if praying—or pleading—facing out into the street.

Facing me.

After an initial mild discomfort with the eerily familiar feeling of the displays, I realized that what they reminded me of was Wiggy's habit of stretching her back legs straight out, in what I called *the drumstick effect*, with front paws placed on either side of her sweet, snuggled little head. My mild discomfort at the pink piglets morphed into something closer to horror. All I could visualize was my beloved Wiggy on a plate. That night's dinner was fabulous, although there was no part of any pig on my plate. The restaurant was dark and almost medieval, full of old wood and stone, mysterious passageways, winding steps, and flickering, low-slung lanterns.

I'd recommend my dinner to anyone passing through that part of Spain. It's even worth a detour. When you dine in Segovia, just ask for *Alubias Segovianas*, i.e., the local beans.

Within weeks I was back to my pork-loving ways. Just as long as I didn't have to see the pork in any drumstick-effect splendor.

WHEN I WAS A KID IN MY MOTHER'S rigidly snobbish household, which masqueraded as bleeding-heart liberal, Television Was Not Watched At Dinnertime. Walter Cronkite's CBS News was the only exception; when I was introduced to him outside Romeo Salta restaurant in New York in the early seventies, I said, "I feel like I grew up having dinner with you!" As a consequence, all my life I have shamelessly adored watching TV with dinner. Ideally with dinner trays.

I brought this cherished and naughty activity—never mentioned when guests were around—into my marriage. During the first two years we lived in Spain, English-language television was limited to Gibraltar TV, which every night broadcast reruns of *Coronation Street* and half an hour of BBC news. Gib TV was on the air from 5:30 to 7:30—long before any respectable resident of Spain would even begin to consider dinner. Imagine my delight then, when I was finally able to coax enough people in our little 20-house *urb* to team up and purchase a satellite dish.

And now, after eight or nine years watching nothing but great British programming, I discovered re-runs of an American show called *China Beach*. Living in Europe for so long, I'd missed out on my country's cathartic process of coming to terms with the Vietnam War. As a result, I consumed any book, movie, or TV show that addressed the experience. After writing my thesis about the post-war Vietnamese diaspora, this felt personal. I read Michael Herr's *Dispatches* five times and watched *The Deerhunter* over and over, vainly trying to divine my displaced spot in the story of America and Vietnam. The week-nightly reruns of *China Beach* assumed mythical importance in my evening routine: Dinner must be ready and on trays, and butts must be on the sofa, when the first strains of the theme song, the Supremes' *Reflexions*, wafted from the big TV in the tiny living room, within view of Morocco's flickering lights.

One night, *Platoon* was broadcast. I'd never seen it, lagging behind my home culture once again. This was 1990; it had come out in 1986. As we sat side-by side on the sky-blue sofa with our dinners, Joffrey asked me, "Why didn't you Yanks just nuke Hanoi?"

I turned slowly and looked at him in full profile—not his most flattering angle—he had virtually no chin. He didn't appear to be joking. Joffrey had always wielded his knife and fork in proper English fashion, but there were times when his Twickenham roots showed. As an American, I was *supposed* to be immune from England's rampant classism. I'd been mystified when some of his friends whispered cattily that Joffrey had "married up." When he had first introduced me to his City buddies—the ones he lunched with at "Titty Circle"—one or two had said, "That's a lovely bit of crumpet you've landed there, mate." Inquiring minds were not highly prized assets among investment banker's wives.

Suddenly I wasn't sure who, in fact, I had married nine years before. Earlier that month, he'd espoused a mass sterilization scheme for women in over-populated African countries. Who was this guy? I was a liberal with a proud family legacy—even if Uncle Pat, the only Democrat other than JFK to defeat Richard Nixon in a general election, had tainted himself with his almost thirty-year affair with my mother. *Our hearts bleed, damnit.*

IN MY SPANISH GARDEN

while you were sleeping

SUMMER ARRIVED ON THE COSTA DEL SOL, and with it the influx of friends from London, welcome demands for more and bigger catering gigs, and the annual parade of Moroccans on their way home from Paris for the holiday. Scruffy vans carrying a minimum of seven people and towering dangerously high with parcels and carpets careened down the most dangerous road in the world, the *Autoroute del Sol*, on their way to the ferry at Algeciras. Locally it was understood that the carpets accompanied their owners every year because they were too valuable to leave behind in Paris, even for a few weeks. Waggish expatriate myth also claimed that, if a grandparent died during the previous year in Paris (home of infidels), the body would be preserved and then returned home in August—*inside a rolled-up carpet*—for proper burial.

By the end of August, I'd amassed a nice little vacation fund from my catering. Rather than take Joffrey on a jaunt to, say, Greece, where he had proposed to me—he had, after all, missed out on the Italian journey last summer—I went off to Los Angeles to see my mother. Alone. For three weeks. In retrospect, this may not have been a wise decision for a woman who was intent on making her marriage work. It was, however, a good trip. I reconnected with a few old friends, and at least partially soothed the maternal hurt caused by my absconding back to Spain the Christmas before. I reveled in the culture of my hometown twenty years after I'd left for boarding school at the age of 14—never, I'd thought, to return.

When I went home to Spain once again, I brought with me a cassette tape of KMET, my favorite L.A. radio station, to play—over, and over, and over—in the little Peugeot, a new slalom ski for our peaceful early-morning skis around Puerto de La Duquesa, and the kind of snow-blindness that can only be excused by the presence of snow.

AS HE BECAME MORE AND MORE comfortable with his role as tennis pro at *La Duquesa* country club, Joffrey had begun to spend a lot of time at a tennis club just a few kilometers away in our resort-y community. He signed up to play with various partners and started to regain the pride he'd once felt about his tennis prowess. I never once went to watch him play. There was always something more deserving of my attention.

The mostly sex-free culture of the marriage had not changed. The well-traveled bed still had its two distinct person-shaped hollows. Sometimes, my hand would creep across the sheet in his direction, only to be rebuffed and sent scuttling back to its own side.

"What's wrong?"

"Nothing, I'm just tired. Really, there's nothing wrong."

We were like comfortable siblings who shared a bed.

When I'd discussed this with my father years before, he had made it clear that he felt that a marriage was not a full one—that life, for a woman, could not be full—without a rewarding sexual component. When we'd had our Big Conversation in Venice, this was still a concern to him as he took his non-dad-like position of encouraging me to dump my husband.

Deep down inside though, I had my suspicions. *Am I a ball-breaker, a judgmental bitch whose standards are so high that no man's masculinity can remain intact?* When Joffrey couldn't keep up with my thought processes or my college-bestowed knowledge of history and civics, I not-so-gently ridiculed him. I had *sworn* never to treat my husband the way my mother had treated my father. But there were times when, in spite of well-meaning efforts, I was unsuccessful in veiling my contempt for him. *Am I just like my mother? A fate worse than death.*

Perhaps I emasculated Joffrey just as she had emasculated my father, and this sexual purgatory was my punishment. Revisiting my mother's revelation to me at age 11 that my father was impotent, I suspected a possible new cause for his condition.

ONE NIGHT ON THE WAY DOWN the railing-free half-stairway from the kitchen to the living room, right on time for the evening's planned TV viewing, Joffrey's wine glass spilled all over his dinner plate on the carefully balanced tray. He erupted into a biblical rage, directed at me, that shook windows for kilometers. After repairing his plate, he again descended, and dined. In complete silence.

At some point I ventured a prodding, wifely statement: "If we keep up at this rate, we'll end up divorced."

"I do think we need a bit of a break."

I turned off the TV.

He needed "time to think," he said. "Perhaps it's the old 'seven-year itch,'" he said.

Ha ha. Wait—what?

He went on, while I sat with my jaw several inches above the floor. He had in mind a three-month separation.

I feel like I've never laid eyes on this person in my life. But as he is speaking, something begins to rise inside me. I hope it is a wall to protect me from harm.

He would rent a small flat down the coast a bit, he said, and at the end of this hiatus, we would go on a second honeymoon and begin again. After the trauma of his firing and the loss of his old life three years ago, a re-evaluation was in order, he claimed.

I am eager to believe his words because to not believe them is to admit defeat. My blinders are securely in place, and I totally skip the denial and anger phases and agilely pivot to acceptance and even support.

"Sure, honey, I understand; perhaps this really is for the best. We've been through a lot, but we'll get through this together."

A week later, I packed some pretty napkins and decent wine glasses for his new, temporary flat.

He simply *must* move out on Saturday, he insisted. It is perhaps a good measure of the vast depths of my naïveté that I accepted whatever excuse he offered up. The next morning, a Sunday, his mother called as usual.

"Didn't he tell you? He's renting a flat down the coast for a couple of months."

Marjorie's voice, already shrill, ascended several octaves. No, in fact, he had not told her.

Our across-the-road neighbors were in London for a few weeks, and Joffrey had been assigned their pool-keeping duties. After hanging up with Marjorie, I crossed the road and peered behind their bungalow. Their pool was green. I suppose it was at this exact moment on that Sunday morning that I finally began to smell the rat that had been rotting under my floorboards. I took strange care with my outfit and makeup that morning, paying far more attention than one might normally, early on a Costa del Sol Sunday when most of the population was still sound asleep.

I drove down the coast toward Marbella, to his flat, then knocked at the glass door that led into a vestibule; I didn't have a key. The door of his flat was at the far end of the building's hallway. I could see him open the door and walk slowly towards me, proceeding at about the pace at which a rattlesnake swallows a mouse. His usual costume of blindingly white tennis shorts was augmented by an untucked, unevenly buttoned shirt. *One of the many I've been ironing weekly for nine years.*

He opened the door. "You can't come in, because you will jump to conclusions."

"There's someone in there, isn't there?" *Clever repartée, no. Clearly, I have not rehearsed for this. This is actually someone else's life. Or a movie.*

He stammered, trying to explain the presence of a slim, long-haired and fashionable blonde woman now peeking out of the door behind him. She was wearing a knitted V-neck tunic not unlike mine, and she was very pretty. Even in that surreal, compressed period of time I could sense in her a hint of that *sang-froid* with which certain Englishwomen are born. I hoped to discern some other universe in which this event was not happening to me. As if, by getting angry, I could somehow make it not true.

"It's not what it looks like!"

"Are you fucking kidding me?! How could it be anything else? How could you *do* this to me?"

"You need to calm down so I can explain!"

"What is there to explain? You are a cheating, lying asshole and everyone in London and Spain will know it! I will ruin you! None of your friends will ever speak to you again!"

I did not throw anything yet, mostly because there was nothing throw-able in the hallway. The slim woman wisely decided that this was our family business, not hers, and started to leave.

As she walked out, she said cinematically, "Your keys are here, Joff."

Joff?! Who says Joff? Bitch. Marjorie had drilled into me years ago that The English Simply Do Not Do *Diminutive Names.* But beyond the nickname, signaling some element of domesticity, her actual statement was far worse than her being in the flat so early in the morning, clearly having slept there. Put together with the "Joff," it signified some level of logistical arrangement—I had not been the only one making sure the flat was well equipped for his stay.

That someone else should be intimate enough with *my own husband* to discuss keys to his flat—this took my breath away and left a sucking vacuum where my heart was supposed to be. I barged down the hall and into the flat; looking around, I saw the domestic little scene: the two washed wine glasses on the drying rack, the carefully made bed, cup of tea on the nightstand, *just like the cup of tea he's been bringing me every morning for nine years.*

Like some diminutive, hysterical version of Sherlock Holmes, I ripped back the coverlet and examined the sheet. It told me nothing I didn't already somehow know. *I am not trying to prove myself betrayed here but rather to prove myself not betrayed.*

Once we were alone, my anger ramped up to cataclysmic force. This gullible little thing, always so afraid of expressing a strong opinion because it might be seen as "too American," let loose with all barrels of the scathing, condescending, and destructive language I'd tried in vain not to learn at my mother's knee. But nothing I said, no matter how cutting, how justified, could alter the reality of this moment. Denial was now in the past, left behind in a cloud of radioactive vitriol. The last man standing in my life had literally left the building.

I went home, up the coast to Wiggy and my sunny, empty house with its riotous geraniums, turquoise pool, and vegetable garden full of zucchini, arugula, and nasturtiums. The house of new beginnings, of fresh hope. In an inspired gesture of empowerment, I threw his good tennis shoes into the pool. Then I got out the frozen vodka and fired up the new fax machine.

"Joffrey has been having an affair. Expect my imminent arrival," I faxed to my mother. It was way too early and far too expensive to call Los Angeles. *Why was my first impulse in this crisis to reach out to my mother, she of the long history of blaming me for any troubles I encountered?*

My friend Dan, summoned down from Sotogrande in a frantic call, arrived to assist me with the vodka. I now sported two lines of liquid mascara, one traveling lazily south on each cheek. Into each small glass of vodka, I carefully placed a twist of cheerful lemon zest—ever the hostess. The relentless mid-day sun beat down on the whitewashed house. As we drank together and I wailed, Dan gently told me that I was the last to know about "Them."

This word doesn't sit at all well with me. "They" had been seen together all up and down the coast for months; they'd been in the tennis club together three or four times a week and everyone thought they were engaged. *Remember: I never wanted to go and watch him play tennis. And then: Why didn't anyone tell me?* It was like sipping, thirsting and trusting, from a bedside glass of water in the dark of night and then waking up to find a dead slug floating on the surface.

The next morning, my glance carefully avoiding the small glasses of clear, lemon-tinted liquid on the mantle, I called London. After almost ten years in Europe, it was where virtually all of my good friends lived. The English are far more sanguine about extra-marital affairs than Americans—this comes from centuries of *noblesse oblige* and the maintenance of stiff upper lips.

My very best friend Jane, ten years older to the day, counseled, "Darling, I know this is difficult, but let's not throw out the baby with the bathwater, shall we?"

Later that night my mother faxed back: "Hold hard, Harry." She, too, wanted me to reconsider instant flight. I gazed out at the sparkling Med, unable to appreciate the silver path of the moon across the still water that had always filled me with joy. I was alone in the little whitewashed house on the hill. I faxed an old college friend in Los Angeles—a lawyer, now—for some legal advice; he faxed back the text of a standard financial separation agreement. On the sage advice of a local friend, I called Midland Bank in Jersey, in the Channel Islands, and froze our joint account.

"From now on, two verified signatures will be required for any and all transactions." *This guy will never know what hit him.*

Later that day, Joffrey showed up at the house without a warning.

"For what it's worth, I never set out to hurt you."

Although my heart should be breaking, I am angry with him, so very angry.

"You can stay in the house as long as you want, and I'll pay all the bills," he said.

"I'll be leaving Spain as soon as I can." He appears shocked at this. *What the fuck else do you expect, lover-boy?*

"It's all Morgan Stanley's fault. They did this to me." *Wimp. But still; my wimp. Or at least he used to be.*

"I'll be taking Wiggy with me."

He starts to cry. *Oh, you can cry for Wiggy but not for me?*

A little corner of my heart wants to cry out "All is forgiven." and carry on with the sparkling marital narrative as if this never happened. *But the maggots are out, and they have formed a festering colony in my brain, where the fear of humiliation—of being fooled, lied to, taken advantage of—is wielding all the control now. Tenderness is a weakness from my past that I can no longer afford.* The lies were stacking up like the woodpile that once signaled the approach of a safe and cozy winter season. And yet I demanded details. *A form of self-torture. Got a scab? Pick it off and make it bleed again.* I wanted to know who this unspeakably evil homewrecker was, still not getting the fact that the homewrecker here was a he, not a she.

"Joff" was not forthcoming: "There's no point in talking to you, because you won't believe anything I say anyway. I wish I could turn back the clock. Maybe I need professional help. I don't know why I did it."

He signed the faxed separation agreement, which specified a simple 50/50 split of all assets.

"I do think the house is overvalued here," he protested.

Oh well.

He left.

I watched a *China Beach* rerun, alone.

The next morning, I awakened full of self-recrimination, doubts. *Have I brought this upon myself by being overbearing, just like my mother? Perhaps I have been too demanding—just like my mother. I may have banished her from my heart, but does she still have her bloody hooks in my brain?* I sat bolt upright, alone in the marital bed below the mosquito-blood spatters on the ceiling that had once seemed so funny. I screamed, loud and long and piercing. Wiggy licked away my tears.

As a young adult, I'd had no shortage of sexual partners—at least during the five and a half minutes I was single. And on a few rare occasions, even when I was not. But after the wedding I suddenly got all traditional. I firmly believed in fidelity, despite, or perhaps because of, my mother's affair with the Governor and the behavior of Hollywood's denizens in general. In my childhood, infidelity had been normalized. I had put as much distance as possible between me and Hollywood's lax moral compass, but it had followed me like an abandoned dog. During nine years of marriage, not only had I not strayed, I had not even been tempted. *I reject this reality with all of my being. I have left behind the kind of tools that might equip me to even conceive of this happening to me.*

In the weeks that followed, mom and I burned up the international fax line. Reaching out to her immediately with news of my betrayal had *not* been a mistake, as I'd feared.

To my surprise, she hadn't said, "What did you do to deserve this, you selfish little girl?" Suddenly she became a wise and empathetic correspondent. Every evening, I sent off reams of handwritten doubts, questions, pleas for explanation from the woman who had given me life. For the first time in my 33 years, she offered perceptive and even sympathetic wisdom in return. When I awoke every morning her densely typewritten answers were spilling out of the fax machine. They were like a security blanket I'd never known was available to me.

MY DAD TAUGHT ME TO PRUNE. He was heartless. But the plants always came back, greener, more vigorous, and well-shaped. I'd look at a plant he had just pruned and tear up. But then, miraculously, a month later it was suddenly glorious. Today, I attacked the overgrown pink geranium on the tiny patio outside the living room. When a geranium is in flower, you don't want to cut it back to the soil—it's not necessary. Judgment calls have to be made, again and again: Is this stem sturdy enough to stay, or should I take it back and let the next one remain? All the dead leaves, of course, must be ferreted out from the massive tangle, and as I worked, I began to see the shape that the plant would be in a month or so. *Where will I be?*

My left brain was writhing like a butterfly pinned alive to a specimen board. But over in my right brain, the über-capable captain of crisis-management was dusting off her tools. It had been in hibernation during the three years since our hasty retreat from London. Clearly, I could not stay in Spain. It was an unhealthy place to be single and far too small a town to share with Joffrey and Sharon— whom I now knew to be *the other woman*. My recent life in England was the closest, and London an almost peerless center of culture, happily within shouting distance of France and Italy. These were big pluses. But the idea of navigating a single-life in that class-saddled society did not appeal. Also: the weather. Next up was New York. I had family in the Northeast, and many friends still in New York City. But the idea of a non-triumphal return nine years after my hopeful departure reeked of failure. Also: the weather.

In the end, despite the presence of my mother in Los Angeles, California beckoned me with that sort of sunny, wide-open idealistic Western promise that had lured generations of pioneers. I had always been an only child; now I would be an only woman.

It was terrifying.

WITH WIGGY TWO WEEKS BEFORE MY DEPARTURE FROM SPAIN

the prodigal daughter

SPAIN AND LOS ANGELES, 1992

I WAS TRYING TO GET COMFORTABLE in the Peugeot at 3 a.m. with my worn old Camp 7 down mummy bag, a relic of a more American life that would be incomprehensible to my English friends. In February, the nights in Spain are cold. I was staking out what I believed to be the flat belonging to Sharon because Joffrey had told me that their relationship was just a short flirtation. I had put my move to California on at least a temporary hold while we tried a reconciliation with the aid of a marriage counselor down in Torremolinos. I *so* wanted to believe him, but the lies kept on rolling. Once my nose had caught the scent I was like a bloodhound, looking desperately for something I certainly didn't want to find. I excavated lies from the past—where was he *really* the night my dad died? In this small expat community—yes, Dad-in-heaven, you were right, it is vacuous and shallow—lies were easily uncovered.

But on that cold, dark, and really—hellooo?—*pitiful* stakeout, I did not, in fact, see his truck.

Joffrey wanted to start the process of getting himself a green card. *Of course, he does, and why exactly am I enabling this? Because let's face it, I am desperate to make all of this go away.* We drove up to Madrid, to the American embassy, and filled out the application. On the drive back from Madrid the weather and traffic were atrocious going through Malaga. Both of us were irritable and I started peppering him with questions about all the stories that didn't add up. His answers were typically evasive and self-deflecting, always making me doubt my own sanity and, paradoxically somehow, my actual right to know the truth.

Do I not deserve *the truth?*

I sent a letter to the First Congregational Church of New Milford, Connecticut, whose priest had officiated at our wedding, for a "true" marriage certificate. The green card was going to be a long process despite the length of the marriage, but it had begun. He continued to live in his separate flat as we navigated these deceptive rapids. One of us was lying to the other, and each had a vastly different agenda.

My old cooking-school-days friend Ronda wanted to come down from London, where she was wrapping up her *second* marriage to an Englishman. Her heart and spirit were broken; when I picked her up from the airport I was shocked at the pale, wan version of my boisterous friend. It was either a very good time for us to share stories and woes, or an awful time. One night, we went into Estepona Old Town for dinner at a one-man, hole-in-the-wall restaurant where the specialty was simply grilled langoustines. This was a favorite dish for both of us—one I could never indulge in at home because of Joffrey's fear of seafood. Unlocking the front door upon our return, I looked down at my left hand and saw the Tiffany setting of my engagement ring, naked and empty. The gold claws were reaching out like a desperate praying mantis with nothing to grasp onto.

"It's a sign," I wailed to Ronda. "All this effort will come to nothing, there is no way my marriage can be saved."

She wailed along with me, mourning her own broken heart and all the hearts that have been ripped asunder by men who were incapable of keeping their promises. An hour later as I was pulling wet clothes out of the washer in the kitchen, I suddenly spied the little diamond, sitting saucily on the terracotta tiles.

"It's a sign!" I crowed, snatching it up, giddy with happiness.

"Yes!" she cried, "A sign! Everything is going to be Okay."

We sobbed and sniffled and laughed together as we hung the washing on the rooftop clothesline, Africa crouching on the horizon.

The following Sunday I was having a beach-bar lunch with my friend Diane when her daughter blazed in.

"I've just seen Joffrey's truck all smashed up by the side of the *Carretera*! He's not in it now, but there was an ambulance pulling away!"

Panic.

I rushed to the hospital, heart in mouth, but Sharon—still just as effortlessly stylish as the day I'd caught her in his flat—was already there.

He had called her first.

He was badly bruised, but okay. *You, my dear Brigit, are a ridiculous, gullible, naïve idiot. Fool me once, shame on you. This was number two.*

The twisted three-month game of faux reconciliation had come to an end, and I was the loser. I dusted off the separation agreement and called the movers.

On moving day, Joffrey was there early to co-sign the bank transfer instructions.

I watched him watching the movers haul out the furniture we'd shared for what seemed like a lifetime and load it all into the big Maersk container.

"Why did this have to happen?" I asked tearfully. He seemed to have a tear in his eye. Or maybe it was the dust. It must have been dust rather than emotion or even regret. In the end he placed the blame squarely on my shoulders.

"I don't know, why did your father dump your mother?" *A low blow, and ever so telling.*

"But I *didn't* want a divorce!" he said, "I was devoted to you for eight years." *Helluva way of showing it, mister.* "I always knew you thought I was a nobody. You stole my confidence, and that's why I lost my job at Morgan. Morgan did this to me, and I want to *make them pay*."

It is as if he is jumping precariously from boulder to boulder like we used to do in Sedona when I was 16, but below him is an oily, treacherous torrent, not the pristine waters of Oak Creek. "I guess people just change, Brigit. You helped me get a green card, so you must believe I'll come after you. For what it's worth I never set out to hurt you. I'm sorry for what I've done."

And finally, this: "I *will* come to California someday. Shall I look you up?"

The scorned woman inside me came up with this: "If I find out you've gone back to Sharon, I won't testify or help you with the court case against Morgan Stanley." *This seems to shock him. There is a brief flash of naked anger, a hint that this would be an inconvenience in his Machiavellian scheme.*

Not long before I was due to leave, I went down to the mini mart in Sabinillas to secure some *pinchitos* for my solitary dinner amongst the half-packed boxes. *Pinchitos* are tiny cubes of pork that have been bathed in a marinade of smoky paprika, flavor-forward olive oil, and intense garlicky-ness. All you have to do is thread them onto a skewer and broil or grill them up. One *could* dice the pork and make the marinade yourself—and I'd done so many times—but I'd lost any urge to cook for myself; I wasn't worth the effort. Luckily little neighborhood Spanish markets on the coast are well supplied for the I-don't-care-to-cook brigade.

The garage sale was over, all my precious Chinese language books shipped off to the daughter of an English couple who had been browsers at my sale; they had *oohed* and *ahhed* over the once-precious books. "Our daughter is studying Mandarin at Bristol Uni, but she could never afford those fancy dictionaries with all the complicated characters in them!"

"It would be my pleasure to gift them to her, and I wish her all the best luck and excitement going forward with her studies—she will have a brilliant time learning Mandarin." *I am bequeathing my spent passion onto a younger generation. Perhaps she will do more with her Mandarin study than I did.*

To get myself into an L.A. frame of mind I started listening to my recorded snippets of KMET radio on the Peugeot's cassette deck. The music was evocative of Southern California at its best: the Beach Boys, Steely Dan, Fleetwood Mac, my discarded heritage coming to life even as I lamented the end of my European sojourn about fifty years too early. My huge shipping container had departed for Los Angeles—next I would follow it. I had packed every single existing photograph from nine years of marriage. *If you choose to erase me from your life, you are going to be left with no records at all of our time together.*

Full disclosure: part of me was beyond excited to go home, to the country I'd left ten years before, but I was also feeling exceedingly sorry for myself. Mom had uncharacteristically offered her home in Brentwood as a sort of halfway house as I set out to build a new life, but Wiggy wasn't invited. According to my mother, her dog Piglet would likely kill Wiggy on sight and she didn't want the weight of responsibility in case that were to happen. Until I had a job and a place to live, Wiggy would stay in Spain with friends at their dog-loving compound in the hills instead of at the family home with Joffrey, because he "won't be around enough." *Asshole.*

I was about to be one hundred percent alone in a new country that did not feel like home, near a mother whom I'd spent much of my life considering a low-grade enemy. The remaining few members of my family lived on the East Coast.

Our little tile-roofed mini-villa, with the sparkling lights of Morocco in the distance, had been a good port in a storm and I'd poured love and care and sweat into making it a welcoming nest. It was to be my nest no longer.

But Joffrey *must* take me to the airport, I insisted, wanting to rub it in his face that I was truly leaving. I closed the front door to my home. I would never see it again. After leaving me at the airport, he would return and re-claim it as his own.

"You'll never believe how sorry I am." He sobbed.

"You're right, I won't." I was stoic, an ice queen.

"I've lied to you so much. It's all because of Morgan Stanley."

"That's a convenient excuse."

"You would have been better off if you'd never met me." *Likely true.*

"If you file for divorce, the day it comes through would be the saddest of my life," he continued.

"Too bad."

"I don't know why I turned out like this."

"Let me know if and when you figure it out."

"If I come to L.A., will you see me?"

He must honestly believe that he can stay here and carry out his sordid little affair until it ends of its own accord, and then come running after me—to take advantage of the new life I create in a new land after he's fucked up the last one. Will I? Will I create a new life that might include him? No matter—now he has to be strong and risk rejection like the rest of us. I will not give him one shred of encouragement. *I've already given him more chances than a cat has lives.*

Wheels-up as the jet ascended into the sky above Malaga, I felt like my intestines had been left behind on the tarmac, discarded, dusty and leaking essential fluids. Three months of painful negotiation, attempted reconciliation, marriage counseling, and eventual, exhausted acceptance stretched out behind me like a ripped and discarded snakeskin.

The Med glittered carelessly to the left of my window, but my tear-filled eyes were blind to its siren call. No more would I waterski in the dusky early morning on the glass-like sea in Puerta de La Duquesa harbor. The bougainvillea-draped little white house on the wild thyme-covered hill was in my past, as was my marriage. Nobody ever gets married thinking they will get divorced, and when it happens the tell-tale heart cries murder most awfully foul. I had been away from America for ten years and didn't have a clue what awaited me on the far end of an eleven-hour flight. I'm embarrassed to admit—even to myself—that I still hoped he would see the error of his ways and come after me. Perhaps it was just a crutch I could lean upon in the months to come. *In the movie of my life, when he comes, if he does, the soundtrack will play the theme song from* Chariots of Fire.

LANDING AT LAX ALWAYS STRIKES some sort of primordial chord in my soul. Memories of returning to my hometown after so many peripatetic wanderings: from Hong Kong, New York, Athens, London, Sedona, Portland, Kuala Lumpur. On a clear night it's like floating down as gently as a feather into a jewelry box strewn with diamond tennis bracelets. For daylight arrivals, a patchwork of jewel-like swimming pools greets your lazy descent.

This view says: Here is an easy place of fortune and security. Here, anything is possible. *No matter that my mother is down there somewhere, lurking and ready to turn on me, to sap my self-confidence and sabotage the sparkling new life I plan to design for myself.* Los Angeles would be a welcome port, but I would not stay forever. No, I was in search of a smaller place, more bucolic, but certainly, always forever; California.

So long a beacon of light on a too-far-away horizon, California would be my home again. The prodigal daughter had returned, if much the worse for wear.

MY MOTHER, AGE 2

MY MOTHER, AGE 21

CHAPTER 25

brown-eyed girl

PASADENA, 1929

IN 1929 MY GRANDMOTHER was a single mother with a 3-year-old child who required a full year's stay in Children's Hospital of Los Angeles, and they were about to experience the Great Depression.

The little girl's first earache hadn't seemed particularly serious. Over the next two years, the pretty, dark-haired baby's earaches got progressively worse; soon, she began to pass out from the pain. The first transfusion came when she was three. She remembered waking up in the hospital with blood-filled tubes sticking out of her wrists and ankles. It was a memory that would never leave her.

The little girl who would one day become my mother was very, very sick. Her mastoids—those are the big bones right behind your earlobes—were so infected that they had to be removed in a risky operation. Today, the surgery is almost never done, but the infection can spread to the brain, so the surgeons essentially carved deep into the bone of her skull on either side, leaving huge holes that would have to be carefully cleaned to prevent infection for the rest of her life. The child had a crush on a handsome surgeon, who had told his tiny patient the surgery wouldn't hurt.

"You'll smell only sweet flowers," he had said. But he was lying. She never spoke to him, never looked him in the eye, again.

As a young woman, my grandmother Barbara Feningston had been a radical; according to chronicles of the American socialist movement, she was never married to Ben Legere, my mother's father, a.k.a my grandfather. A French-Canadian Catholic and unrepentant ladies-man, Ben Legere was a famous radical labor-organizer—member of the IWW (International Workers of the World), better known as the Wobblies—and Communist Party. Evidently Ben fathered several children out of wedlock and, along with many of his compatriots, including Jack Reed and Louise Bryant (see: *Reds*), believed that marriage was a bourgeois institution.

Undoubtably the two young-ish lovers disagreed when real life—in the form of a child—intervened on the utopian scene. Barbara must have decided such liberal ideals didn't apply to parenthood. In any event, she fled the big, communal house on Nob Hill in San Francisco, where the Bohemians—as they were known in those days, long before there were hippies in Haight-Ashbury—had lived together in apparent harmony. They talked of capitalism and revolution late into the night, drinking endless cups of coffee and jars of cheap red wine, and always wearing black. But Barbara's appetite for the liberal life apparently evaporated less than two years after she gave birth to my mother. Ben Legere had been terribly charming, but not the fatherly type. Barbara moved south to Los Angeles with her baby, leaving no forwarding address. From what I later learned of Ben, he would not have tried to follow her. Although she never married Ben, she did take his name, and from then on was known as Barbara Legere, a nice, non-Jewish-sounding name. Ben never provided any child support.

In that one decision in 1927, my grandmother consigned my mother to childhood, and life, without a father. My mother didn't re-meet her father until she was twenty-one. Like most fatherless children, she had romanticized him; since Barbara never once spoke of him, the little girl's fantasies were all she had. When the longed-for event finally came to pass, they met for lunch in San Francisco. Ben talked only of his conquests, and never once asked a single question about young Marcia's life. She never attempted to contact him again.

Soon after arriving in Los Angeles, Barbara became the couture fashion buyer for one of the fanciest department stores in California, Bullocks Wilshire. What qualifications she cited to secure the job are unknown. Her working lair was all Champagne-colored, draped with silk and subtly lit; she traveled to Paris regularly, and her friends were some of the most respected designers of the time: Irene, Pola Stout, Gunn Trigere.

The pressure to provide led my grandmother's career to become all-consuming. She traveled to Paris and New York for buying trips, and on her infrequent days off was often exhausted. She worked six days a week and soon sent my mother off to an expensive private boarding school.

Photographs of my toddler mother and my grandmother, often taken at the beach, show an amazing tenderness and love of the mother for the child. This is painful for me to look at, because it appears entirely one-sided: The child, Marcia, even at 4 years old, seems totally uninterested in the mother, gazing into the distance, away from the doting eyes and looking for, perhaps, another more interesting family not her own.

At boarding school, the lonely little girl who had spent two years of her early childhood in and out of hospitals and convalescent homes hobnobbed with some of the wealthiest families in California. My mother became a bobbysoxer, proud of her luxuriant dark curls, slim physique, and sexy brown eyes. Schoolmates called her "Legs Legere." Since Barbara was so busy working to pay the bills, she couldn't provide child or teencare during school breaks, so my mother spent summers and vacations with the family of her boarding school-friend Lizzie Hollister on one of the family's sprawling cattle ranches. She learned early to appreciate well-designed and well-made clothing and was always the best-dressed girl in her class. She was equally at home in a tailored silk herringbone suit or rough cotton riding breeches on the back of a horse.

But as a result of Barbara's selfless devotion to her child's education, mother and daughter spent very little time together. Eventually their relationship became more like that of sisters. Barbara read cookbooks before going to bed, like novels, but never cooked. She felt intimidated by the Hollister clan and visited the isolated ranch north of Santa Barbara only once. Barbara refused to spend the night because the distance from civilization made her "nervous." Throughout her childhood, adulthood, and declining years my mother referred to the woman who gave her life as "Barbara-Legere." Never *Mom* or *Mother.* Never just "Barbara." Always "Barbara-Legere."

Barbara, who was 25 years old when my mother was born, never married. By the time she was 27 her hair—which had begun to go gray in her late teens—was pure, blindingly white.

Along with taking sole responsibility for raising her child, Barbara harbored that secret that clearly preyed upon her soul: she was Jewish. This secret caused her to constantly fear losing the job that made her daughter's privileged life possible.

The cover-up caused a devastating rift between Barbara and her parents and four sisters. The five girls had grown up together in a solid, middle-class Jewish household in Mt. Vernon, New York; their parents had emigrated from Poland in 1908 to provide a better life for their family and believed that they had done so. Yet all five of the sisters had embraced radical social and economic ideologies, and three of them had gone to California.

As my long-lost cousin Audrey said to me some 90 years later: "Who goes to California?"

When Barbara's parents back in Mount Vernon discovered that she was masquerading as a gentile, they were horrified. As a result, they had no relationship with my mother, their grandchild.

My grandmother communicated her constant, sapping fears and shame to her daughter, who adopted the embarrassment and made it her own. Under the matrilineal rules of Judaism, my mother was Jewish. Carrying on the family tradition, she never told a soul. For eighty-seven years my mother lived in denial of her true self, praying that no one would ever discover the dreadful truth. The very worst, the most unbearable thing, would be for the Hollisters—whom she liked to think of as her real family—to find out. And it mattered little that Ben Legere had been a lapsed Catholic, because according to Jewish custom, Marcia Legere was Jewish, too. But it would be many years before I discovered their heritage. Their shame-fueled cover-up was successful for almost two generations before my father revealed the secret to me.

In her freshman year at the University of Wisconsin at Madison, the leggy, brown-eyed, brown-haired girl with the too-stylish wardrobe set her sights on the swankiest sorority at the school, Kappa Kappa Gamma. As the editor of her high-school newspaper and a clearly confident social butterfly, Marcia was considered to be a great catch.

"All the sororities" pursued her, and she could have had her pick, as she recounted it. In my mother's telling, "Kappa" was the tip-top and only choice. When relating this story to me, she sang a sad little jingle, "Kappa Kappa Gamma ... "—to demonstrate something, I'm not sure what.

One day in her shared dorm room, the giggling pearl-and-twinsetted girls received a visitor.

"Hi, Marcia, guess what? We share an uncle!" trumpeted the unknown girl to my mother, in front of her three stunned roommates. According to my mother, the girl was "very Jewish-looking," and my mother shut her down cold, exhibiting what was later reported back to the family in Mount Vernon as appalling rudeness. Years later she apologized to the family, but the damage had been done. In one fell swoop her hopes for a swanky sorority were dashed; each and every one of them dropped her like a rock.

When she told me this story multiple decades later, her manner still dripped with resentment and regret. But her regret was *not* for the way she'd treated her cousin. With a sad bitterness that flirted with blame, my mother said, "My life was never the same."

JOACHIM SPLICHAL'S

Patina Cookbook

Spuds, Truffles and Wild Gnocchi

POLENTA

Brigit Légère Binns

Photography by Deborah Denker

MY FIRST TWO COOKBOOKS

home alone

LOS ANGELES, 1992

MY MOTHER *ACTUALLY* PICKED ME UP AT THE AIRPORT! My feelings about rooming, even briefly, with this lifelong antagonist, were mixed. In our flurry of faxed correspondence prior to my arrival, she had been uncharacteristically supportive. After first counseling me to stay and work it out, she'd become convinced there was no hope for the marriage. The plan was for me to stay with her until I got a job, and then find a place to live and bring Wiggy over.

I didn't have much time to wonder if cohabitating with my mother would work, because four days after I arrived, she took off for a month at her barnhouse in New Milford, Connecticut.

The day after my mother flew east there was a 6.1 earthquake. As a native Californian this did not dent my enthusiasm, but I did wonder if it might be a portent. My English and Spanish friends called, full of concern.

I allayed their fears: "It's not a big deal; they happen here all the time."

After the 50/50 split, the little money I still had in the bank in England—leftover from the sale of the London house—would last a good long time only *if* I quickly found another source of income.

I desperately missed the comfort of Wiggy's solid little brindle body and liquid brown eyes.

I must find a job.

In the first week, I had lunch with Ellen Rose, owner of the Cook's Library. It was our first meeting in person after several years of correspondence.

"I'm looking for a job," I admitted. Ellen, who had somehow been under the impression that I owned a winery in Spain, seemed a bit shocked, but almost immediately offered me a job in her bookstore. *Eureka! I have a job! Okay, it's only $10 an hour a few hours a week, but I get to talk about cookbooks—heavenly!* Ellen was friendly, enthusiastic, helpful, and full of bright ideas. I had the sense that, even if this was not a forever job, it was the beginning of a beautiful friendship. I had also applied for a job at Gault-Millau, the venerable culinary guidebook producer then publishing *The Food Paper.* This was a short-lived food-focused tabloid centered around the culinary scene in Los Angeles, the scene I'd been watching jealously from afar for as long as I could remember. Miraculously, I was offered a job as a junior editor.

But on April 29, 1992—the weekend before the Gault-Millau job was to start, my entire, newly-re-adopted city shut down completely. No one was going anywhere for quite some time, new job or not.

Sitting alone in the rambling house in Brentwood with only her dog Piglet for company, I gazed up at the phalanxes of military helicopters heading towards South-Central to quell the riots that had erupted after the four white police officers who had brutally beaten Rodney King were acquitted of any crime. I watched in shock as Reginald Denny was dragged from his truck and beaten to within an inch of his life. My friends in England and Spain called again, worried about this crazy place I was attempting to call home.

"Are you sure it's safe there, Brigit?"

After leaving for boarding school number two in eighth grade, I had not spent more than a week at a time in Los Angeles. Even if I was temporarily sleeping in the canopy bed in my childhood bedroom, it was another city, not my own. And it was turning out to be a very scary place to be. But my privileged problems paled in comparison to the anger and despair playing out on the streets of this odd schizophrenic community. The kids I went to school or camp with long ago were no longer in evidence.

As the city slowly calmed itself, I sent out resumes to every chef I could think of, offering to help them write a cookbook: "London-trained chef with catering experience in Southern Spain is available to ghost-write your cookbook."

About a month after my arrival, I had an interview with the chef at the multiple-award-winning restaurant Patina, Joachim Splichal. I met Ellen for an early breakfast at Il Campanile and she graciously bestowed upon me much valuable insider wisdom about the culinary community in L.A. I looked at myself in the mirror in the restroom before heading over to Highland Avenue for the meeting.

"Today may change your life," I said to my hopeful image.

I sensed that these were portentous days. The idea that Ellen Rose truly cared about my progress gave me a feeling of being cherished, appreciated, supported. She was the first of several generous women to help me find my feet as a culinary writer. My mother, however, was never one of them. According to her, all my writing was self-centered and trite.

Now I had two great jobs, a smile on my face, and a little money in the bank. Soon, because I had a job, I also had a little rented bungalow in Mar Vista with a Cadillac-sized turquoise Gaffers and Satler stove, plus room for a vegetable garden and a dining area in the backyard. I attacked the chore of fitting into a culture I'd left behind ten years before. Steve Martin? Who is Steve Martin? What is *Saturday Night Live*? Why is everyone adding "like" to sentences where it doesn't belong? Bagged, perfect salad greens and cordless phones seemed like magic. I hadn't been on a date in ten years. I still had an old friend or two from college here, and they had friends. Soon, I had a date. I had very little recollection of the correct way to behave at such an event. But evidently it was like riding a bicycle, and I got right back on, pedaling furiously to make up for lost time. *I want to run around the house naked and have someone besides me enjoy it.*

Joachim Splichal's secretary called about a week after our interview, and suddenly I had my first cookbook job. I had zero experience writing cookbooks and had cold-written to him. Ten years in Europe and professional cooking school must have popped out from my resume. Venerable writer Charles Perry, formerly of *Rolling Stone*, would be writing all the text; my job was solely to re-interpret Patina's recipes for the home cook. Chef scribbled recipes on cocktail napkins and passed them to me. I sat at a brand-new Apple computer and typed up my best interpretation of the recipe in home-cook-speak, then assembled a "shopping" list and faxed it to my assigned contact in the Patina kitchen.

On testing days, I turned up at the back door of the Patina kitchen early and collected my box of expensive, exotic ingredients, then went to the Splichal's empty house in the Hollywood Hills and cooked all day. At the end of the day, I left the plated dishes on the counter for Chef's critique, alongside the printed recipe with my own notes scribbled in the margins. The next morning I'd return and attempt to decipher Chef's notes and diagrams, peppered with occasional German words. These painstaking steps eventually produced finished recipes. Even if they were not particularly user-friendly, they were guaranteed to work. That is, if one had a large disposable income and no day job.

Chef's English was still patchy, and sometimes when he was deep in the weeds during service, he would whirl around and point accusingly at one of his devoted, deer-in-the-headlights kitchen brigade and scream: "GIMME THE—GIMME THE—THE *THING*!!!"

HERE'S A TYPED NOTE FROM my assigned kitchen-contact at Patina that was included in my box of supplies one morning:

Brigit, This is the new recipe that Joachim wants in the basic recipe section of the book. Check it out and make sure it is user friendly.

Preparation: Morels

3 shallots, finely minced

10 oz fresh morels, cleaned

2 oz butter

___ chicken stock

Soften the shallots in the butter, add the morels and sweat to release some of its juices, about 5 minutes. Make it sweat like it just came out of a step aerobics class. Then give it some water because it will be thirsty, and then feed it some frozen yogurt and cook it til it is pink and juicy. Put it in the microwave and nuke it til it starts smellin' funny. And then stick your head in there to make sure it is done.

IF I STOOD ON MY TIPTOES, I could see a tiny sliver of glittering Pacific Ocean from my back stoop. It couldn't match the view from my kitchen window in Spain, but it was all mine. When the big Maersk container arrived and began disgorging my cherished pots, pans, plates, glasses, books, and furniture, the overachieving whirlwind that was me turned it into a humble oasis of beauty and calm. Waiting to meet the unknown, I was proud, excited, tentative.

Finally, it was time to bring Wiggy over. Joffrey was too cheap to purchase an approved dog-carrier from British Airways, so he hired a local carpenter to build one out of scrap wood and metal mesh. We communicated by fax about her travel arrangements. When the day of her departure dawned, he drove her to Gibraltar, loaded her into the crate, and sent her off. If he was sad about this, he didn't let on. The plan was for her to spend one night at the quarantine kennel at Heathrow Airport and then fly on to Los Angeles the next day. When the airplane's cargo hold was opened in London, Wiggy was sitting proudly at the huge door because she had chewed her way out of the wooden box.

As the worried mom, I called the quarantine kennel in the morning to check on her. The impersonal voice on the other end demanded an "airbill number," and my stomach dropped. *Is this some sort of huge impersonal facility where my baby is lonely and unloved?* After a few moments on hold, the voice returned: "Oh *yes*, that's the sweet little Staffy! She's just had her breakfast and a tummy-tickle!" Saved by the Brit.

For the momentous arrival at LAX, my mother came along as my co-pilot. In the vast lexicon of things we did not agree on, the litany of past disappointments and failed rapprochements, the love of a good dog was one thing we both valued above almost anything else. It was a bond that held us together while others were left to slowly fray.

I had a handful of documents allowing me to import a dog into the USA, and we were told to wait behind a yellow line outside a massive empty airplane hangar for her crate to be offloaded. Acres away across the huge expanse of asphalt, I saw a massive door slide open, and a forklift began to make its slow and wavering way across toward us. Eventually, I could see that it carried a large official airline crate—some kind person at British Airways in London had given us one. As it meandered its way closer and closer, suddenly I could see those sweet, dancing brown eyes looking out the grill of the crate. Moments later that solid little body was in my arms, wriggling and licking me and suddenly rendering my fractured life complete. In a rare moment of shared emotion, my mother and I both shed tears. But first, the paperwork.

A block away at the office of live animal imports, an official stamped my papers and asked me, "Is it alive?" My glare alone could derail a train.

Ellen Rose had, not unkindly, let me go from my Cook's Library job, saying I was vastly over-qualified. *The Food Paper* folded. Two jobs down in only six months, but more work was on the horizon, and the Patina book was underway. At lunch one day, Ellen said, "You know, there's a polenta book just waiting to be written. People suddenly love it and no one has done a book yet."

Ellen would have liked to write the book herself, and in fact for about five minutes we collaborated on a book proposal, until her workload led her to hand the project off to me. Ellen had been in touch with an editor at Chronicle Books in San Francisco about the possibility of such a book. When she handed me the idea for the book and the chance to make it my own, she also graced me with an introduction to the editor. *Is this the small beginning of something big?*

I sent the proposal off to San Francisco with my usual internal mini-prayer and prepared to hear nothing about it ever again. A few weeks later I got a call from the editor's assistant, who told me that Chronicle Books would be thrilled to publish *Polenta*, by Brigit Binns. I was over the moon. I literally cried with joy. *My dream. The pinnacle of my hopes. Is this even real?*

At around the same time I took another part-time job testing recipes for the eminent cookbook author Diane Worthington. Diane was an ex-editor at *Bon Appetit* and the author of iconic books *The Cuisine of California, The Taste of Summer,* and *Seriously Simple,* plus several titles for Williams-Sonoma. She sat upstairs in her home office writing recipes for her new book, *The California Cook,* while I prepared them in her kitchen. We'd then taste the dish together, make notes, and she would amend the recipe to reflect the results. I learned everything about recipe testing from Diane. One eye-opening moment: she came down to taste a rice and legume salad and found the dressing to be totally wrong. Instead of starting from scratch, she rinsed off the grains in a colander, shook them dry, and we created a new dressing. We'd avoided both a waste of food *and* of time. It was a revelation.

The Patina Cookbook: Truffles, Spuds, and Wild Gnocchi, by Joachim Splichal with text by Charles Perry and recipes by Brigit Binns, was published by HarperCollins in 1995; a year later *Polenta* came out from Chronicle Books. The soothing rhythm of the alliteration was almost as empowering to me as the idea that I'd published two real, actual cookbooks, and was working on a third: *The Jody Maroni Sausage Kingdom Cookbook,* by Brigit Binns.

It was a world I'd been peeking in at for decades. Now I lived in it.

An attempt at Détente

fool me once

LOS ANGELES, 1992

SEVERAL MONTHS AFTER WIGGY'S triumphant arrival, I found my-self having a quiet dinner with my mother at her home. We were still basking carefully in the warm backwash of her supportive help getting me settled in my new country. Suddenly, out of the blue I remembered my dad's announcement about our Jewish heritage, when we were in Venice together shortly before he died.

"What's this about us being Jewish, Mom?"

It was as though a bucket of ice-cold salamanders had been dumped over her head. Through gritted teeth: "How did you find out?"

"Dad told me."

"He must have truly, truly despised me, to tell you that," she stammered. My mother didn't stammer.

I couldn't believe what I was hearing. She came up with a raft of ex-cuses, but I was having none of it because this cover-up made absolutely zero sense to me. I was raised to be a bleeding-heart liberal—largely by her. I went to bar- and bat-mitzvahs, attended temple in Beverly Hills with school friends, and was taught that all religions and races are equal.

"You don't understand what it was like then!" she wailed.

What, in the fifties and sixties? The Civil Rights era? My grandmother's generation had to contend with systemic anti-Semitism, yes, but where did my mother get this imperative to urgently and fearfully deny her 50 percent Jewishness?

"Why didn't I know this? I thought we were liberals! How could you have kept this a secret?" My gut instinct was to blame my mother but I soon, grudgingly, realized the obvious: The secret-keeping had begun with my grandmother.

"You don't know what it was like in the twenties and thirties. Your grandmother worked at Bullocks Wilshire—as WASPy as they get. If they'd found out she was Jewish, she'd have been fired. She was a single mom with absolutely no support from my deadbeat dad, just doing the best she could for *me*!"

Would she really have been fired? Does it matter? Did my mother believe it?

Many nights Barbara Legere came home from work, my mother said, and stared into the mirror, white as a sheet, whispering, "They're going to find out I'm Jewish. I'm going to get fired." In light of what was happening in Germany and Europe at that time, perhaps her fears were not entirely unfounded. But in her drive to provide what she thought was the best for her daughter, my grandmother worked herself into an early grave; she died at 63 of a stroke or heart attack. I was six at the time. Barbara had loved me deeply and to distraction.

Barbara left behind a well-educated, self-involved daughter who was alternately convinced of her own invincibility and petrified that she would be "outed" as Jewish. Marcia was a very unhappy woman who could hold a circle of martini-clutching men in the palm of her hand, and often did. Barbara also left a granddaughter with a lifetime's worth of unanswered questions.

"Don't let them Jew you down on the price," my mother had heard one of the Hollisters remark, and apparently from that moment on, feared that every social ladder she'd climbed could be rudely jerked out from under her if her true identity were known. *From a purely selfish standpoint, one of my reactions is this: Wait, you mean I could have had a bunch of fun cousins instead of my lonely-only existence?*

In bringing this subject up at our quiet dinner, it seems that I had derailed a plan she'd long cultivated: To erase all stains of Jewishness from her family tree in just one generation.

The researcher in me now wanted nothing more than a full reckoning of this mysterious family history. The only live cousin I knew about on the Feningston side, Carlota Shipman-Smith, lived in San Antonio.

But my mother stopped stammering and became steely: "You Will Not Under Any Circumstances contact your cousin Carlota. I will not give you her phone number." *She talks in capital letters too, as well as writing in them for emphasis. Like fingernails on a blackboard.* My regard for my mother, always on the verge of contempt, took a nosedive over the closest cliff. This stunning development marked the end of our *glasnost* phase.

Over time, I gingerly shared my discoveries with my mother. My grandmother Barbara (born "Bruschka") Fenigstein was the youngest of five Berlin sisters; when they emigrated from Poland in 1909 and settled in Mount Vernon, New York, they changed the family name to Feningston. Another branch of the Berlin family stayed in Poland and perished in the Holocaust.

My mother did not appear to have known about any of this fascinating and heartbreaking history and seemed genuinely sad. She was in fact guardedly, bashfully curious, as if poking a hornet's nest that might have a diamond ring hidden inside. Most of this information came not from Carlota, who had by then passed away, but from my long lost and many times-removed "cousin" Audrey in Chappaqua; she'd turned out to be the passionate but unofficial keeper of the Berlin and Fenigstein/Feningston legacy.

I loved hearing about these characters who were family, but not family. If only my grandmother had been less embarrassed about her heritage, if only my mother could have bravely broken the bonds of shame. Instead, I was deprived of my own rich history and a whole host of relatives. In the end there was my mother, and there was me. That's it. A pairing made somewhere north of Hell, but one that was rapidly losing its ability to cause me pain and shame. Just like the riotous bougainvillea vines so emblematic of Southern California, I began to blossom.

Outside the back door of my Mar Vista bungalow there was a covered patio. By removing every other board from the lanai and populating the space with a teak table and a jumble of potted geraniums, I made a sun-dappled dining terrace almost as lovely as the one left behind in Spain. What it lacked in terracotta (the floor was concrete) and whitewashed clay (the walls were stacked raw concrete blocks), it made up for in soul. I began to entertain. It was a good way to make friends, and soon I had a few. Apparently, most of the locals didn't cook. Anything I did seemed like magic to them, and I was having more and more fun. I relaxed into a style of entertaining all my own. Me, Brigit. No husband in sight.

At first, I recycled old favorite dishes from my years in England and Spain: duck breasts with Cassis, lamb and artichoke heart brochettes, salmon *en papillote*, herb-flecked potato gratin. My new friends seemed surprised but grateful at this sudden home-cooked bounty.

Later I started to include some of the foodways of the writers and chefs I worked with: Diane Worthington's "Orange-Chive Aioli" opened a whole new world of aioli offshoots. Joachim Splichal's recipes were far too complex for casual entertaining, but I did learn to pull out sub-recipes that shone brightly all alone. "Sea Bass with Creamy Lentils and Garlic Infusion," although it sounds simple enough, was a three-day project. The creamy lentils all alone took up a permanent spot in my repertoire. "Roasted Medallions of Rack of Lamb with Fresh Peas, Pearl Onions, Chanterelles, and Roasted Yukon Potatoes" became a standard on Thanksgiving menus—without the lamb medallions. But the best part of cooking in my new-old home was the abundance of excellent ingredients—fennel, kale, citrus, micro-greens—plus the sudden freedom to cook as much fish and shellfish as I liked, now that I was happily unburdened of Joffrey.

I even began to forget about my broken heart; it had been months since any communication had arrived from Joffrey. One morning an exceedingly early phone call informed me that he was on his way to L.A. "to talk." He was "very, very sorry about everything that has happened," and wanted to attempt a reconciliation (and incidentally secure my help in finalizing the green card application, so he could "stay there if things work out"). That I'd needed six months to establish legal residency in California before filing for a divorce seemed to be on his mind.

The phone call came six months to the day after my arrival.

"That was my husband," I said, in a tone equal parts incredulous and blasé. Michael, a forty-something, earthy-swarthy Venice Beach architect—with a golden retriever and a fruitful vegetable garden—whom I'd been seeing for a couple of months, rolled over.

"What the hell does he want?"

"He doesn't seem to want me to rush into filing for a divorce."

"Asshole."

Over the next six weeks, I received regular phone calls and long, navel-gazing faxes from Joffrey. He wanted to explore what had gone wrong with us, and how it could be fixed. Usually he called from a telephone booth late at night, Spanish time; not because he didn't have a home telephone, but because by then he was living with Sharon and her two children.

"I still blame Morgan Stanley."

"I can't live with the idea of never seeing you again."

"I need to come and talk to you in person."

My response to this unexpected onslaught was guarded. When my plane had lifted off from Malaga I'd been convinced he would eventually come after me. Now, it seemed he was setting out to do just that, just when I was finding my feet with a few great jobs and even better prospects, a picture-perfect lover, and a healthy social life.

I examined my feelings carefully. I wrote *reams* of self-examination. *I am, most certainly, flattered; it is hard to underestimate the value of this level of flattery to a woman scorned.* But what if this evaporated just like all the mixed messages during the three months before I'd left Spain? *What if I wanted it to evaporate? What* do *I want?*

I certainly wasn't going to make it easy for him. But the lure of a healed marriage was strong, too. I didn't want to end up like my parents had, bitter and angry. I kept extending an olive branch even though its leaves were now yellowed and frail.

"Don't let life happen *to* you—blaming this on Morgan isn't fair," I told him. "Stand up and take what *you* want from life. Probably yes, I would see you; but it all depends on your situation when you get here." And because it seemed relevant: "Why are you still living with Sharon if you feel this way? What about her children? Haven't they become attached to you?"

His familiar, circular answers did not bode well.

In early December, Joffrey landed at LAX with a small suitcase and an apologetic-seeming grin. *He uses his grin like a power tool.* My mother offered him my childhood bedroom for a week; she supported the effort at reconciliation although she had also voiced doubts about Joffrey's character.

We met for tea, and lunch, and endless conversations punctuated with "gee-whiz" moments on his part: Wireless phones! Freeways! The beach in Santa Monica!

My relationship with Michael-the-architect did not thrive during this week, but I was not making any commitments to anyone yet. It was good to be wanted. It was unfortunate that Michael's birthday fell during this week. That I did not attend made him very angry. *I'm selfishly thinking only about myself? Yeah, dude, get in line behind my mom.*

When Joffrey returned to Spain (and to Sharon), nothing was resolved. It was time to move on. Two weeks later I filed for divorce and sent a registered letter to Joffrey in Spain—papers requiring his signature. The details were all reproduced as in the agreement we'd both signed way back before I left Spain.

Joffrey was not eager to sign the papers and stalled me for more than a month. He continued to insist that we could work it out and was full of excuses. Curiously, I still had not figured out that he was not a stand-up guy. I was loathe to admit that I may have wasted nine years of my life with a loser.

In a previous incarnation of her peripatetic life—strangely parallel to my own—my old friend Ronda had worked for L.A. Chef and restaurateur Evan Kleiman, owner of the iconic Angeli Café and its successful offshoots. Based on that connection, Evan offered me a part-time job as her assistant, and also introduced me to her agent. Selling the *Polenta* book meant that it was suddenly possible to actually *get* an agent! Evan, who has a heart of gold, was one of my early friends and mentors in this strange land. I'd left for boarding school at 14, so wasn't quite the L.A. native I'd have liked to be.

"Evan, my lawn is sprouting all these cool-looking mushrooms! Can we eat them?"

"No, Brigit. Don't you think if those mushrooms were edible there would be an annual L.A. Lawn Mushroom Festival? Instead, every couple of years you see a story "Entire Vietnamese Family Sickened after Eating Lawn Mushrooms.""

My agent (!!) began to bring me other projects. I sold my second solo cookbook. I did not immediately recognize these baby steps as a green flag signaling my accelerated run towards an independent life and career. I continued to engage in an endless round of faxed navel-gazing with Joffrey. *He insists that he really* can *change,* can *be a good husband.* Soon after the Splichal project I wrote books and learned priceless skills from two other male chefs in Los Angeles, Hans Röckenwagner and Jean-Francois Meteigner, but it was the women I worked for in L.A.'s culinary world who selflessly provided invaluable support, advice, and direction. Joining Ellen Rose, Diane Worthington, and Evan Kleiman were Laurie Burrows Grad, Ilana Sharlin Stone, Marilyn Lewis, Susan Feniger, and Mary Sue Milliken.

Joffrey insisted: "Come to England! We will meet there, hop over the Channel for a few days, and talk about what our future might look like."

When I asked about Sharon, he prevaricated. He insisted he had moved out of her house and back into our old house, which had been rented for six months. Yet when I called one night, Sharon answered the phone. He grabbed it away from her and I heard yelling, then a dial tone. The next day, he insisted she was just there to drop off some of his things.

"At dinnertime?" I visualized the little living room with my old no-longer-sky-blue sofa and view of Africa.

"Yes, I *promise*. Don't worry, you can totally trust me." *I am unaccountably assuaged.* The kid in me is myopically eager to erase and replace the failures of my parents.

And yet, there I went. *Gullible's Travels.*

In England, we saw old friends—justifiably confused, but supportive—and revisited old haunts for a day or two, then hopped the car ferry over to Boulogne. We stayed, together, in a dingy French hotel. Back in the room after dinner, Joffrey moved toward me with a distinctly amorous look on his face. I recognized the look from many years before—those twinkly blue eyes, that fetching smile, just a bit turned up on one side in a kind of a smirk—but it wasn't something I'd seen much of in the latter part of the marriage. As he advanced, I backed away, afraid of rejection, afraid to get my hopes up, but Joffrey had been infected with a new self-confidence. *Should I thank Sharon for this?*

It was immediately clear that this was not the same asexual creature I'd lived with for nine years. He was still largely unaware of a woman's physical needs and desires but found his own to be admirably met by the act.

"Amazing!" he trumpeted after we'd made love. *Is this love? Can you just make it happen like that? And who is this person again?* But the conversations had taken a turn for the better. I returned to Los Angeles and the torrent of faxes continued.

Two months after the trip to London and France, Joffrey landed at LAX.

We were officially going to try again. I'd added a paint-it-yourself cupboard to the guest room, for him to store his things. A shipping container containing all his worldly goods was on its way from Malaga to Long Beach. *He is very confident.*

At work in a little bungalow/office behind Evan Kleiman's house on the day of his arrival, I was consumed by debilitating self-doubt. My co-workers watched my psychic contortions with amusement. At one point I was under my desk hyper-ventilating. *Why did I agree to this? It's going to be a disaster. Why do I not learn from my mistakes? How can I be so ridiculously needy?*

FROM DAY ONE IT FELT AWKWARD. *Joffrey* was the one who was needy, a fish-out-of-water; the self confidence found in France evaporated. I resented his demands upon my attention, the need to re-arrange my social life to accommodate this interloper. I suspect I did not make it easy for him; I was also convinced I was *not* doing this on purpose, for revenge. Naturally I lost Michael-the-architect in the general upheaval, but this was already in the cards. My calendar for the following two months was virtually devoid of social plans. I was suddenly ashamed of Joffrey.

Six weeks after his arrival, I was sitting in a large booth at a trendy hot-pot restaurant in Koreatown. On one banquette: me and Joffrey; on the banquette opposite: two of my dearest friends, one of whom I'd known since college. Three of us were bantering about the great food, the vibe, the ultimate cool factor of dining in Koreatown in the midst of one of the most ethnically diverse dining cities in the world. One of us did not participate in the banter. Overhead, chandeliers glittered. At the table, we swished paper-thin slices of beef in hot oil and piled on the lip-scorching condiments. There was an ocean between me and Joffrey.

The next day, I asked him to move into the guest room and to contemplate, eventually, a plan to seek a job and another place to live. This came as a profound shock.

"But there's nothing *wrong*! We're getting along! I'm *trying*!"
I have made a horrible mistake.

He registered for a paid medical trial and spent a week in a Culver City hospital being shot up with God knows what. His application for a Series 7 securities-trading license evaporated like the morning dew on a broken promise. But he did follow up on his green card application.

Two months after his arrival, Joffrey had given up. I dropped him at LAX for the return trip to Spain. As I pulled away from the curb, I could see him crying in the rear-view mirror, his face all squinched up and as bright as my red VW Rabbit convertible. I discovered later that Sharon was ready to welcome him back with open arms and, I guess, no questions. The shipping container sitting on the dock in Long Beach returned to Spain without ever having been opened. Alongside it on the Spain-bound cargo vessel: a 15-year-old Alfa Spider I'd bought for him with his/my money. Inside the Alfa, I belatedly learned, he had crammed tennis rackets, a barbecue, water skis, life jackets, and a ski rope. I would spend the next five years fielding calls about the credit cards he'd defaulted on after charging all this swag; he had given my name as a reference.

Drunk on my own independence, I danced around my little living room in Mar Vista throwing air-punches while belting out Gloria Gaynor's, "I Will Survive."

If Wiggy missed Joffrey, she didn't let on. I finalized the divorce.

Photo credit: Ronda Kamihira

OUR FIRST CHRISTMAS BACK IN CALIFORNIA

CHAPTER 28

heal thyself

VENICE BEACH, 1994

ONE EVENING IN LATE JUNE, when the sun was playing glittery games between the slats of the lanai and pieces of garlicky chicken sizzled gently on the grill, a new French friend told me that my backyard was like a little corner of France in Southern California. "*Un petit coin de France.*" It was one of the nicest things anyone had ever said to me. I had a good job and my culinary career was continuing to show signs of promise.

All communication with Joffrey had ceased.

In familiar fashion, the tenuous detente with my mother had failed. The first nail was the "We're Jewish?" conversation. Then, she became angry that I wasn't always available for her frequent and fraught airport runs on the way to her time-share in Maui and her Barn in Connecticut because: job(s), life. I refrained from reminding her about the time she couldn't arise before noon to collect me from LAX after many months in Southeast Asia. It was as if she resented the fact that I'd settled in so quickly and was no longer a fish out of water in my once and current hometown. The valley of vitriol separated us once again, but now it was deeper and wider than ever. Once again, I was "selfish and trivial."

My mother was fond of regularly repeating the story that, in Puerta Vallarta when I was three years old, we had seen some friends approaching along the beach. I'd said "Oh! They'll be so happy when they see that *I'm* here!" From that moment on my mother was convinced that, because of this statement, I was a selfish and self-involved person.

I was three years old.

All her life-long contempt for me apparently stemmed from this moment of youthful self-confidence. Once again she was full of disappointment, blame, and recriminations. These were not helpful ingredients in my effort to build a capable and proactive new life in a new land. My mother asked if I would attend therapy with her, to discover the reasons for my "deep hatred of my mother." I was more than willing.

"You go alone for the first six sessions," I suggested, "and then I'll join you." I figured this would allow her to get the therapist "on her side" before we began the joint sessions.

After a few sessions together, Kate the therapist told my mother, "Your daughter has always felt like an employee who could be fired at any time." This was clearly not what my mother was expecting, but I felt a sense of vindication.

My mother called off the therapy. "That wasn't the right therapist."

We didn't find another one, but I continued alone with Kate. It was this hard work, over months, that finally allowed me to cast aside my mother's scathing opinions of me and emerge with a growing smidgeon of self-esteem. The elephant that had been squatting on my shoulders for decades had disappeared.

IN VENICE BEACH

un petit coin de france

FRANCE, 1994

A JOINT BIRTHDAY APPROACHED—that of two good friends—and I was ready to flex some culinary muscle. Ten people would sit around the long teak table I'd bought to grace my little backyard paradise. I resolved to feed them something really fabulous. *But what? A grand roast beef is so last marriage, so pitifully English.* Still fresh from the chest-swelling experience of being told my backyard was like a little corner of France, I settled on escargot. Garlicky, butter-drenched, and oh, so *chic, n'est ce pas?*

That's sixty snails. And sixty snail *shells.* And, um, I hesitate to mention this lest I come off as insane: It was summertime. Not exactly escargot season. *No matter! Remember Gloria Gaynor? I will survive.*

The day of the birthday party dawned, and I pulled two pounds of butter from the fridge to soften. The snail butter—that concoction in which garlic, shallots, and parsley combine in a celestial troika to create The Most Delicious Substance on Earth (dipped into which even a piece of cardboard would taste heavenly)—was supposed to have been made the previous day. Instead, my day before had been spent driving all over Los Angeles County looking for sixty packaged (i.e. perfectly clean and sterile) snail shells, ten snail-grabbers, and ten snail forks.

Due to the heat, the butter softened almost immediately (it was just 9 a.m.). After only a moment in the food processor, I had my big pot of green-flecked elixir, ready to stuff. First, you rinse the canned snails under cool running water. *These rubbery little gastropods comprise all manner of nooks, crannies, and disturbingly shaped protrusions. Fine, I'm a big girl, I've gutted fish, boned ducks, touched a piece of cooked okra. Get on with it.*

Then you begin to stuff.

I had chosen a low-maintenance main course; I popped a rose-mary-spiked leg of lamb into the oven at noon, about halfway through the snail-stuffing marathon. *For maximum butter-bathing, you've got to put some butter into the shell behind the snail. Then you smash the snail in and cram some more butter in on top of him/her/it/them. (Because Life Is Short, I'd decided to put two snails into each shell.)*

The guests and birthday couple arrived. I was dressed in white jeans with a bare midriff. The theme cocktail of the event—a French 75, for continuity—was on the outdoor sideboard. Ten white porcelain snail dishes, each containing six stuffed snail shells, sat patiently in the fridge. The lamb that had been relaxing in the low oven smelled beyond heavenly and was now beginning to resemble butter as well. Baskets of crusty sourdough bread dotted the well-dressed table and my date for the evening poured water at each place, using one remnant of the posh English years that had made the pilgrimage from England to Spain to California: an ornate, solid silver carafe.

My date, an impossibly tall Icelandic architecture student named Ivar (roll the "R" when you say that) drove a sky-blue Thunderbird and sported chin-length salt-and-pepper hair (although he was substantially younger than me). He seemed to think I was the bee's knees, or however you say that in Icelandic.

The great big turquoise Gaffers and Satler stove was pretty as a picture, but the broiler compartment was the size of a toaster oven;

it proved to be capable of broiling only two snail dishes at a time. To achieve authentic escargot-ish effect, the butter must be really sizzling, and the door would not close during this operation. So, during the approximately forty-five minutes it took me to, two by two, bring five batches of snails to the perfect serving point, I hovered just outside the broiler door. The dishes had to be turned occasionally to insure even heat exposure, which put me in full directional blast of the heat emanating from the gas jets and the sizzling and spitting butter. Ferrying two dishes at a time outside to the waiting diners, I was able to achieve a remarkably Impressionistic grease-spatter pattern on my white jeans. It was like painting the Golden Gate Bridge: by the time I got to the end of the table, the first two diners were looking hungry again. I snatched a snail and darted back to the kitchen.

Over in the oven of the hulking stove, the lamb had been slow-braising for almost seven hours. I served the spoon-tender meat with a mustard-kissed green salad and more crusty bread, then briefly assumed an unruffled air. For dessert, I'd chosen a Champagne sabayon, to be ladled over bursting-ripe fresh figs. Sabayon is the French cousin of *zabaglione*, in other words one of the most labor-intensive last-minute desserts in the lexicon of last courses. It was ethereal, the eggy foam sending a sort of signal to the primordial mind that, yes, we will indeed survive.

I looked around the messy table and saw raw happiness.

Later in the evening Ivar, trying to show off by juggling with my silver pitcher, dropped it, denting it beyond any hope of repair. *Is this an omen?* I performed a post-mortem on the party and found it to be largely successful. The lamb had been a huge hit and the guests had enjoyed themselves enormously. So what if I'd had to work hard to make that happen?

I had learned long ago that for me, the most important thing about cooking was making diners happy. But I decided it was time for a few changes. For one thing, I didn't need a boyfriend. Men are highly overrated. Wiggy and I were fine on our own. In fact, we were more than fine.

It was time to just relax and let life happen on its own terms.

MOTHER AND DAUGHTER

epilogue

I CALLED IN HOSPICE CARE ON LABOR DAY, after my mother's primary doctor said to me: "She is in too much pain to stay at home. Either she goes to the hospital, or you call in Hospice."

"I am *not* going to the hospital," the patient pronounced to the doctor and everyone else within earshot or telephone's reach.

Plus, thus spake forcefully her Advance Directive: "No hospital, over (her) dead body." I had no choice. A fall in the bathroom a few days before had left her unable to walk, sit, or even move in the bed without intense pain. A deeply black-gray-purple bruise covered the whole expanse of her hunched, bony, and misshapen back. All her disks had long ago begun collapsing like an exhausted accordion, leaving little room for her internal organs, which were now engaged in slowly forcing themselves out the front.

Because it was Labor Day, it took an inconceivably long and torturous eight hours for the morphine to arrive. With the first vial, she went to a far more peaceful, but also way less perceptive state. It was like watching a light go out, very slowly. The two dogs, my second Staffy Stella, and mom's beloved Piglet, were quiet guardians, each curled at one corner of the big medical bed in her blue and white bedroom. ("It's got to be *Matisse* blue!" she would cry when selecting paint colors or fabrics.)

As I rolled all 90 pounds of her over to replace the diaper and plastic sheet, the dogs were stationary and silent yet with eyes wide and watchful. When situated again, she peered up with myopic fascination at her "Rottenkid," me, who for several years now had been the arbiter and executor of her care.

For seven excruciating days, neither dog seemed to need a bathroom break—or if they did, I didn't notice. They were *always* there. I existed in a state of heightened awareness incongruously combined with a kind of sleepwalking. I made momentous decisions with impunity. For once it was good to be an only child.

At night I was alone, camping out in the blue and white toile chair by the French doors—through which she'd pointed the rifle at my stomach—always ready for disaster. But during the days there were times when the long-time caregiver, a hospice nurse, the pool-house tenant, and an old family friend were clustered around the head of the bed.

"I don't think I'm *dying*!" Mom once shouted to the general atmosphere. No one answered, though we may have exchanged guilty looks in our complicit silence.

I was able to get my mother's old college boyfriend, a once-and-forever-friend to her and still sharp as a tack, on the phone. After filling him in ("I hope you are doing *everything* possible for her," he intoned sternly, as if perhaps I would not.) I held the receiver up to her ear so they could talk.

At one point she blurted into the phone, "Guess what? My *Rottenkid* turned out to be not so rotten after all!" Then immediately, "Oh shit, she's standing right here."

During "the surge" (it is real) toward the end of that endless seven days, Mom had a few hours of amazing clarity, a true gift for those about to be left behind, even though we know it's almost certainly a harbinger of death.

"My beautiful daughter," she exclaimed. "Why did we waste so much time being angry with each other?"

* * *

THANKSGIVING IS MY FAVORITE HOLIDAY of the year. I let my inner overachiever out of the stockade where she's locked up most of the year. I pull out Barbara Legere's delicate white bone china and my mother's full set of Italian majolica, collected on our family trip to Italy in 1969—a huge splurge for her. My you-won-the-lottery husband of twenty years requests a sit-down soup every year and makes some mean mashed potatoes. My turkey is legendary.

When the carving begins I look around in vain for my dad and his pronouncement, "The skin people can come in now."

In a prominent niche on the bookshelf sits the *TV Guide* picture of three-year-old me salting the frozen steak as my apparently doting parents look on. By using their dishes and serving pieces I celebrate the two imperfect women who came before me, showing me the way to live— and the way not to live. Their flaws and unique spirits lead me always onward like a trail of golden crumbs stretching back across 120 years to Poland and Pasadena, New York and Mount Vernon, through the place where the adults become the children and the children, the adults. It's a dance where partners may be mismatched and tempers run high, but there is priceless knowledge to be found in legacy. The trick is to drain off the anger and vitriol, and retain the tasty, nourishing nuggets.

The trick is to survive.

OUR LAST PICTURE, WITH STELLA

Photo credit: Casey Biggs

A SKIN PERSON

recipes

WEENIE N' EGG

Age 5: Get dad to do it.

Age 25: Are you kidding? Babe, grow the fuck up. Bottomless mimosa brunch at 11 a.m. with the girls.

Age 60: Place one Hebe-Nat (hot dog) into a medium sauce-pan three-quarters-full of cold water and bring to a simmer. Meanwhile, warm a small, pretty bowl in a low oven. Place a cutting board and a folded kitchen towel adjacent to the stovetop. When the water has been simmering for one minute, *very* carefully use a small spoon to lower one large, cage-free brown egg into the water next to the hot dog. Remove the pan from the heat, cover it, and let stand undisturbed for 3 minutes. With tongs or a fork, retrieve the dog and quickly slice crosswise about 1/3-inch thick; quickly transfer slices to the warm bowl. Moving fast now, use the spoon to transfer the egg to the kitchen towel and let it shed its exterior water for just a few seconds. Crack the egg in half with the edge of the spoon and scoop the warm jelly-like egg into the bowl over the weenie slices. Top with 1/2 to 1 teaspoon of top-quality tamari sauce (to taste). Gently stir the contents of the bowl. Serve yourself and immediately return to childhood.

BINNS' BREASTS

Collect $1 from each of your six hippie-ish off-campus house-mates. Lace up your Wallabees and head to Fred Meyer. Buy bone-in, skin-on chicken breasts. Take 'em home and stick 'em on a piece of foil. Preheat the broiler (does it work? Lucky you!). While it's preheating, clean up the dog poop on the stairs even if your dog didn't do it. One for all, and all for one. Melt a stick of butter in the dented, lid-less aluminum saucepan. Dump in a bunch of soy sauce. Find a pastry brush (that's not paint, right?). Brush the butter mixture on top and bottom of each breast. Broil until they seem like they're probably done, brushing a few more times if you remember. Do not burn them. Let somebody else worry about the salad and brown rice. Pop a half-gallon jug of Almaden White Burgundy. Serve.

THE EVOLUTION OF MR. BEEF

There has always been a "Mr. Beef" in my life, but it hasn't always been the same Mr. Beef. To qualify as Mr. Beef, the dish must be very special. It must be a holiday-special occa-sion-impress-your-friends kind of dish, and so far, there have been four, but never at the same time. As my life has changed, so has my definition of Mr. Beef.

1. The first Mr. Beef was a fat cat. Times were swell, I was living in England (the temple of roast beef), and due to the weather tended to entertain indoors. Thus, number one was a seven-rib standing rib roast, which the butcher in our village would chine for me. He then re-attached the chine bone with a little skewer which, after roasting, could easily be pulled out to ensure stress-free carving.

Roasting with the chine bone attached was crucial since, as every meat man (and woman) knows, the meat closest to the bone is the tenderest and most flavorful. I can only read in horror of the three years not long after I left Europe, when beef "on-the-bone" was banned. *Les pauvres Anglais!* A black market flourished, but still.

2. Times became, quite suddenly, quite lean. The excessive cost of the first Mr. Beef was deemed to be, well, excessive. The London Evening Standard provided a solution, which for about five years was known as "The New Mr. Beef." The Italian dish Beef in Barolo has been around for a long time, but when attempted with chuck roast, my results had never been prepossessing. It took English food writer Sophie Grigson (daughter of the famous Jane) to suggest making a similar dish using brisket. To prevent dryness during the long cooking, the beef is larded with strips of bacon and studded with garlic cloves. An entire bottle of wine is required, but I'm here to tell you it needn't be Barolo. Actually, Zinfandel works quite well, but since the tenure of the second Mr. Beef included three years in southern Spain, the dish was most often executed with a mid-range Rioja. It takes three days to produce optimum flavor in this dish but, since the truism, "Money but no time, or time but no money" was never truer than in my case, that wasn't a problem.

3. In later years the pendulum swung again, perhaps not so high as during the time of the first Mr. Beef, but to a place that was sweet, calm, happy—perhaps the best word is mature. My home state of California provided the weather for outdoor cooking, and life brought me a wonderful man who loved nothing more than nurturing coals and lighting myriad candles and fairy lights while I create the

less fiery ambiance that will be eaten. The third Mr. Beef involves six pounds of boneless rib eye, which is studded with garlic and bits of mild, white anchovies. Impaled on a spit and basted with butter, it turns slowly over the coals and, towards the end, receives the secret crust-building treatment. In a surprisingly short time, the result is ready for its close-up (after a decent rest, of course). Crusted a deep, dark brown on the outside and perfectly pink and yielding inside, this is a very fine iteration of Mr. Beef. Try as I might, I've never been able to stretch this quantity of meat to satisfy more than four people.

4.   But as I've grown older, the siren lure of fat has faded, and the "fun" of hovering over a hot rotisserie basting while my friends are sipping Prosecco has also lost some luster. The fourth Mr. Beef is lean and cool, perfect for the 100°-plus temperatures on California's Central Coast where I finally landed. A whole beef tenderloin is dry-brined for 24 hours, then smoked for about 1½ hours until the temperature at the interior reaches 128°. Immediately after its time in the smoker, Mr. Beef IV is dusted with pepper and seared in a cast-iron pan, bathing briefly in sizzling-hot butter. I give it about 1½ minutes on all four sides, to develop a lovely crust. Then, it's into the fridge with him! After a nice overnight rest, Mr. Beef and I are ready to roll with virtually zero effort. We are both competent and cool. Sliced and served nice and chilly, the rosy, gorgeously tender meat is perfectly accessorized by a large dollop of horseradish-laced mayo.

This is by no means the final Mr. Beef, that much I have learned. To assume that life will remain the same would be naïve.

Snails From My Garden

Serves Six

This recipe marries a bit of my Greek influence with the quintessentially French presentation of escargots within "their" shells. Angling the shells as you eat, for maximum butter deployment is half the fun of this dish, but remember, you will need to secure all the correct gear in advance. That's six metal or porcelain snail dishes, each with six small depressions; 36 perfectly clean, packaged snail shells; six snail forks (2 skinny prongs); and six snail-grabbers. Also: the snails.

Tips:

*You will have plenty of garlic butter left over, but it is a wonderful thing to have on hand. Spread any leftover green butter (softened) in a line down the center of a long sheet of plastic wrap, roll up to enclose the butter tightly, firming and smoothing into a cylinder with your hands on the outside of the plastic wrap. Freeze for up to 4 months. Unwrap and slice straight from the freezer for topping grilled steaks, grilled or poached fish, poultry, or vegetables.

*You will likely need two racks in your oven to accommodate six snail dishes; if you are pinched for space or do not wish to buy six one-purpose pieces of kitchen equipment, you can always spread a layer of rock salt in a rimmed half sheet pan and nestle/balance the snails with the opening fully upright. OR find six gratin dishes and use the rock salt method in those.

For the Green Butter:

1 pound cultured unsalted butter, cut into chunks, at room temperature

3 large shallots, trimmed, peeled, sliced, and minced

9 plump cloves garlic, peeled and minced or pushed through a press

1 teaspoon fine sea salt or 2 teaspoons lemon flake salt

1/2 teaspoon freshly ground black pepper

1 cup (loosely packed) flat-leaf parsley leaves

1 tablespoon vegetable oil

Half a small yellow onion, finely chopped

Half a small fennel bulb, finely chopped

1 stalk celery, finely chopped

¼ cup ouzo

1 cup dry white wine

Four 200-gram cans Escargots de Bourgogne (from France, not China) or other Helix snails, each containing 18 snails (72 total), well rinsed and drained

2 cups water

Juice and zest from 1 orange

2 tablespoons fresh lemon juice

2 sprigs rosemary

Kosher salt and cracked black pepper

Hunks of crusty bread, for serving

1. In a food processor, combine all the ingredients for the Green Butter and pulse on and off, scraping down the sides, until the mixture has turned an even, bright green color. Use within 1 hour, or wrap as described in the note above and chill for up to 2 weeks, or freeze for up to 4 months.

2. In a large skillet, warm the oil over medium-high heat. Add the vegetables and wilt for 3 to 5 minutes without browning. Deglaze the pan with the ouzo and white wine and immediately add the snails, water, juice and zest of the orange, lemon juice, and rosemary. Season generously with salt and pepper. Bring to a boil and reduce the heat slightly. Simmer briskly, uncovered, for 35 to 40 minutes, until the snails are tender. Drain the snails well, separating them from the veggies, which by this time will have released all their flavor and may be discarded, along with the poaching liquid.

3. Assemble the drained snails, Green Butter, and empty snail shells. Put on Pink Martini and get to work. Using a very small rubber spatula or mini-palette knife, smear a small lump of butter into the first empty snail shell and shove it way in. Shove in a snail, another small clump of green butter, a second snail, and a final smoosh of green butter. (That's right, two snails in each shell, surrounded by butter on all sides.) Continue with the remaining snails, butter, etc, placing each well-stuffed shell in its position on the snail dishes with the opening facing upward. When you are finished, you can chill the six dishes until roasting time if there is room in your refrigerator. I suggest you do not let them wait for more than a few hours.

4. Preheat the oven to 400°. Cook until the butter is sizzling, about 10 minutes; remove from the oven. Carefully carry each plate (now swimming with sizzling butter) to the table. Serve the snails with crusty bread on the side and be sure to alert your guests to the thrilling presence of two snails in each shell.

about the author

The prolific author of almost 30 cookbooks, **Brigit Binns'** books have sold over 100,000 copies. The most recent, *Cooking in Season*, is one of eleven titles she authored for Williams-Sonoma. She's also helped some of the USA's most respected chefs, like New York's Michael Psilakis and Los Angeles' Joachim Splichal, turn their cookbook dreams into reality. Binns has ghost-written books for many celebrities as well as editing over 40 cookbooks and developing 400 recipes for Weber Grills. Brigit has been featured several times on *The Today Show* and wrote 90 shows for the Food Network series *Too Hot Tamales*. A graduate of England's Tante Marie cooking school, she ran a catering company in Spain and served as editor of the Costa del Sol's English-language magazine before returning home to California. In a previous life, she worked on Wall Street for one of the world's foremost investment banks, and has walked from one end of the Grand Canyon to the other carrying a 60-pound pack. She now lives full-time in California's Central Coast wine country with her fabulous dogs and third-and-final husband, the actor Casey Biggs.

Enjoy more about

Rottenkid

Meet the Author

Check out author appearances

Explore special features

acknowledgements

In 2009, I set out to spend a month alone in Marfa, Texas, to begin working on the concept that eventually became this book. I reasoned that the solitude, together with all the creative energy flowing in Marfa's dry and rarefied air, would set me on the road to writing well. My friend, the excellent writer Linda Ellerbee, gave me two bits of advice: "Verbs are always better than adjectives," and "just try to write one good sentence every day." Instead, the clanking of my split heat pump convinced me that the Texas Chainsaw Massacre was going to take place in my bungalow, and I didn't even begin writing until twenty precious days had passed. After that month, I packed up the notes and diaries into a plastic box; they stayed there for over ten years. It was only the pandemic that finally pushed me to sit down and resume writing. During that time I published ten cookbooks, moved across the country (again), and lost my mother.

The fact that this book ever got written is due to so many colleagues, friends, family, editors, readers, and just all around excellent supporters.

Several professional editors labored with me over this material in all its many iterations: Jaime Lewis, Franz Wisner, Lily Binns, Vicki DeArmon, Joanne Hartman, and Julia Park Tracey.

Kind and patient readers, both early and late, helped me get over my bloated nothingness and—never unkindly—pointed it out wherever it still lurked: Ilana Sharlin Stone, Casey Biggs, Susan Bass, Nancy Binns, Judy Binns, Mary ("Zak Hart") Robinette, Anita Grinich, Evelyne Penia Fodor, and Jean Pedigo (for correcting my Chinese).

AND THESE WONDERFUL SUPPORTERS, REPRESENTATIVES,
FRIENDS, AND TEACHERS:

Joe Regal, one of my strongest supporters for decades, whether he was representing me or not.

Reed Maroc, my brother-from-another-mother; we navigated the dangerous reefs of childhood and then adulthood in spite of our parentals.

Michael Flamini, my forever friend, for publishing *The Relaxed Kitchen* and thus allowing me for the first time a writer's voice that was not exclusively about recipes.

Linda Ellerbee, for always cutting right through the shit to the heart of whatever the Hell it is or was.

Carole Bidnick, the endlessly patient and supportive Jewish grandmother I didn't get to have.

Alison Caine, from the way-back machine, thank you for insights into my childhood.

Elissa Altman for helping me find the permission to tell my own truth.

Miriam Pawel for her endlessly inquiring and razor-sharp mind.

Diane Jacob, for directing me to the savvy editing team of Vicki D. and Joanne H.

My early L.A. mentors! I was a true rube when I got off the plane from Spain after ten years in Europe. These gals showed me the way. Ellen Rose, Laurie Burrows Grad, Diane Worthington, and Marilyn Lewis (for her wisdom and patience during our eye-opening collaboration on her autobiography).

Leslie Jonath, for agreeing to publish my very first cookbook when I was still a total newbie.

Sarah Putman Clegg, for bringing me along with her from Chronicle Books to Weldon-Owen, which led to all the Williams-Sonoma books.

Lorena Jones for her confidence in me and for the many editing and writing jobs she sent my way from Ten Speed Press.

Kim Laidlaw, Amy Marr, Lisa Atwood, Sara Deseran, and everyone (then) at Weldon-Owen for riotously happy collaborations on so many wonderful books. And the San Francisco lunches!

JoAnn "JoJo" Cianciulli for always having my back when it comes to agents, chefs, and publishers.

Maureen Lasher for taking me on as a client when I had exactly zero books under my belt.

To the talented and generous Chefs who helped shape my post-mom culinary sensibilities (in roughly chronological order):

Joachim "BRING ME THE....THE...THE THING!" Splichal; Hans "Crap Cakes" Rockenwagner; Evan Kleiman (also a cherished mentor); Susan Feniger and Mary Sue Milliken; Jean-Francois Meteigner; Jill "Villa Jilla" Davie; Jordan "The Sausage King" Monkarsh; Tony "You got a perfect steak, so whaddaya need a sauce?" Tammero; Ryan "The King of Meats" Farr; Michael Psilakis; Clark Staub; and last but most certainly not least: Meathead.

To the powerful girl gang at Sibylline Press: Thank you for allowing me the honor of appearing in your second-ever release!

Alicia Feltman: the cover—what can I say—you knocked it out of the park on the first draft. Julia Park Tracy: Your patience and sensitive editing made me shine and helped me trim out some real loser sentences. Sang Kim: You are the glue that holds the whole shebang together. But especially to Vicki DeArmon, who helped me bring the manuscript to the finish line as a professional editor, and then, switching hats, mentioned that she'd like to actually publish the book.

Cilla Saunders, thank you for showing me how to keep laughing, snorting, and giggling through all the tears.

Without my local girls, the capricious waves of life, fate, and everything would have sent me to the bottom a looong time ago. Thank you to Pam Barnes, Andrea DeWit, Ronda Kamihira, and Tracy Secchiaroli.

If I have ended up with any style, grace, humility, or kindness, I owe it all to Jane Moore and Mary Robinette. For humor, if any, I credit my dad.

—Brigit Binns

Sibylline Press is proud to publish the brilliant work of women authors over 50. We are a woman-owned publishing company and, like our authors, represent women of a certain age.

Rottenkid: A Succulent Story of Survival
BY BRIGIT BINNS

Pub Date: 3/5/24
ISBN: 9781960573995
Memoir, Trade paper, $19, 320 pages

Prolific cookbook author Brigit Binns' coming-of-age memoir—co-starring her alcoholic actor father Edward Binns and glamorous but viciously smart narcissistic mother—reveals how simultaneous privilege and profound neglect led Brigit to seek comfort in the kitchen, eventually allowing her to find some sense of self-worth. A memoir sauteed in Hollywood stories, world travel, and always, the need to belong.

1666: A Novel
BY LORA CHILTON

Pub Date: 4/2/24
ISBN: 9781960573957
Fiction, Trade paper, $17, 224 pages

The survival story of the Patawomeck Tribe of Virginia has been remembered within the tribe for generations, but the massacre of Patawomeck men and the enslavement of women and children by land hungry colonists in 1666 has been mostly unknown outside of the tribe until now. Author Lora Chilton, a member of the tribe through the lineage of her father, has created this powerful fictional retelling of the survival of the tribe through the lives of three women.

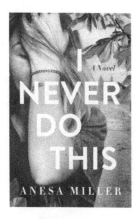

I Never Do This: A Novel
BY ANESA MILLER

Pub Date: 4/16/24
ISBN: 9781960573988
Fiction, Trade paper, $17, 216 pages

This gothic novel presents the unforgettable voice of a young woman, LaDene Faye Howell, who finds herself in police custody recounting her story after her paroled cousin Bobbie Frank appears and engages her in a crime spree in the small town of Devola, Ohio.

The Goldie Standard: A Novel
BY SIMI MONHEIT

Pub Date: 5/7/24
ISBN: 9781960573971
Fiction, Trade paper, $19, 328 pages

Hilarious and surprising, this unapologetically Jewish story delivers a present-day take on a highly creative grandmother in an old folks' home trying to find her Ph.D granddaughter a husband who is a doctor—with a yarmulke, of course.

Bitterroot: A Novel
BY SUZY VITELLO

Pub Date: 5/21/24
ISBN: 9781960573964
Fiction, Trade paper, 18, 296 pages

A forensic artist already reeling from the surprise death of her husband must confront the MAGA politics, racism and violence raging in her small town in the Bitterroot Mountains of Idaho when her gay brother is shot and she becomes a target herself.

For more books from **Sibylline Press**, please visit our
website at **sibyllinepress.com**